IMAGES of America

MELBOURNE AND EAU GALLIE

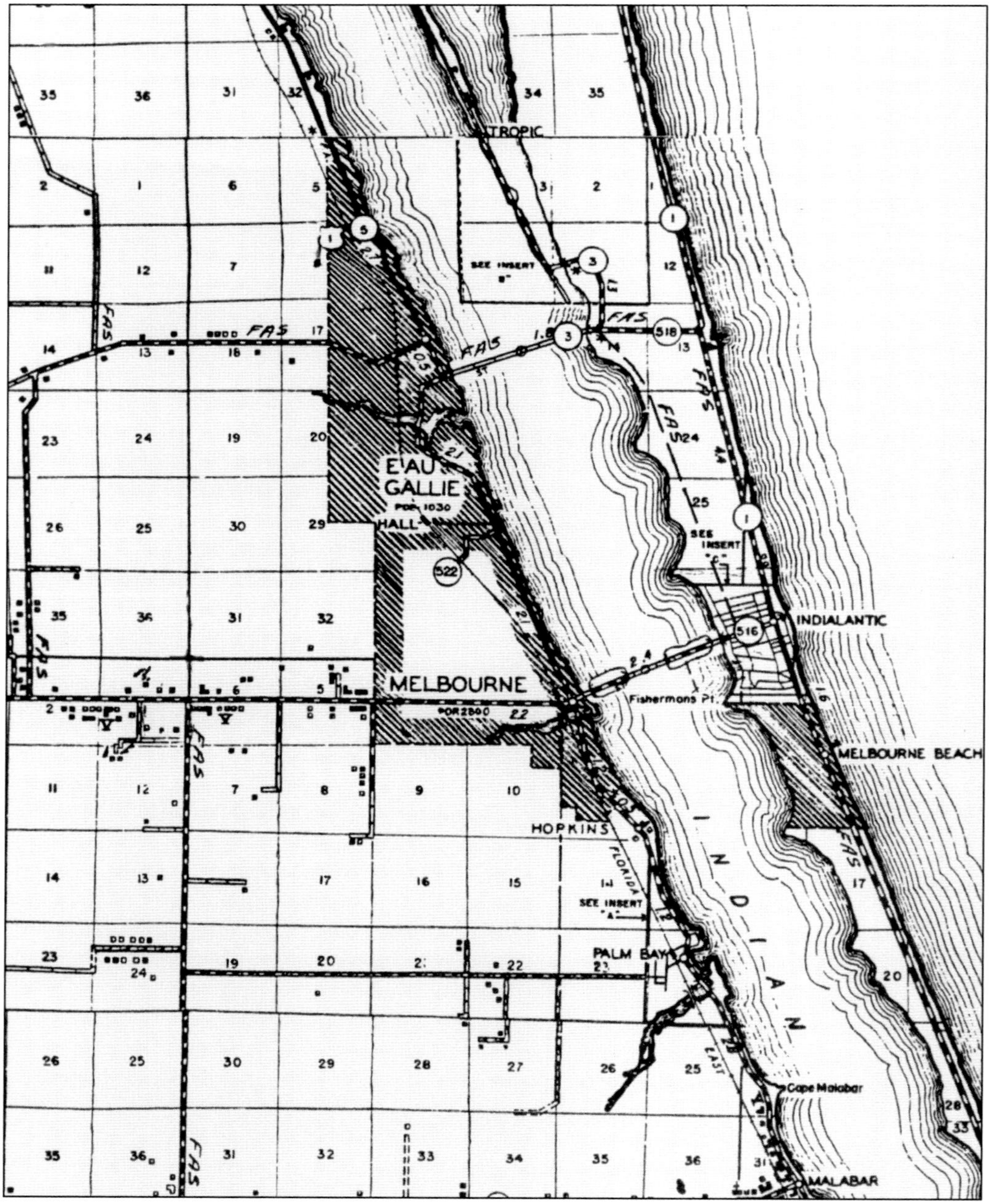

This is the General Highway and Transportation Map of Brevard County from the Florida State Road Department, 1936. Lake Washington, not shown, is to the west of Eau Gallie.

IMAGES
of America

Melbourne and Eau Gallie

Karen Raley and Ann Raley Flotte

ARCADIA
PUBLISHING

ISBN 978-0-7385-1417-8

Published by Arcadia Publishing
Charleston, South Carolina

Printed in the United States of America

Library of Congress Catalog Card Number: 2001098441

For all general information contact Arcadia Publishing at:
Telephone 843-853-2070
Fax 843-853-0044
E-mail sales@arcadiapublishing.com
For customer service and orders:
Toll-Free 1-888-313-2665

Visit us on the Internet at www.arcadiapublishing.com

Dedication

This book is dedicated to our mother, Vineta M. Raley, who has taught us how to live. Her love, support, and inspiration have never failed.

Contents

ACKNOWLEDGMENTS

The following organizations and companies allowed us to use photographs from their archives. We would like to thank the American Homesteading Foundation, BellSouth, the Brevard County Historical Commission, the City of Melbourne, the Florida Historical Society, Honor America Museum/Dorothy Rose Collection, the Florida State Historical Archives, the Melbourne Airport Authority, the Melbourne Police Department, Seabird Publishing, the South Brevard Historical Society/Goode Family Papers, Sterling Photography, the Tampa-Hillsborough Library/Burgert Brothers Collection, Time-Warner, the United States Air Force, and the United States Library of Congress/William Henry Jackson, Detroit Publishing Company Collection. We also wish to thank the individuals who magnanimously made available items from their private collections for inclusion in this book: William Barnett, Teddy Bell, Douglas Hendriksen, Phyllis Jordan, Anne Kaylor, William Lovin, Ada Parrish, Violet Seitner, Monica Tacy, and Peter Zies. Additional images are from the authors' collection.

Many other people generously provided us with historical information, photos, and much-appreciated assistance. They made our work enjoyable. We extend our heartfelt thanks to Chuck Baird, Gayle Baker, Gary Blackburn, Bobby Bowers, Betty Brown, V.C. Brownlie, Jessie and Hazel Buggs, Cammie Donaldson, Rachel Felton, Diana Flett, Bob Garvin, Carol Glanton, Amy Glaser, Spence Guerin, Mary Hayward, John Hiott, Pat Howlett, Drew Huy, Charles Jerry, Kathryn Kyzer, Betty Jean Maxwell, Dennis Meehan, Mike Moore, Ellen Wargelin Noyd, Betty Preece, Vineta Raley, Johnise Sapundjieff, Nancy Sewell, Yvonne Shingler, John Short, Francis Snow, Dan Striby, Philip Williams, Nick and Debra Wynne, Cathy Wysor, the staff at A Better Copy, and numerous others. We are especially grateful to Jim Culberson, Bob Gross, Douglas Hendrikson, and William Lovin for their help and suggestions.

Finally, we would like to acknowledge our debt to the following historians who have recorded their memories and research: Jim Ball, Thomas Barbour, William Barnett, Bobby Bowen, Weona Cleveland, Jim Culberson, Jonathan Dickinson, Ray Fagan, Vera Ferguson, Roz Foster, Lansing Gleason, Harry Goode, Bob Gross, Miriam Hicks, Fred Hopwood, Phyllis Hoskins, Georgiana Kjerulff, Stephen Kosinski, Elizabeth Nutting, Steven Olausen, Irving Rouse, Betty Shanks, Jerrell Shoffner, Elaine Stone, Frank Thomas, Ed Vosatka, Joe Wickham, and Vera Zimmerman.

Our special acknowledgement is to Weona Cleveland who has devotedly investigated and written the history of South Brevard for over 30 years. Through her numerous interviews of old-timers and her persistent combing of records, she has provided an incomparable gift for the people of this area to share with one another.

Introduction

Melbourne and Eau Gallie are two Florida river towns that were established in the late 19th century and came of age during the hardships and booms of the 20th century. Bound together by a river, railroad, highway, and a regional economy, the towns were both neighbors and rivals. While they were still young, the little cities argued over which one was bigger, better, or more virtuous. One journalist compared the number of churches and bars each had and concluded that Eau Gallie was a more upstanding place to live! Competitors in sports and business, the two towns were also linked by social and family relationships. In 1969, the old rivalry was stymied with the unification of the two cities under one government. The residents voted to keep Melbourne's name, but the new city would grow beyond the identities of the two older towns. With a population of over 71,000 people today, Melbourne is a composite of many neighborhoods, old and new.

Geographic location and the natural environment were critical to the character of Melbourne and Eau Gallie. Both towns were settled at the junction of large creeks and the Indian River, a lagoon where salt and fresh water mix. Early survival depended on the river as a source of both sustenance and transportation, and the river provided amply. The land was also rich in wildlife, and farming was not difficult. Mindful of civic improvement in their close-knit communities, the settlers built churches, schools, and public services. By the late 19th century, Melbourne and Eau Gallie were growing frontier towns with viable social, political, and economic structures.

When the railroad came in the 1890s, it pushed the little towns along Florida's east coast into the mainstream of 20th-century America. Efficient rail transportation made large-scale agriculture, timber operations, and tourism feasible. The railroad caused a significant increase in the populations and economies of the two communities, which ended their isolation and slow pace. The advent of railroad travel did not immediately render river traffic obsolete, however, and the towns kept their Indian River identities. They chartered yacht clubs, improved their harbors, and wooed the winter visitors from the northern states.

Melbourne and Eau Gallie were like other Florida towns during the booming 1920s, and large Mediterranean Revival hotels sprang up on their main streets. The Dixie Highway (US #1) was completed from Miami to Jacksonville and began to compete with the railroad as the most important influence on the area's economy. Tourists took to the road as mass production made motor vehicles available to ordinary people. Real estate schemes and housing construction increased rapidly during the 1920s and automobiles, telephones, plumbing, and other modern conveniences changed the way people lived.

Because Melbourne and Eau Gallie were located midway between Jacksonville and Miami, they became ideal refueling and overnight stops on the new Dixie Highway. In the 1920s, the two towns sprouted campgrounds, motels, and gas stations. Oil companies built large tank facilities, and their local agents prospered. Tourists, winter residents, and beach visitors were suddenly just as important as the citrus and timber production, and US #1 was their thoroughfare.

The bottom fell out of the Florida Land Boom well before the famous "Crash of '29." Real estate schemes collapsed with a national decline in new construction by 1926. That year, two disastrous hurricanes helped push the Florida boom into history. Successful businesses failed and the Great Depression left the big hotels empty. The little cities suffered, and Eau Gallie was forced to declare bankruptcy in 1938, defaulting on a debt of nearly $400,000. With the war came a reversal of fortune when the Melbourne and Banana River Naval Air Stations were built. In the 1950s, this military and aviation presence blossomed into the United States Space Program.

The space industry had the greatest impact on the area from 1957 through the mid-1970s, and local population soared. In one year, Melbourne grew from 5,000 to 15,000 residents. This rapid influx of people occurred at the same time the Baby Boom children across the country were creating a need for more schools. With federal assistance, Brevard County expanded its roads, educational systems, utilities, businesses, cultural amenities, and housing. Growth was extraordinary and, to save on duplication of services, Eau Gallie and Melbourne merged in 1969.

This volume takes us from the earliest times along the Indian River and the founding of Melbourne and Eau Gallie through their first hundred years of social and economic maturation. As we end our story in 1970, the newly unified City of Melbourne was poised for even greater development during the last quarter of the 20th century. Its major industries—technology, tourism, and retirement living—and its modernized infrastructure would combine with natural and cultural amenities to make more expansion in the 1980s inevitable.

One

Along the River

Unspoiled scenes, very similar to the ones the first inhabitants saw, still exist in places along the Indian River. This view of birds nesting in the mangroves that grow along the shore is typical of the area. Mangrove roots provide a nursery for a multitude of marine creatures, and their branches provide nests for the birds. The Indian River is a long, narrow lagoon fed by fresh-water creeks and salt-water inlets. An ecological treasure, the Indian River has always been known for its abundance and variety of marine life and birds. Its shores teemed with game and offered good foraging to the early humans who came to the area. After the Haulover Canal connected the north end of the Indian River to Mosquito Lagoon in 1854, moderate-sized boats could journey south from the Halifax River, which ended the seclusion of the Indian River area. Today, the Indian River is part of the Intracoastal Waterway and a channel runs the length of the shallow lagoon.

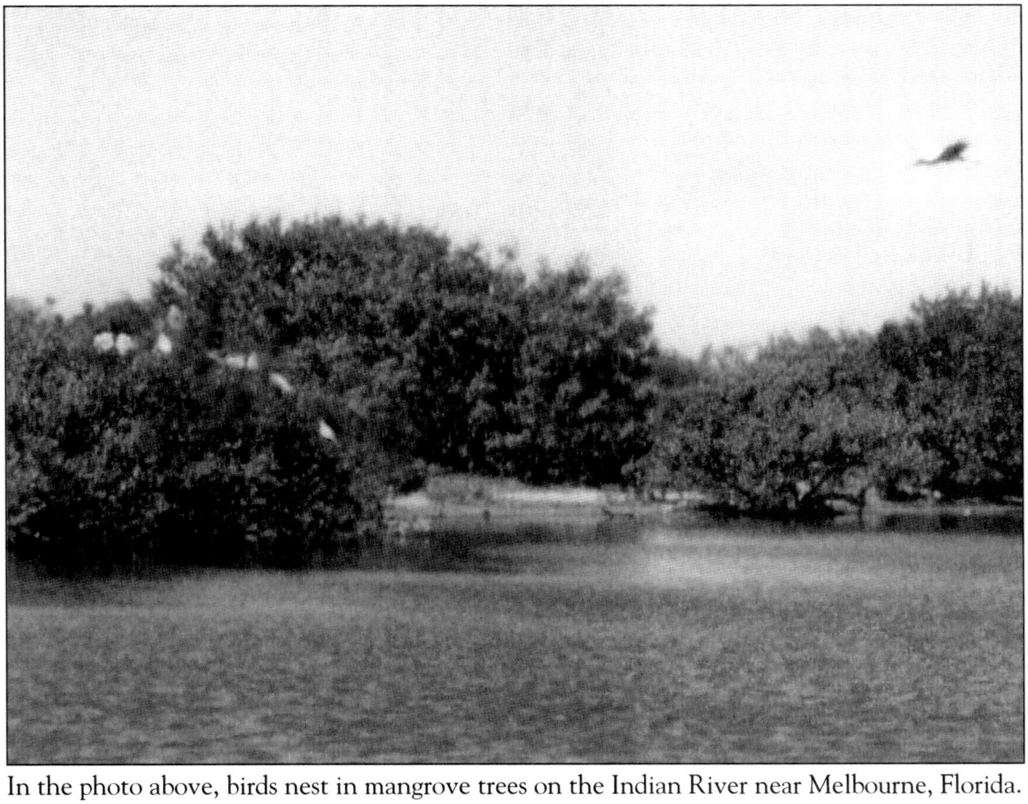

In the photo above, birds nest in mangrove trees on the Indian River near Melbourne, Florida.

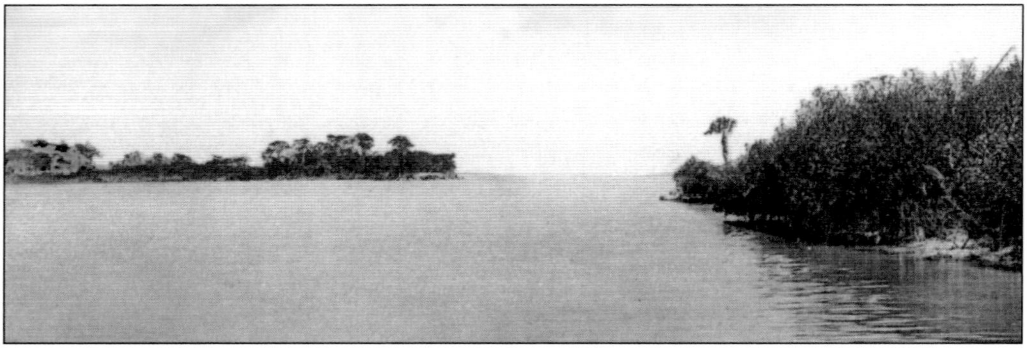

Before the Spanish arrived, the Indian River area was inhabited by the Ais people. The winter site of their village, Pentoaya, included the southern end of Merritt Island, shown on the right above, and the opposite shore of the Banana River, on the left. In the summer, Pentoaya moved to the north shore of the Eau Gallie River where US #1 crosses today. The Ais fished, hunted, and gathered plants. They plied the waters in dugout canoes and built houses of thatched palm. The Ais produced woven clothing and baskets, plaited mats, clay pottery, bows, arrows, spears, decorative items, and musical instruments. They had local governments, religion, medicine, and a network of trade and cooperation with other peoples. On occasion, the Ais resisted Spanish intrusion. By the 1760s, deaths from European diseases had taken a severe toll, and the few Ais who remained joined other groups and moved away from the area.

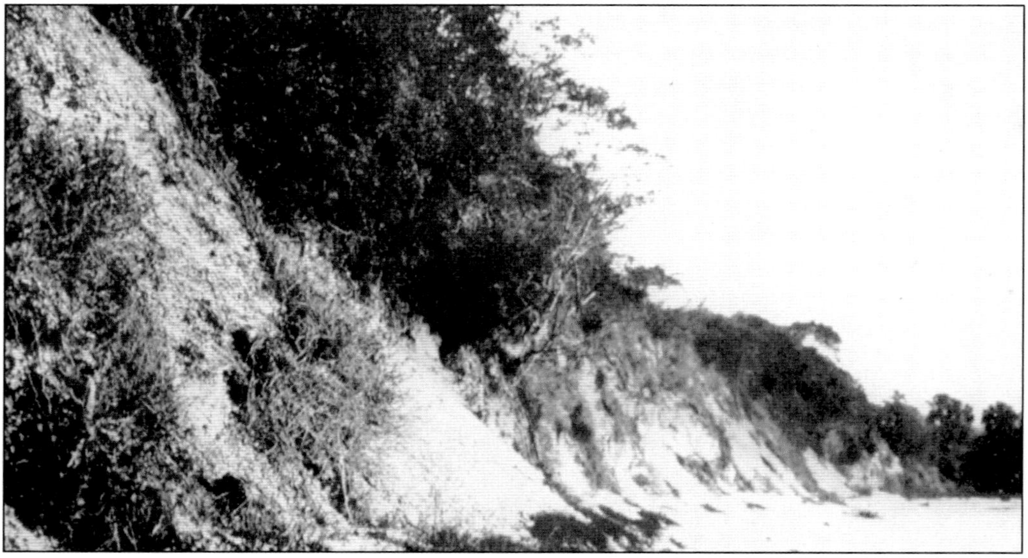

The Ais left behind mounds of shells and other discarded items called middens. Most of these have been dismantled and used as road pavement. Shown here is the 30-foot Ais midden that stood on the east shore of the Banana River opposite the tip of Merritt Island. In 1912, naturalist and sometime Eau Gallie resident Thomas Barbour found artifacts, shards, bones, and shells there. Today, the land is covered in homes and yacht anchorages. The mound has been removed, but its lower level is still obvious on the remaining undeveloped lot. Other Native American sites in the area include a midden in Melbourne at the end of the river bluff, just north of New Haven Avenue, and extensive diggings at A.T. Anderson's South Indian Field at the west end of Malabar Road. The most celebrated find of Indian remains in Melbourne was the unearthing of the fossilized bones of the "Melbourne Man" in 1925–1926 at the Golf Course. Archeological excavation there ended in the 1930s. The sites along the river are almost entirely unexplored.

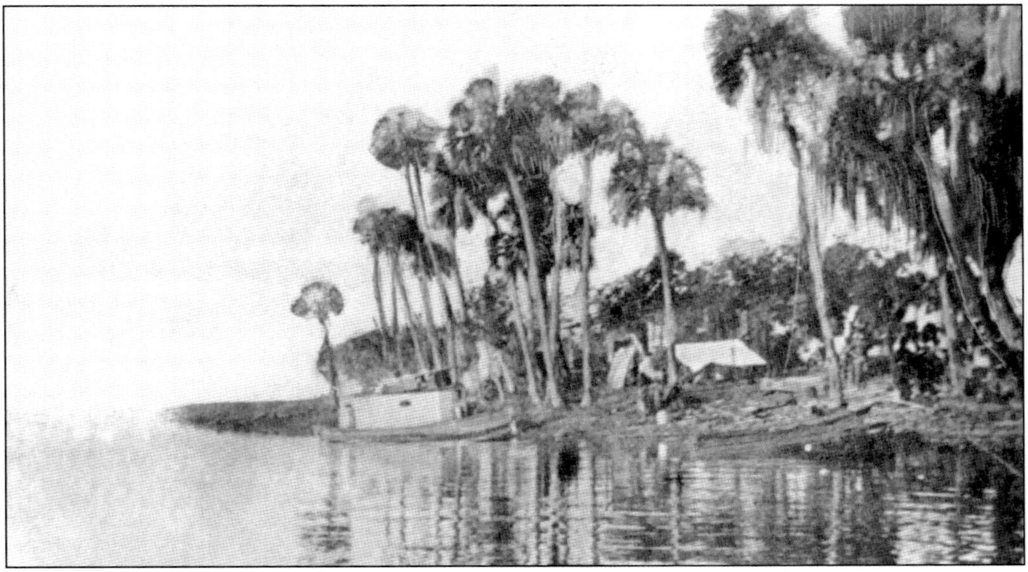

The photo above is a late 19th-century view of early settlers or campers along the shores of the Indian River. In the early years of the 19th century, Florida became a haven for runaway slaves and native people who were seeking safer ground. After the Civil War, both whites and freed slaves homesteaded in Florida, typically erecting a chickee or palmetto-thatched structure to live in while they built a log cabin. Later, they might cover the cabin with clapboard siding or build a larger house of sawn lumber.

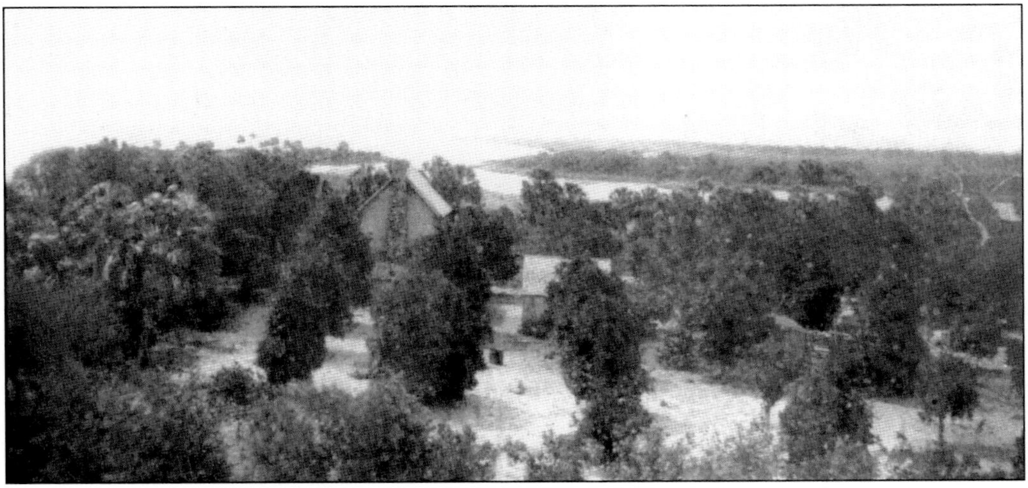

The first settlers at Melbourne (then called Crane Creek) were three freedmen—Capt. Peter Wright, Balaam Allan (or Allen), and Wright Brothers—who arrived in 1867. Allan and Brothers became citrus growers and Wright became South Brevard's first mail carrier. He sailed from Titusville to St. Lucie twice weekly to deliver the mail. This view of Peter Wright's house, c.1886, shows some of his plantings, probably citrus trees. The house stood just west of the river bluff between present-day Strawbridge and New Haven Avenues. Wright's land and that of Thomas Mason, the first white homesteader, became the heart of the town of Melbourne. Balaam Allan and Wright Brothers homesteaded large parcels of land that were south of the creek. In 1885, the Allen, Brothers, and Lipscomb families organized the Allen Chapel AME Church.

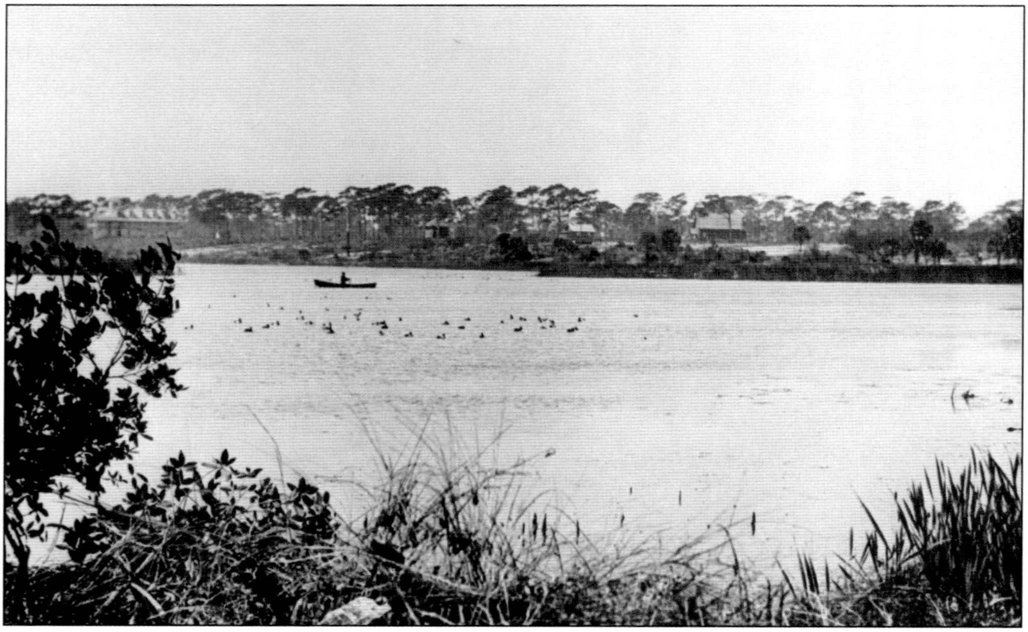

This view shows Melbourne's Crane Creek harbor area. Above is "Melbourne Bay" as renowned tourist William Henry Jackson noted when he took this photograph, c.1880. His vantage point is the south side of Crane Creek, near the spot where US #1 crosses today, looking north at a tiny Melbourne on the opposite shore. The Goode House is just visible at the left. The most practical way to reach the settlement of Crane Creek, later named Melbourne, was by boat.

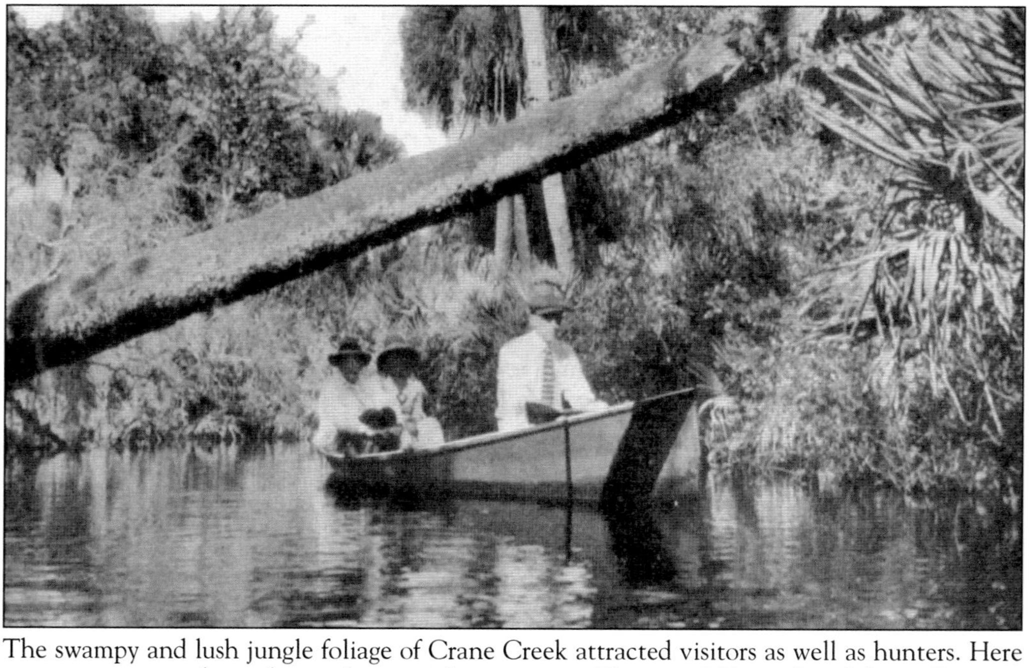

The swampy and lush jungle foliage of Crane Creek attracted visitors as well as hunters. Here a man rows a couple up the creek on a sightseeing trip. They would have found deer, alligators, raccoons, turtles, fish, birds, and possibly even a manatee or wildcat on their trip. In every season but winter, they would also have encountered mosquitoes. The creek retains its aura of unspoiled beauty in several places today.

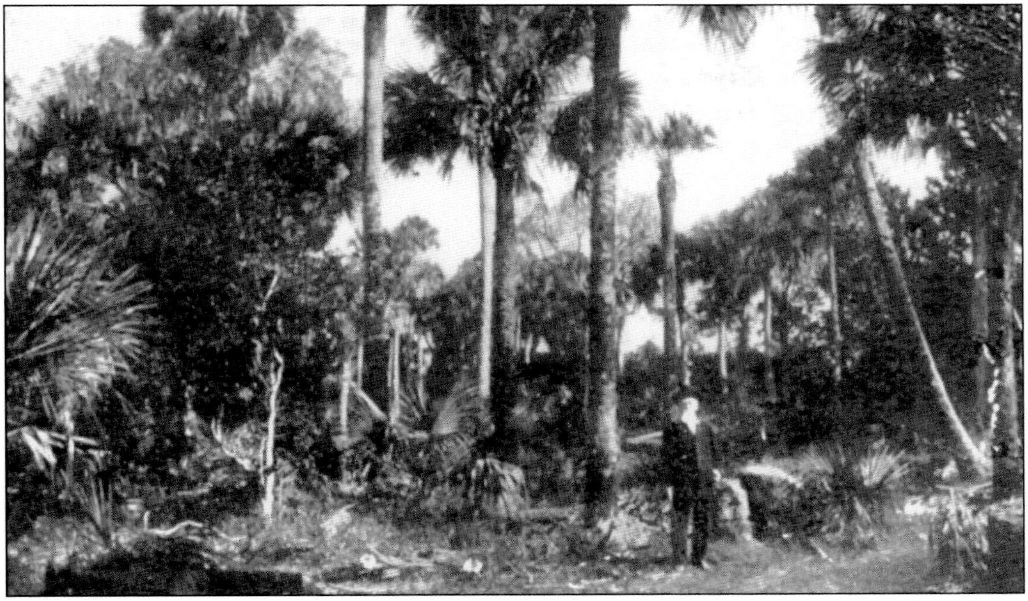

Richard Goode stands on the land he has just purchased from Thomas Mason in this photo. In 1877, Goode brought his wife and three children from Chicago to Crane Creek. Their original homestead was more than 150 acres and included the headwaters of the creek. In 1882, Goode's father, John Goode, brought his wife and two other children to the area and they settled on the south side of the creek. Richard Goode's original cabin was near Roxy Avenue. In 1884, on a site overlooking Crane Creek, Goode built the Goode House, a two-story family home and hotel.

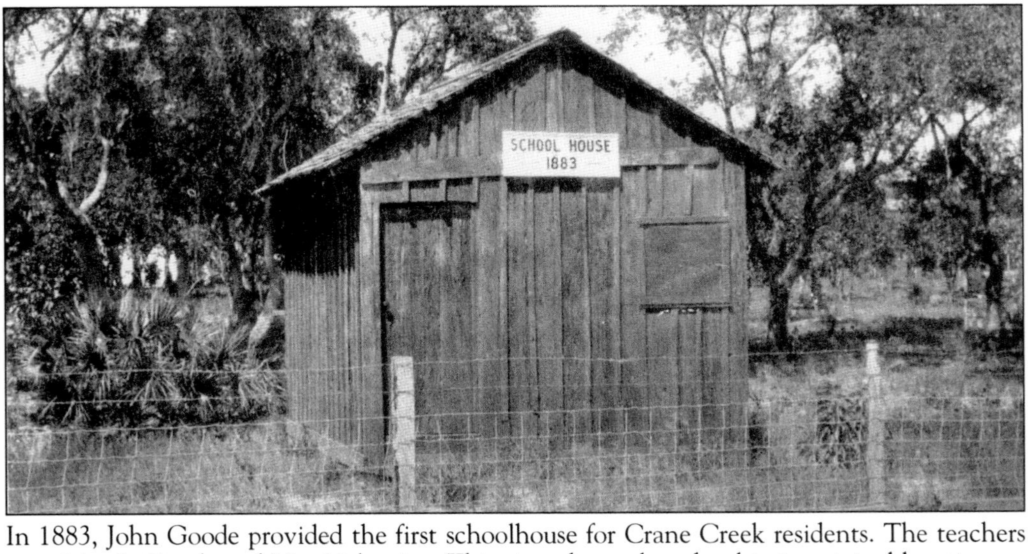

In 1883, John Goode provided the first schoolhouse for Crane Creek residents. The teachers were Maude Goode and May Valentine. This view shows the school in its original location on Riverview Drive. The school was segregated, with white children attending in the mornings and black children in the afternoons. The first students were Grace, Annie, Alex, and Jessie Goode; Fred, Edith, and Helen Valentine; Isabelle and John Clohecy; Lafayette, Balaam, and Susie Allan; Willie Brothers; George Washington Blaine, and Lizzie Trott. The school was moved from this site in the 1950s and became a home in South Melbourne. It has since been refurbished and then moved to the campus of Florida Institute of Technology.

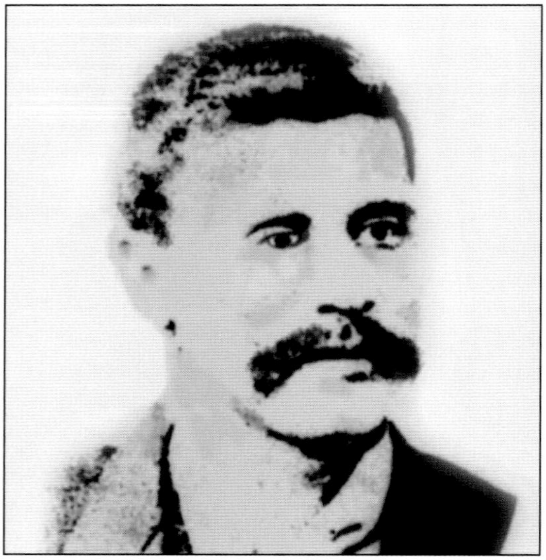

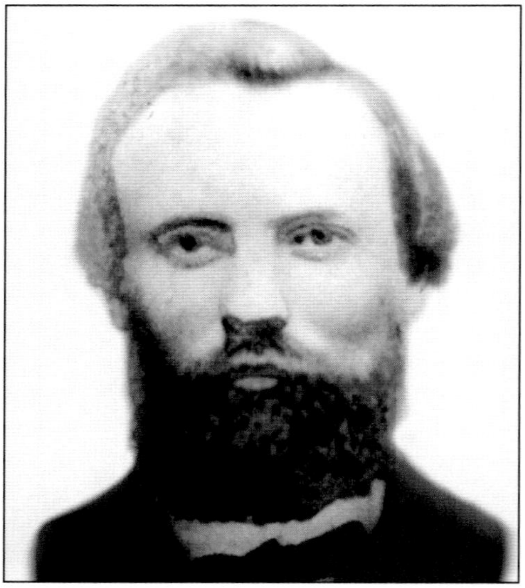

(*above, left*) John C. Houston, with his son and slaves, came down to Brevard County in 1859 to clear and homestead an 80-acre community. Houston called the settlement Arlington and gave Elbow Creek its name because of its shape. His homestead was a world in itself as the group farmed, fished, hunted, traded with Indians, and manufactured their own salt and molasses. (*above, right*) In 1870, William H. Gleason acquired 16,000 acres stretching from the Indian River to Lake Washington. He founded and platted the town of Eau Gallie (Rocky Water) in 1884, which he named for the coquina rock along the shoreline. He dreamed of a canal that would extend the Eau Gallie River to Lake Washington, thus connecting the Indian and St. Johns Rivers. On land Gleason donated for a state land grant college, Florida convicts erected a 10-room coquina rock building on the shore of the Indian River in 1875.

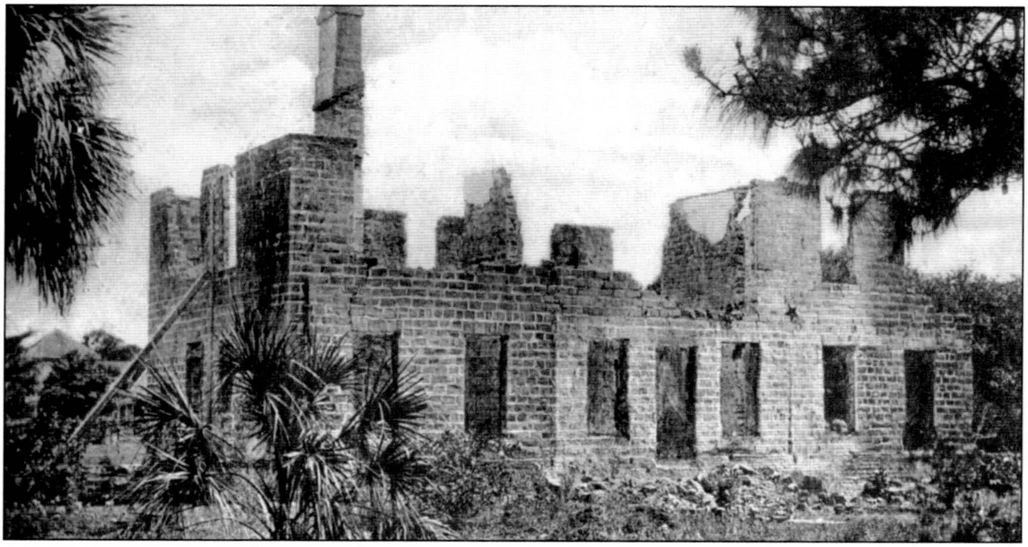

Although Eau Gallie became the county seat, it was so out-of-the-way the state decided to change the location of the college. Gleason moved his family into the empty building and opened it as the Granada Hotel in 1883. Looking for another way to make Eau Gallie accessible, he gave land to the Florida East Coast Railway. The photo above shows the ruins of the Granada after it burned in 1902. The hotel was near the eastern end of present-day Aurora Road.

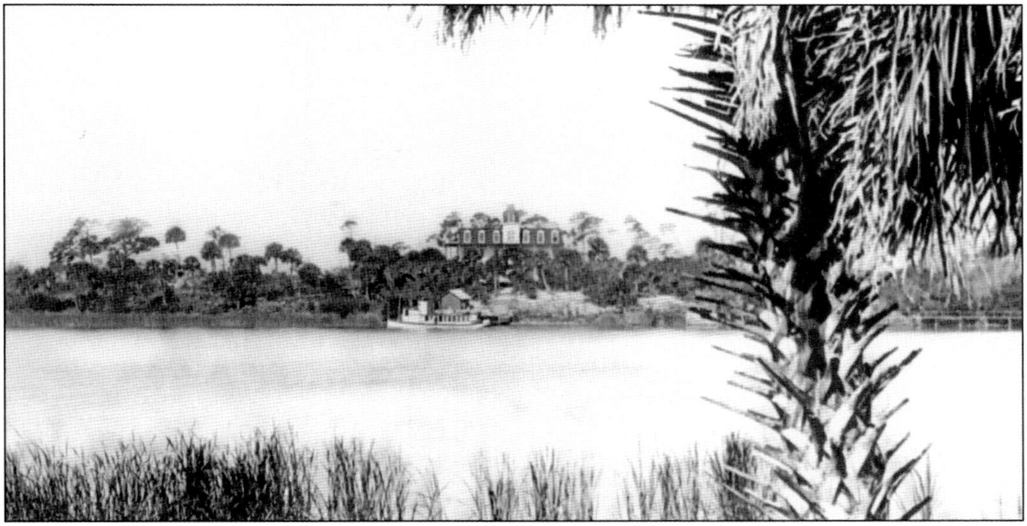

In 1888–1889, William and Albertina Treutler of Chicago built a lovely three-story hotel on the north side of the Eau Gallie River, just east of the US #1 Bridge today. The hotel was popular with early tourists and served as a home for the newly organized Episcopalian congregation. Treutler called his property Hyde Park, and the road leading there still bears that name. The hotel burned in 1893, and the Treutlers built the Riverview Hotel on another site. To get the photograph above, William Henry Jackson stood across the Eau Gallie River and looked north. We can see a launch at the dock of the hotel. In the photo below, two men pose on the front walkway. The man on the right may be Treutler and the man just left of him is probably the captain of the launch seen above.

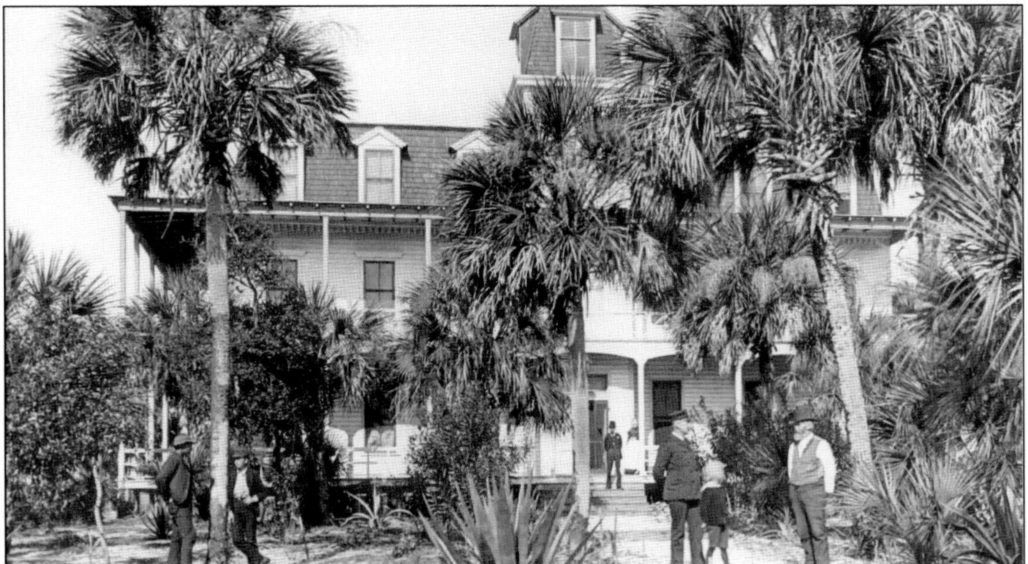

Soon after Houston and Gleason settled in Eau Gallie, the little village had a post office, a school, and a fledgling government. In the 1870s, A.G. Hill and H.R. Olmstead opened stores, and steamers began stopping at the shore. In the 1880s, Gleason platted the town and opened a sawmill. Next came the Hodgson Brothers, who went into business building and repairing boats. Aaron Bennett opened his boatyard in 1896. Eau Gallie had begun to prosper as a river town.

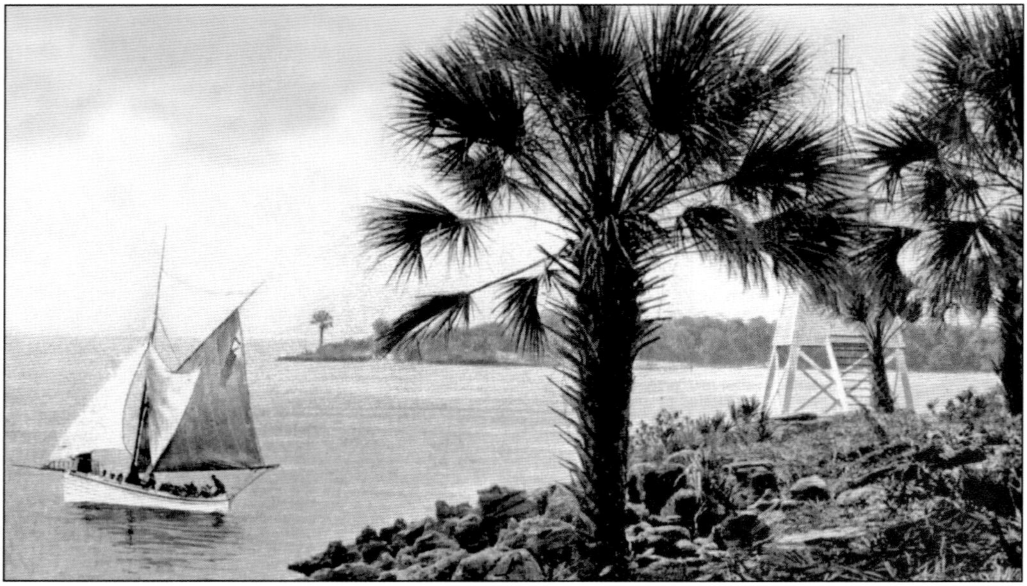

Above is a view of the junction of the Eau Gallie and Indian Rivers, looking south toward Aspinwall (Lone Cabbage) Point. On the right is the Eau Gallie beacon, which was erected on the tip of Sunny Point in 1906. Some of the foundation material for the beacon still exists today. You can see the large outcropping of coquina rock that characterized this part of the shore. The Eau Gallie was dredged and fill deposited on the southern side, creating Ballard Park. So much of the coquina has been removed for building projects that replacement rock has been added to parts of the shore.

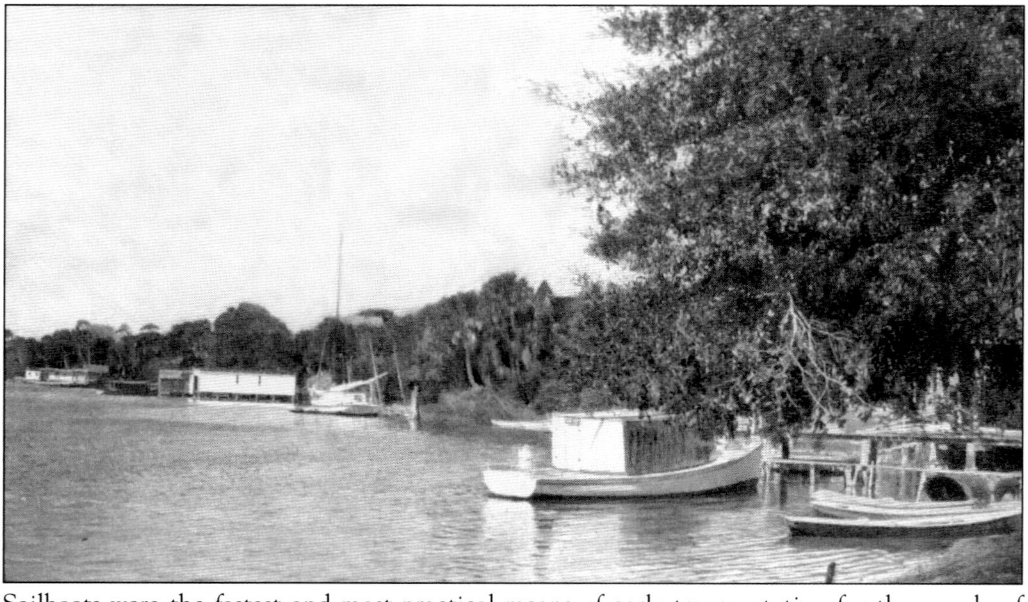

Sailboats were the fastest and most practical means of early transportation for the people of the Indian River area. Boats provided transportation, work, and recreation. People from communities along the river gathered to hold regular sailboat races, and boat building became one of Eau Gallie's major industries. Below is the northern shoreline of the Eau Gallie River. The boats in the foreground are tied up at Hodgson's boatyard. In the distance are Bennett's boatyard and yacht basin.

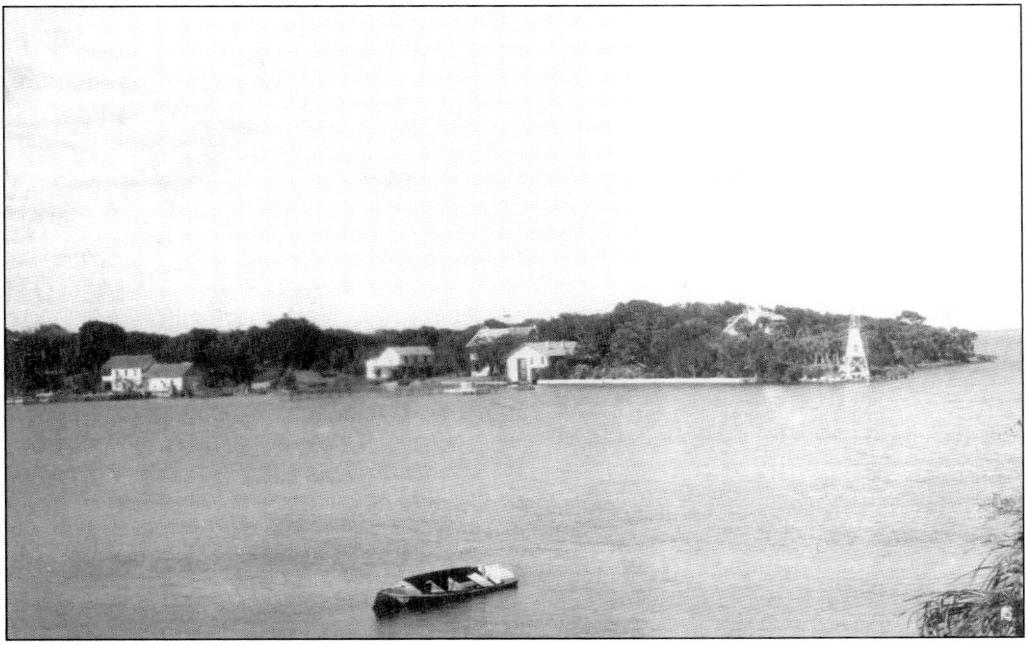

This is a photo of the Eau Gallie River, looking northeastward. In the center are Hodgson's Boatyard and the Eau Gallie Yacht Club. At the far right is the Eau Gallie beacon. Behind the beacon and to its left is Sunny Point, the residence of the Ballards, prominent Eau Gallie socialites. The northern shore, which would later be filled with more boathouses, businesses, and homes, looks quaintly bare in this view.

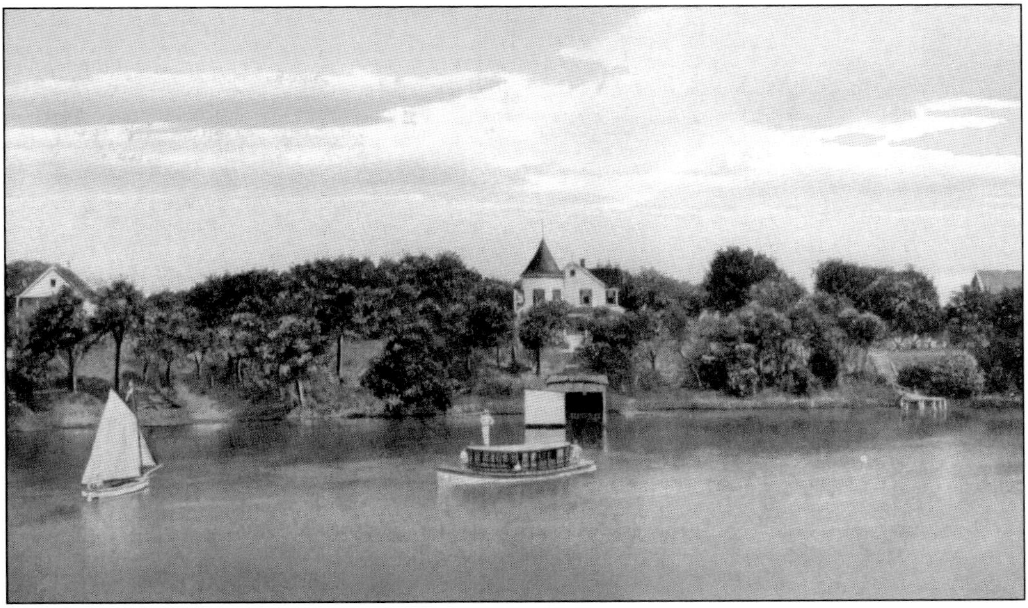

Shown above is a view of the residential section of the town along the north shore of the Eau Gallie River.

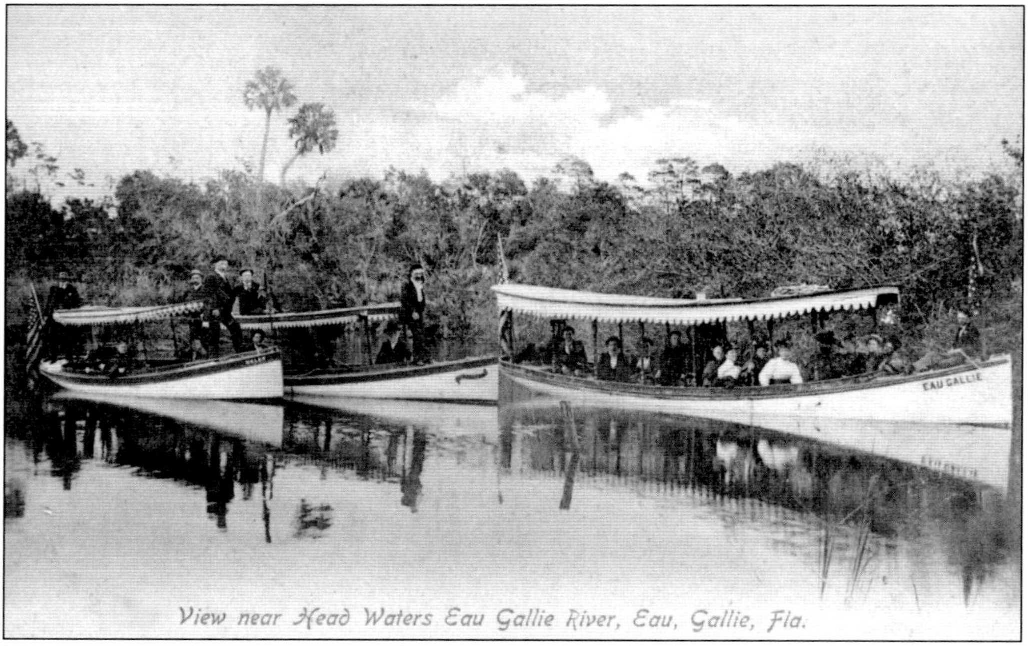

Three passenger launches pause in the Eau Gallie River *c.* 1905. The boat at the far right is the *Eau Gallie*; in the bow is Capt. George G. Gleason and fourth from the stern is George Paddison. Eau Gallie was a growing village at the time and these men were prosperous land and business owners. Gleason called his land along the river "Fountain Heights." Still in family hands, the property contains his little manmade inlet, Gleason's Cut or Gleason's Basin. When Gleason had it designed, it was large enough to harbor modest-sized boats.

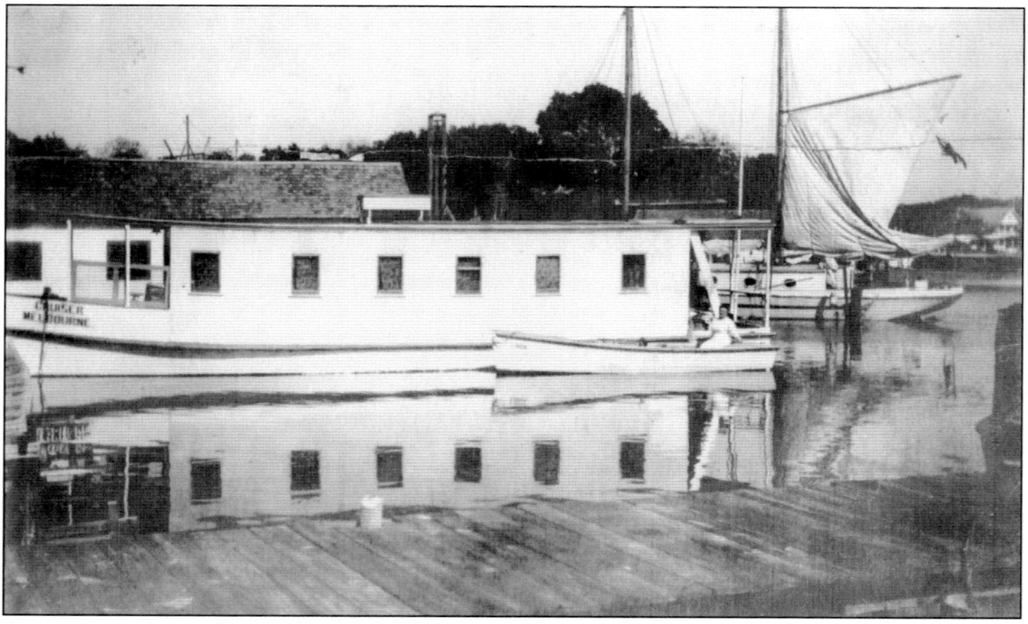

Boats waiting at anchor in the Eau Gallie River include a pretty sailboat and a houseboat named the *Cruiser Melbourne*.

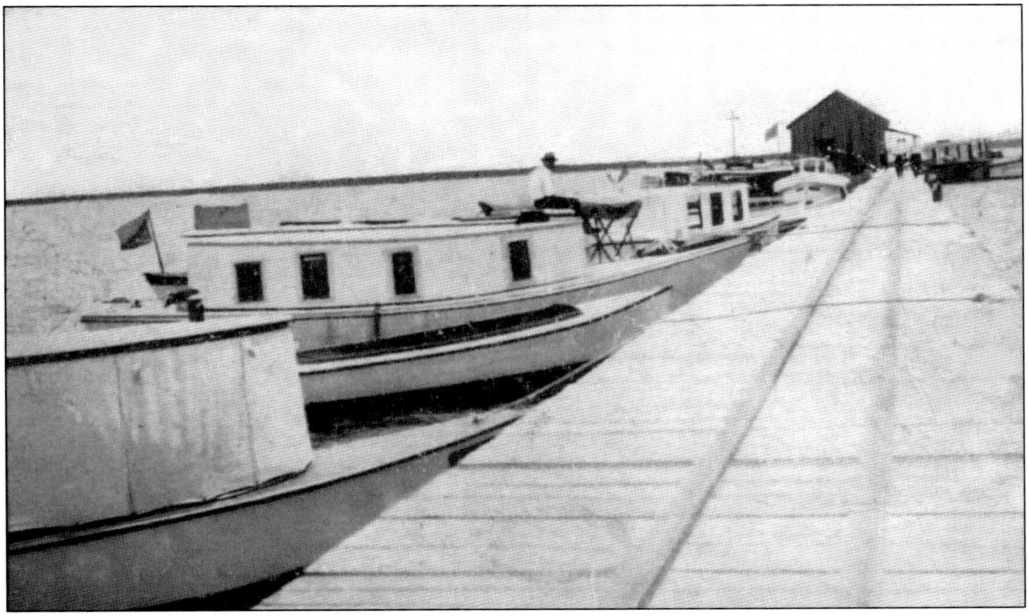

Before the railroad came in 1893, the main means of passenger and cargo transport to Indian River towns was by steamer. The Indian River is so shallow that long piers had to be built out to deeper waters where the steamboats navigated. Melbourne's City Pier, built in 1886, was 1,440 feet long and was located at the north end of the Front Street business district and at the foot of New Haven Avenue. The pier was T-shaped with a freight house at the end. Trolley tracks extended its full length so freight and passengers could be pushed from boat to shore in a handcart.

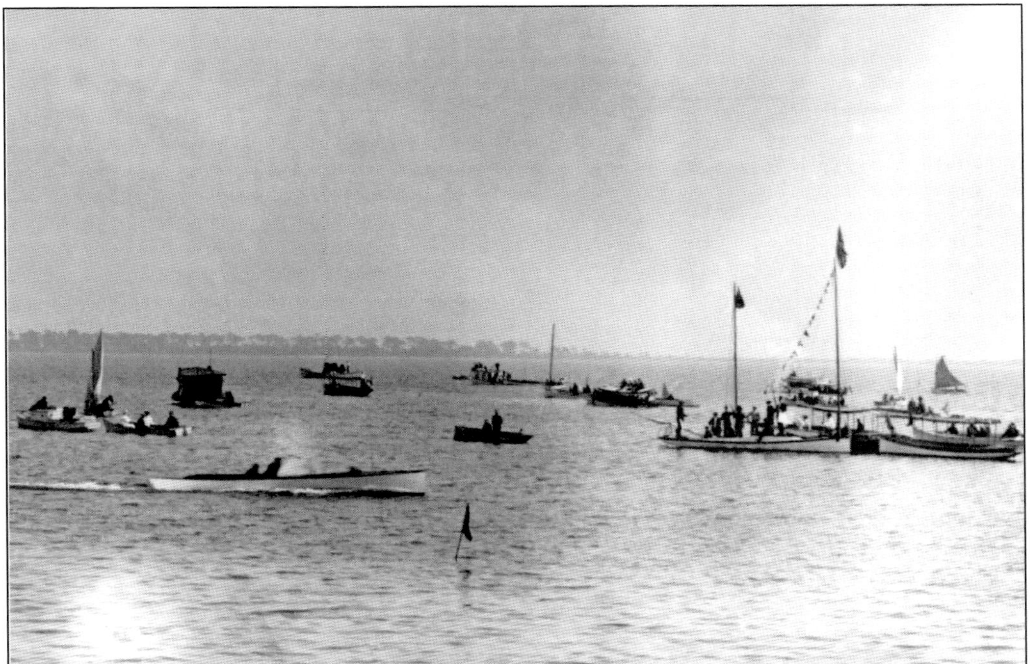

Sailboats seen here are preparing to race in Melbourne's 1902 Regatta. Fisherman's Point or East Melbourne, today known as Indialantic, is visible in the background.

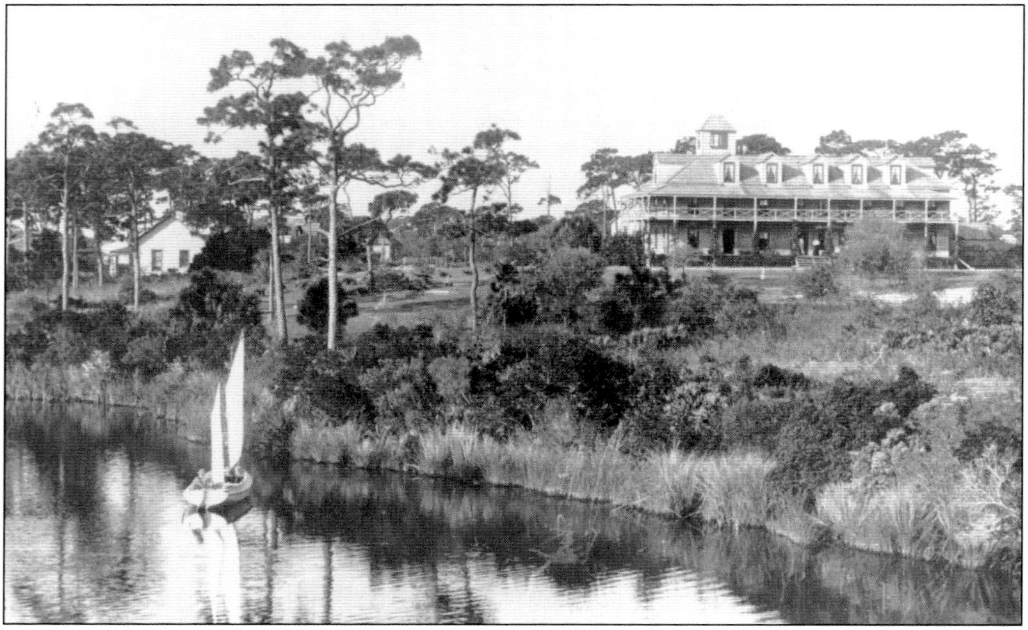

The view above is of the hotel built by the Goodes, later sold to C.J.F. Campbell, whose mother enlarged it and changed its name to the Bellevue Hotel. Later it was renamed the Orange Spot Inn. The hotel was accessible in the early days by boat from Crane Creek, which it overlooked. Many of the best views of Crane Creek Harbor were taken from the upper windows of this structure, which burned in 1927. Today, apartments stand on the site.

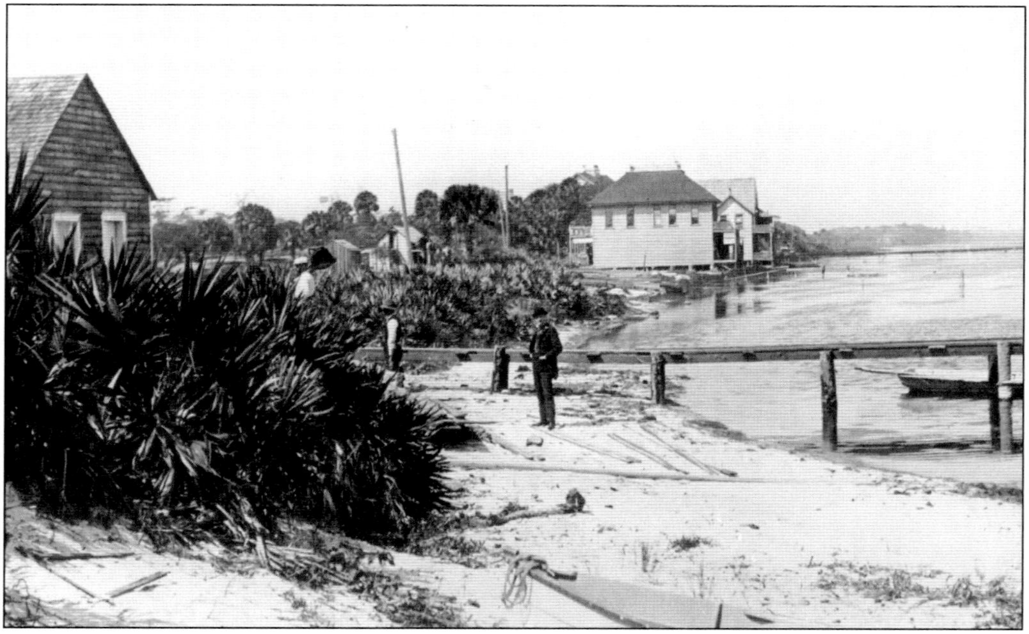

This photo was taken looking north toward Melbourne's business district from Cornthwaite J. Hector's pier. The Front Street stores backed up to the river so freight could be unloaded directly. At the southern end of the point were Hector's home, store, pier, and post office. The little settlement incorporated as Melbourne in 1888, and streets and lots were platted.

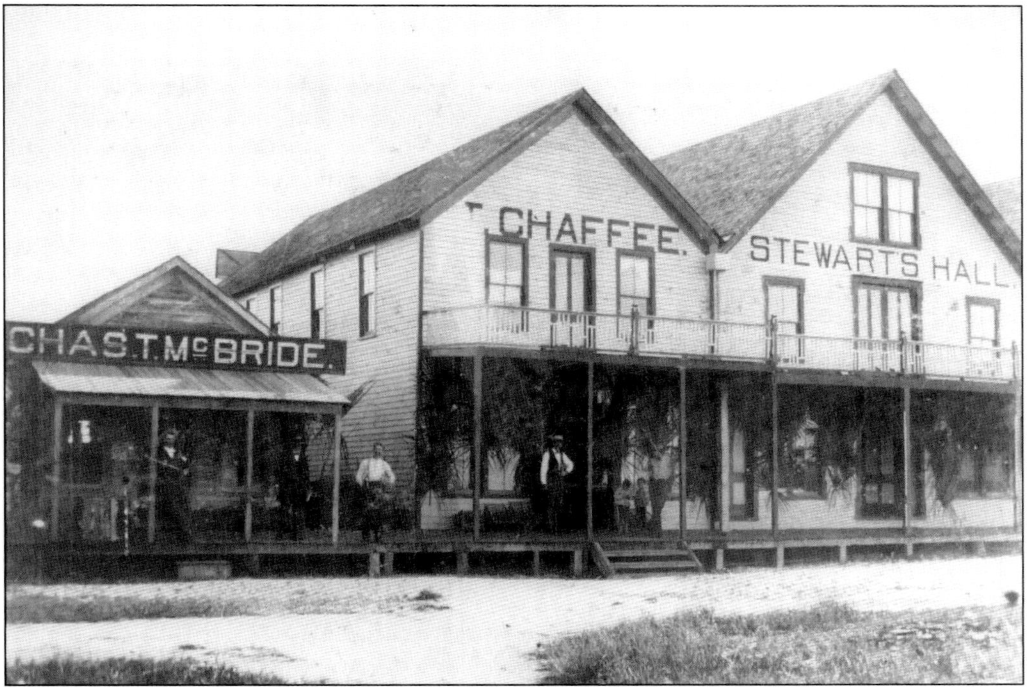

This photograph was taken c.1900 of three stores on Front Street that backed up to the Indian River. Charles McBride came to Melbourne in 1884 and worked for C.J. Hector for 10 years before opening his own store. Charles and Mabel Stewart, who came to Melbourne in 1888, owned Stewart's Hall, a hardware store and funeral home. Stewart and his wife were well-educated, loved books and classical music, but they wanted to be pioneers so they came to Melbourne. Stewart, also a pharmacist, opened the first drug store between Key West and Titusville. He moved his hardware store to New Haven Avenue where he and his nephew, Arthur, continued the business. Other early businesses on Front Street were the Riverside Hotel and E.P. Branch's store, built in 1886. The view below shows Front Street looking south down the path to Cornthwaite Hector's store in about 1900.

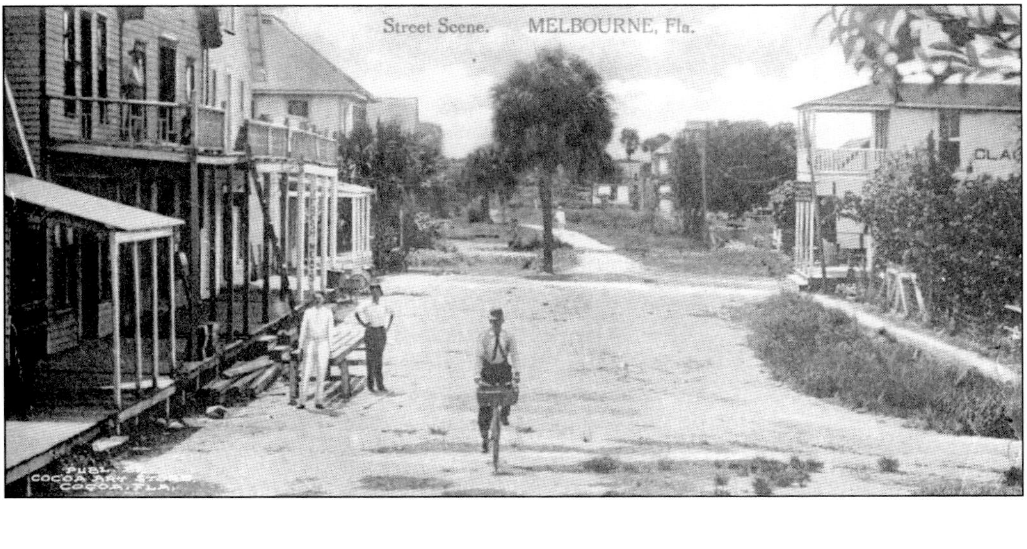

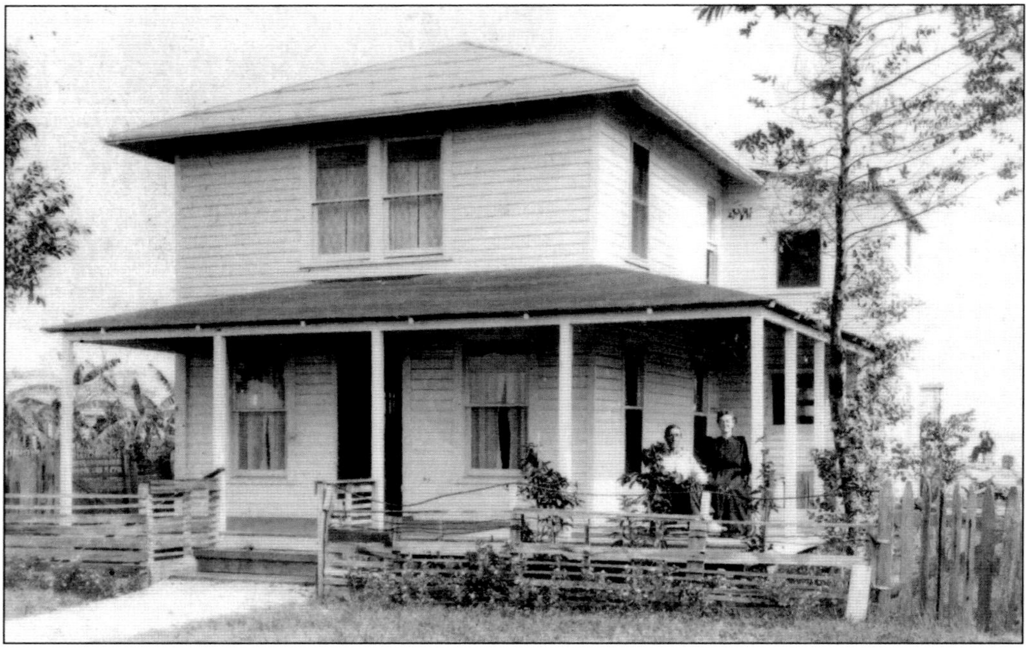

William Scott, Melbourne's harbormaster, and his wife, Mary, sit on the porch of their Front Street home. L.K. Smith built the house in 1888. It was condemned by the city and burned in 1970.

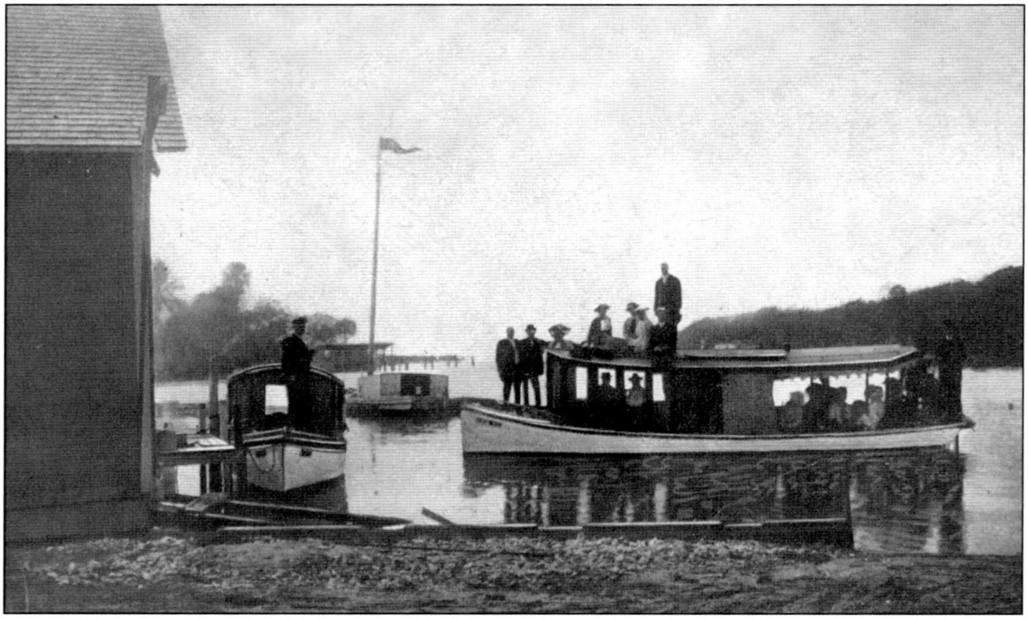

This is another scene in Melbourne's Crane Creek harbor taken before the turn of the last century. These small launches are nosing up to a dock on the north shore of the creek. Melbourne residents built a bridge over the creek near its mouth. It had a hand-operated draw that allowed boats to pass into the harbor. Today this area is desirable riverfront property, and older less valuable structures have been replaced by development that is more expensive. There are two bridges over the creek, and the harbor is filled with large boats.

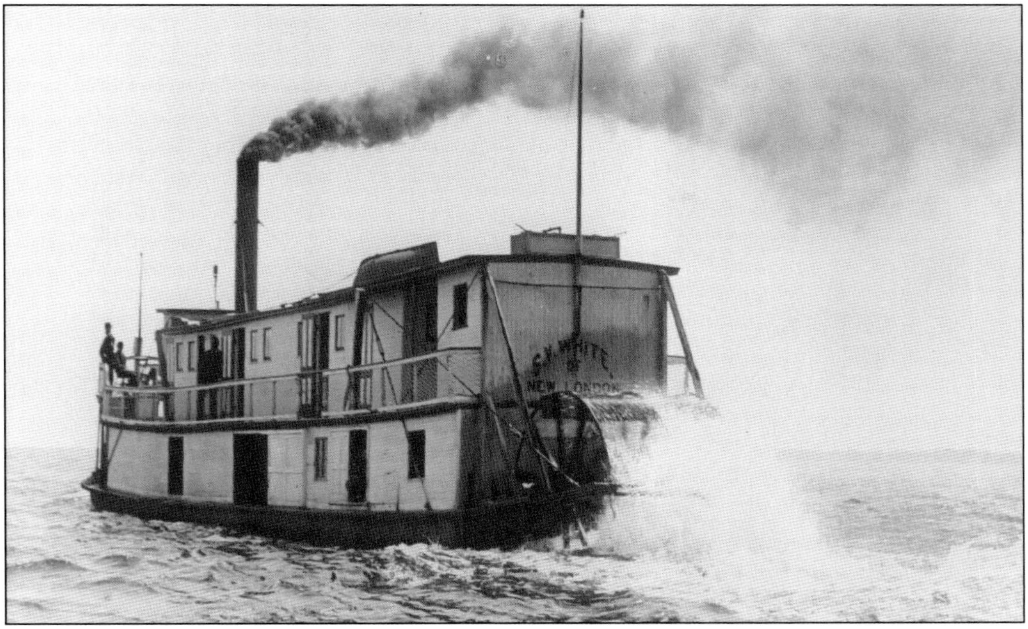

The S.V. *White*, a moderate-sized stern-wheeler, navigates the Indian River in about 1889. Steamers, sailboats, rowboats, and canoes all plied the Indian River and kept trade going before the railroad and good roads were available. The shallow depth of the lagoon made steamers of a moderate size the most practical means of transportation. Capt. Thomas Lund brought the first steamboat, the *Pioneer*, to the lagoon in 1877. By 1884, the Hodgson Brothers of Eau Gallie established a boatyard and telegraph office at the foot of Houston Street. Four years later, they built the steamer *Kathleen*.

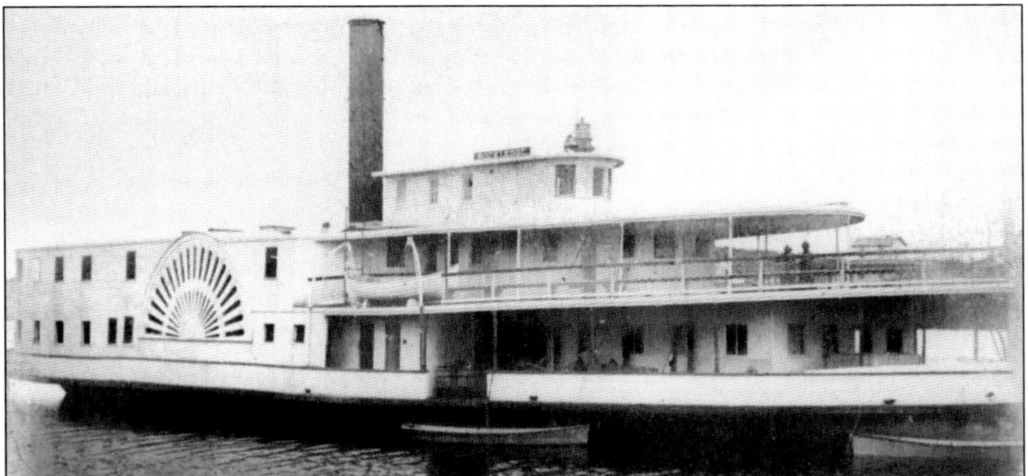

The largest steamer on the river was the Rockledge, brought to Brevard through the Fort Pierce Inlet by Capt. R.P. Paddison in 1886. Paddison made Melbourne her homeport and the Rockledge made daily trips to Titusville, where the railroad terminus was located. Passengers and freight could connect there for the journey north. The *Rockledge*, a side-wheeler, could travel eight miles per hour, no matter which way the wind blew! The big steamer brought daily mail service to tiny Melbourne, whose population was only about 70 people at the time.

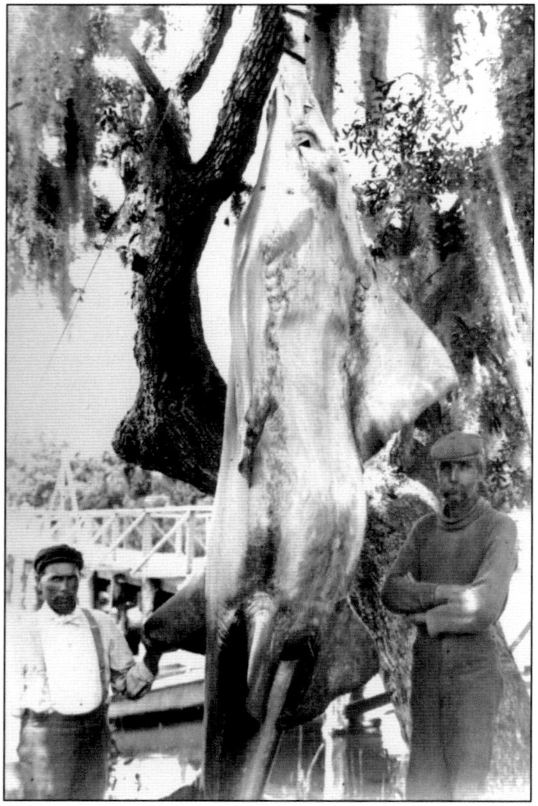

Jim Bird, on the left, and Bob Mattox, on the right, proudly pose with this sawfish, caught in the Indian River in the early 1900s. The river was known for amply providing many different kinds of fish and shellfish. The bridge in the background is the same one that appears on the cover of this volume. It was built in 1886 and connected the north and south sides of Crane Creek. Extending from the southwest portion of Stewart's Point, near the Beaujean and Martin Boatyard, to the Tar Heel residential section, it had a hand draw in the middle so that boats could pass into the harbor.

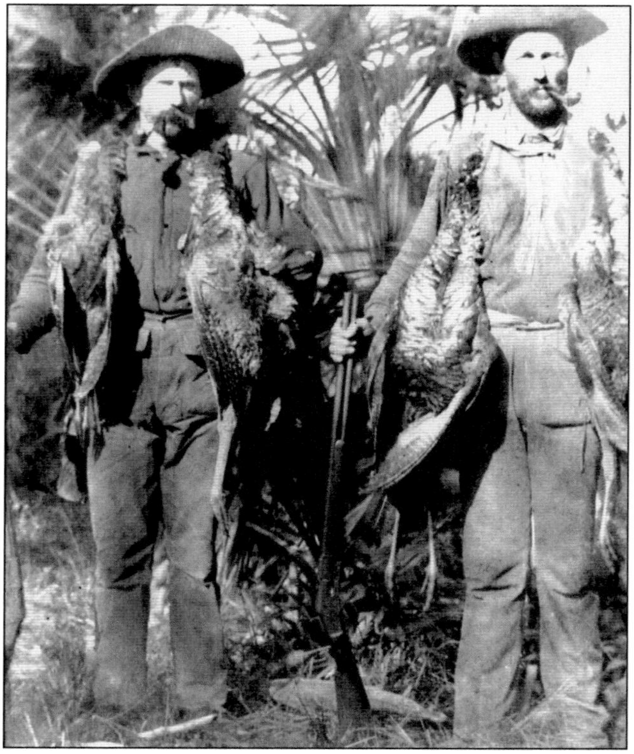

Hunters pose with their kill, wild turkeys. Game was plentiful in the Melbourne and Eau Gallie area and included deer, quail, rabbit, bear, opossum, muskrat, raccoon, wild pigs, land and sea turtles, and alligators. Hunters found the area full of ducks, too, as teal, mallards, ring-bills, peats, and widgeons made the lagoon their home. Hunters and campers had to be wary of rattlesnakes, water moccasins, mosquitoes, "no-see-um" gnats, and the rare possibility of a panther. When Houston first came, there were also wolves in the area.

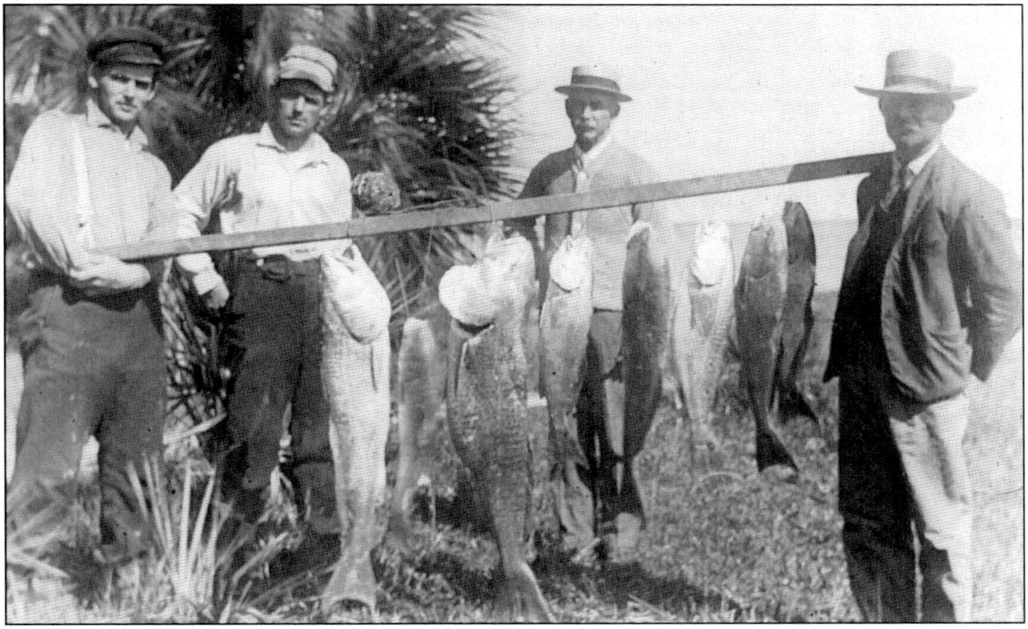

These fish were caught in Melbourne in 1900. Residents and visitors commonly caught large quantities of fish at a time. The Indian River, the Atlantic Ocean, and the freshwater creeks provided a great variety. By 1895, A.M. Sample opened the first fish house in Eau Gallie. He preserved the fish in ice and shipped them out by steamer.

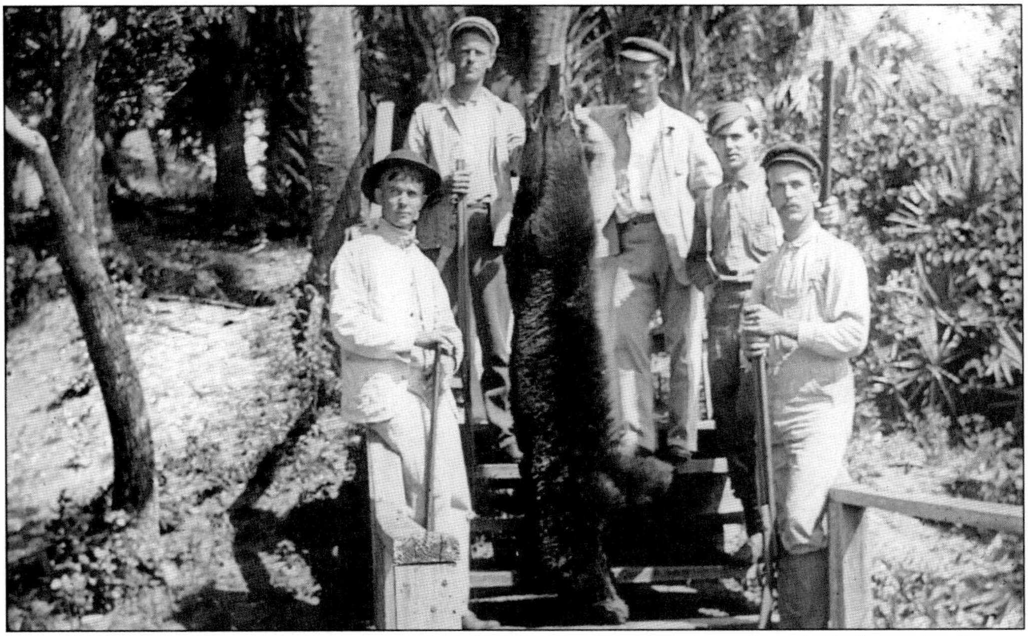

In 1908, Melbourne hunters from pioneer families pose with a large bear killed beachside and brought to the base of the Trysting Steps. The steps, a Melbourne landmark and meeting place, led from the intersection of New Haven and Front Street up to the Bluff Walk. The Bluff Walk, a broad sandy path that followed the bluff north along the Indian River, was Melbourne's most picturesque and stylish promenade. Left to right, the men pictured are Claude Edge, Don R. Beaujean, Alex J. Goode, Smith McFarlin, and Claude Beaujean.

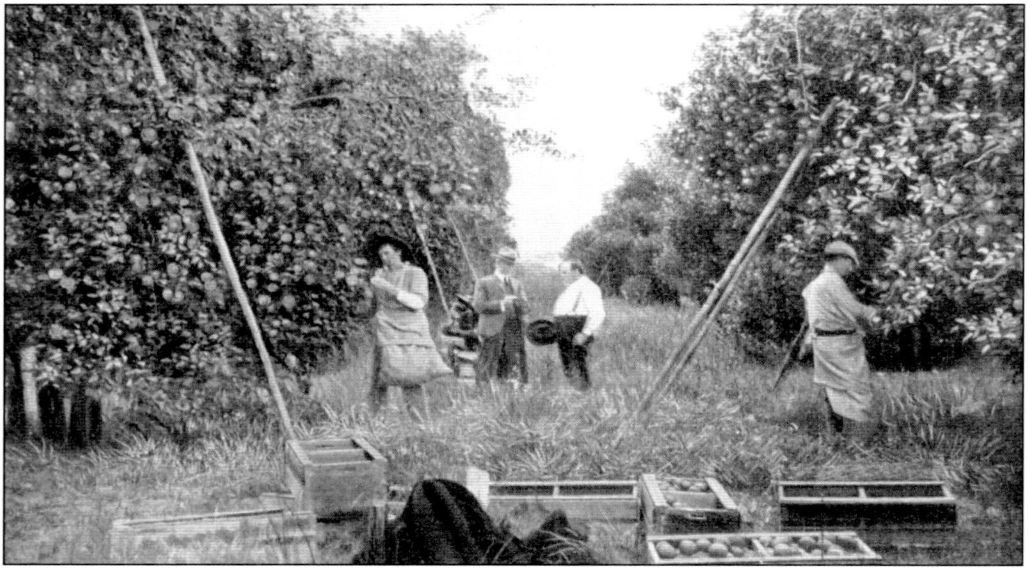

Citrus growing has been a mainstay in the economy of South Brevard County for a century. The Spanish introduced citrus, pigs, European legumes, herbs, and fruits to Florida in the 1500s. From their original stock evolved the famous Indian River Fruit. The biggest problem citrus growers had was the occasional winter freeze. There were bad ones in 1886 and 1905, but the worst came in 1894–1895. People who had moved to Melbourne and Eau Gallie lost their crops and many moved away never to return. Other farmers from tough pioneer families persevered.

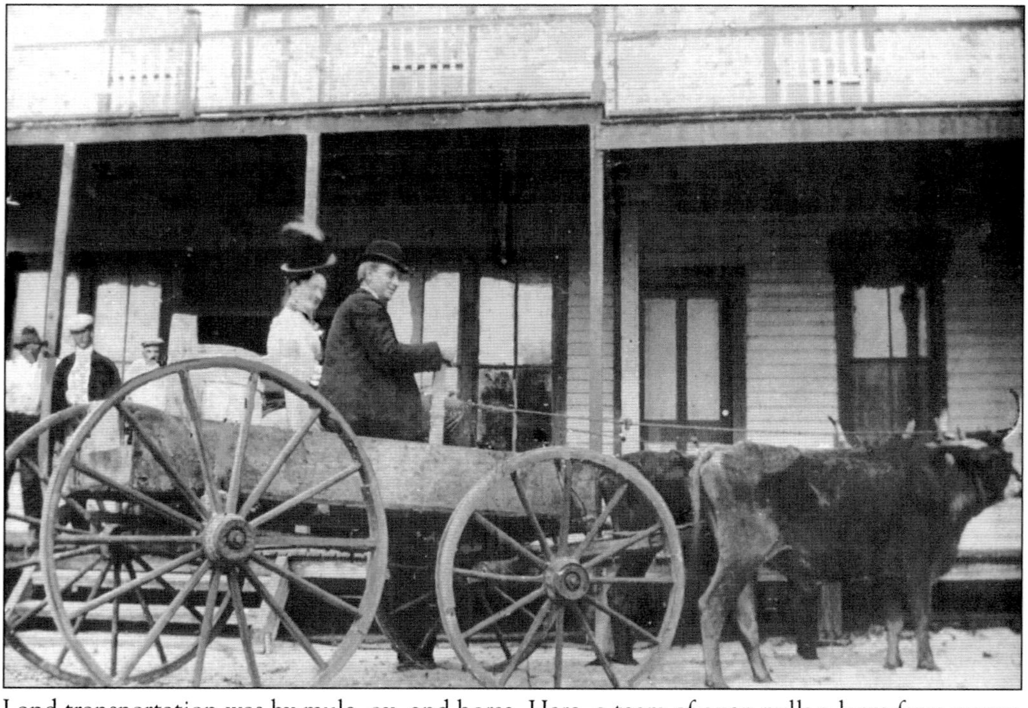

Land transportation was by mule, ox, and horse. Here, a team of oxen pulls a large farm wagon along Melbourne's Front Street. Notice how the couple dressed up to come to town. By the time this photo was taken, c.1891, Melbourne was becoming a financially viable little town with a few successful farmers and businessmen.

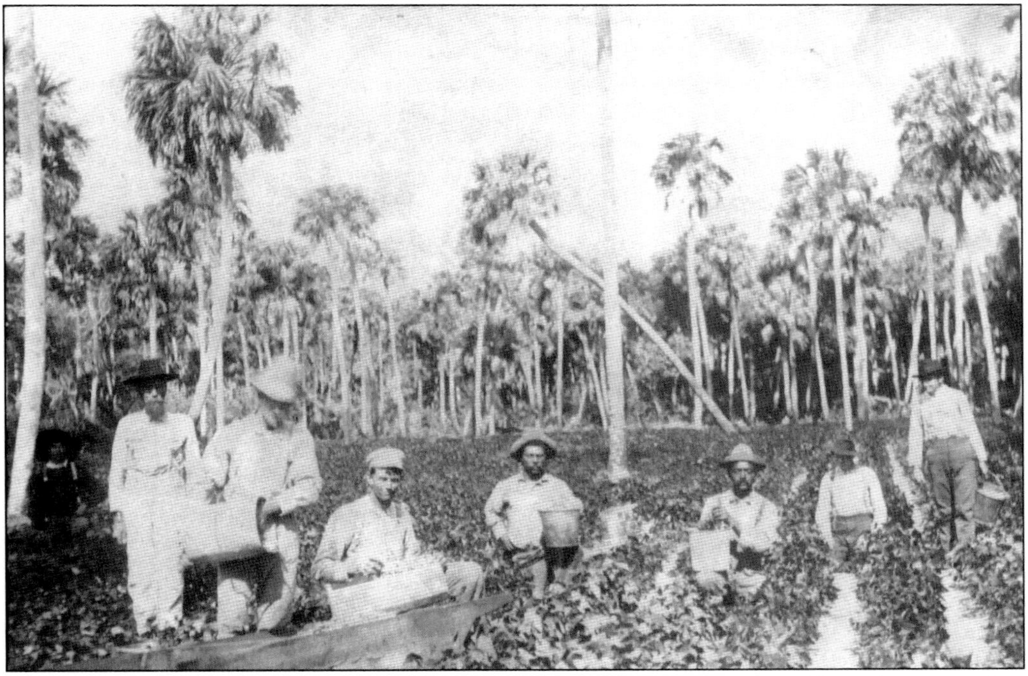

Settlers depended on farming to provide both subsistence and cash crops. Here, farmers gather beans in J.H. Baker's field. Typical crops included potatoes, onions, beans, corn, sugar cane, peanuts, melons, squash, and tomatoes. Sub-tropical foods included citrus, pineapple, bananas, papayas, avocados, guavas, and mangoes. Farmers also raised honeybees to pollinate the citrus.

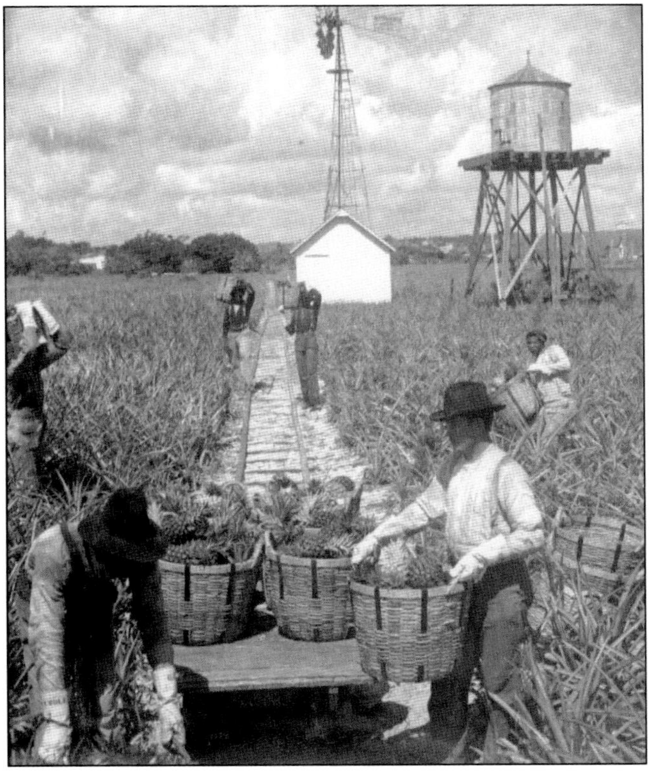

Pineapples became so lucrative that, for a time, much of the peninsula between the river and the beach was covered in pineapple fields. To the right is a view of Indian River pineapples being harvested. Eau Gallie residents John and Juliet Aspinwall lost 150,000 pineapples and over a thousand citrus and other plants in the disastrous freeze of 1894–1895. Like many others, they gave up on farming and left the area. When they returned years later, they lived aboard their yacht, which they kept moored in Eau Gallie's harbor.

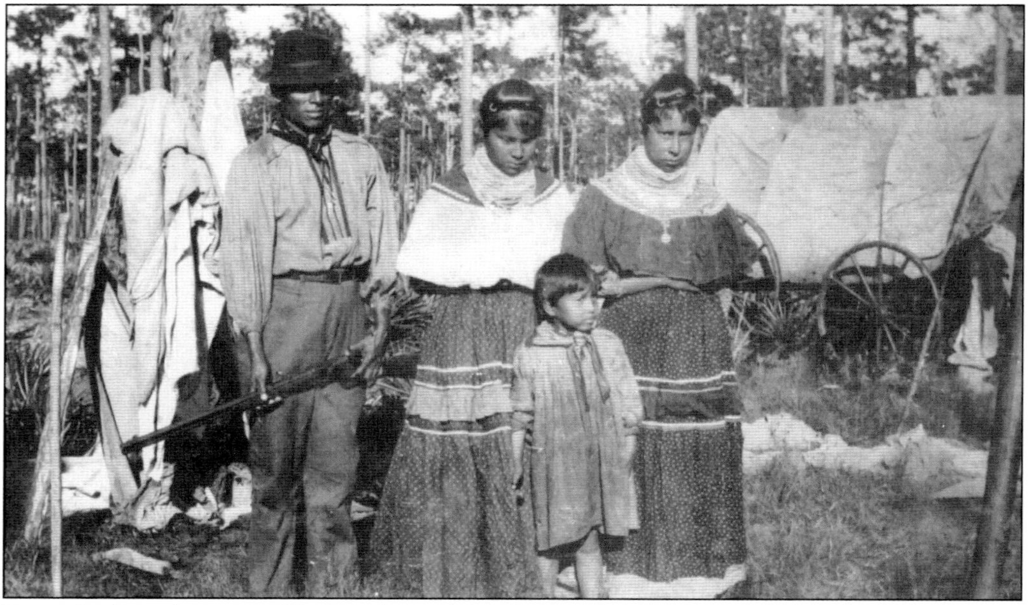

From the Revolutionary War to the early 19th century, the United States engaged in wars against Native American tribes of the Southeast. In the 1830s, the federal government began "removing" them to "Indian Territory" (later Oklahoma). During the Seminole Wars, Native Americans who had originally been Creek renegades moved into Florida to thwart capture and removal. The absence of the Ais and other nations from the area left the country open for the Seminoles. Although they established themselves deep in the Florida Everglades, even as late as the 1920s, Seminoles traveled and camped regularly through western Brevard County. After the Civil War, white and black people moved into the area and the Seminoles traded with them, offering venison and other natural products of Florida. In the photo above, a traveling Seminole family camps with their covered wagon. Below, Seminoles pause for a photographer in Fort Pierce, about 50 miles south of Melbourne. These photos were taken around 1900.

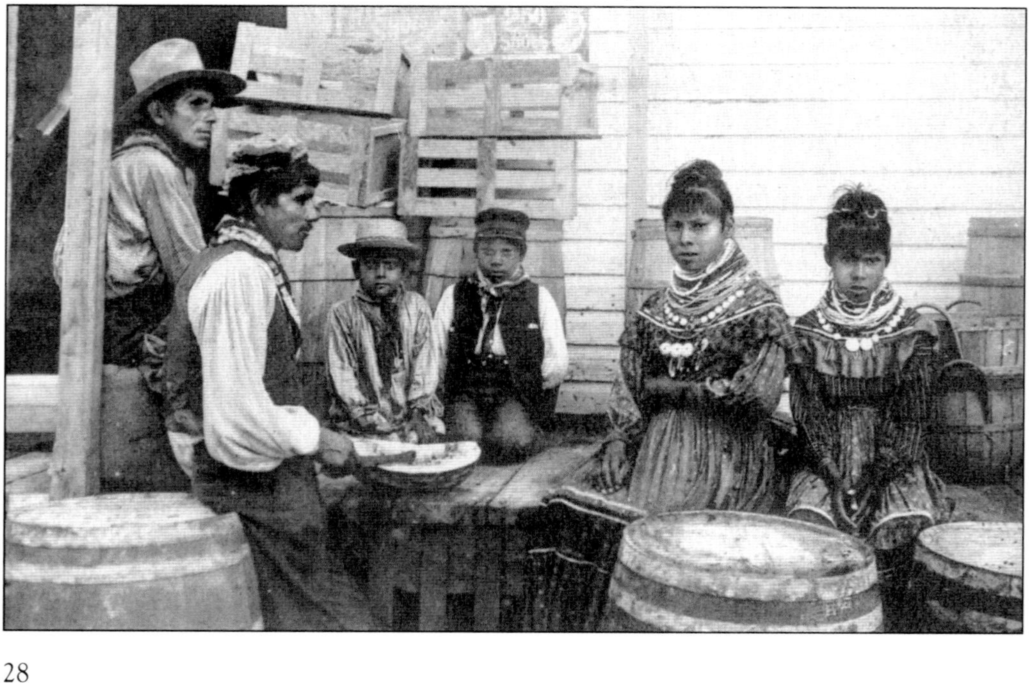

Two

The Railroad Era

In 1893, Eau Gallie briefly became the southern terminus of Henry Flagler's railroad along the Florida East Coast. Railroad literature of the day described the little town as a bustling paradise, touting its natural beauty and commercial development. Eau Gallie did have some commercial development, much of it having to do with the Indian River. Flagler built a spur and railroad pier in Eau Gallie that established the only direct rail-to-water link on the Indian River. Within months, the rail line was extended south through Melbourne and beyond.

As railway transportation supplemented and finally surpassed river traffic, real change began to occur in Melbourne and Eau Gallie. The towns entered a new phase of rapid growth as fast, cheap, and reliable land transportation made distant markets feasible and tourism more likely. Although the railroad would replace the river as the primary means of transport, it would not happen overnight. When the automobile began to compete with rail in the 1920s, the trains kept coming. In 1927, Eau Gallie and Melbourne residents had 14 chances a day to board a passenger train. In the view below, taken in 1923, a train crosses the Crane Creek trestle.

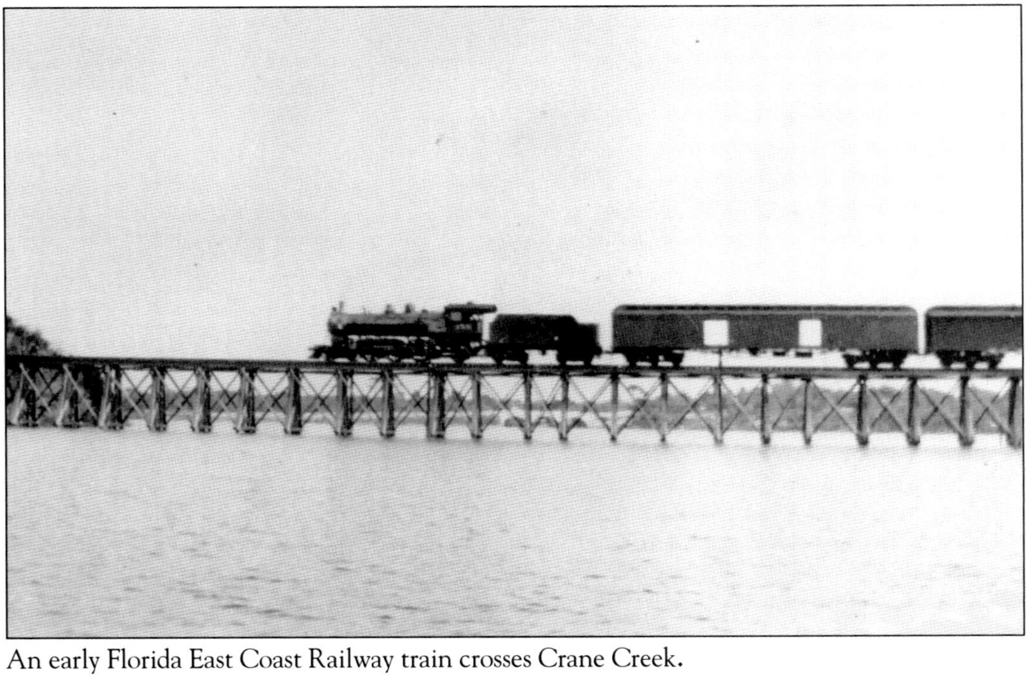

An early Florida East Coast Railway train crosses Crane Creek.

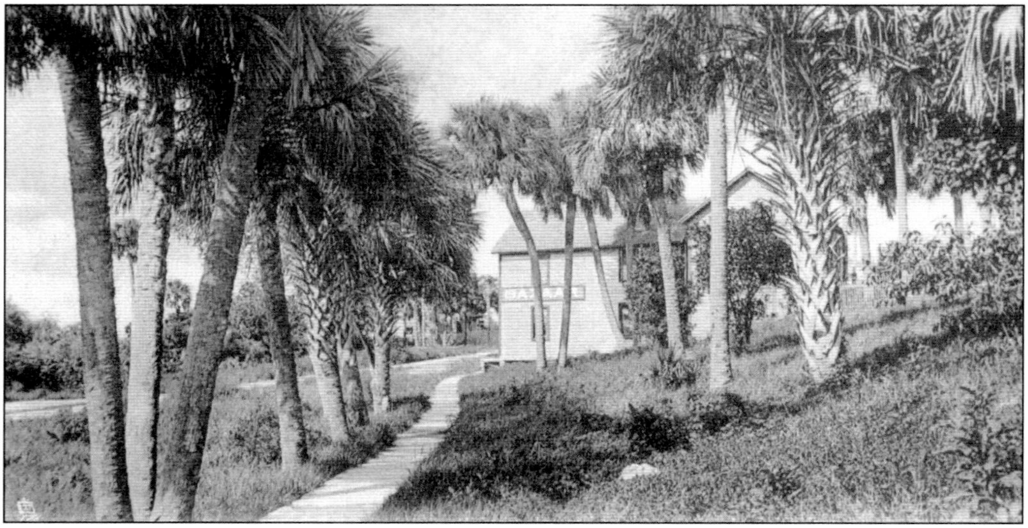

The foot of New Haven, at its intersection with Front Street, was the center of Melbourne from the 1880s to 1919, when a fire destroyed the Front Street district. Up the hill, going west from the river, one could take the Palmetto Walkway to Mme. C.J. Campbell's Bazaar, the wooden building seen in this turn-of-the-century photo. The Bazaar opened in 1895 and remained in business for 27 years. Madam Campbell was an enterprising businesswoman who came to Melbourne with her two sons. She not only ran the Bazaar, but also the Bellevue Hotel (the former Goode House). She published and sold many of the old postcard views we have of Melbourne during the Golden Age of Florida tourism and souvenirs. Melbourne's first library was located at the Bazaar, and her son, John Fraser Campbell, was Melbourne's first mayor.

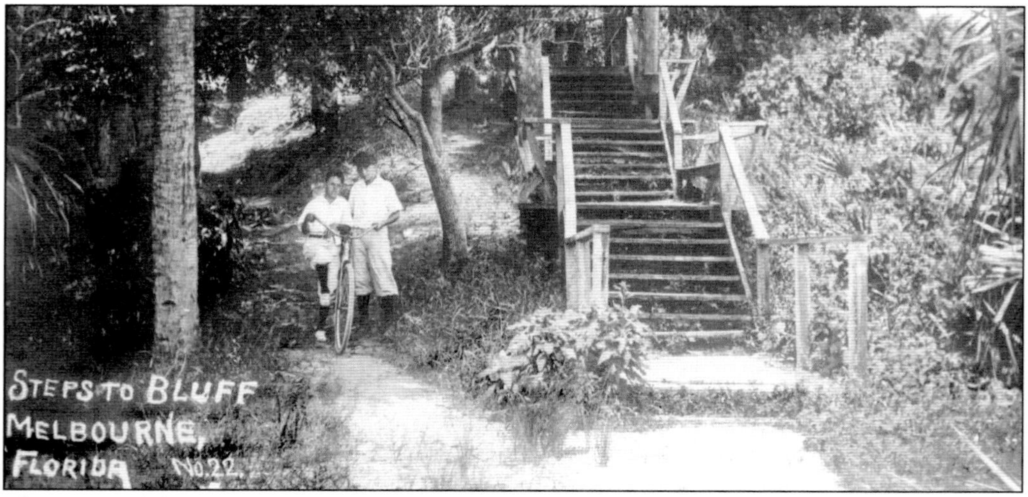

This view of the Trysting Steps (or Stairs) shows their location over an old Indian mound, or shell midden, as confirmed by A.T. Anderson and other archaeologists in the 1940s. The steps lead from the foot of New Haven Avenue north to the lovely Bluff Walk along the edge of the river. The Ais camped here near a free-flowing spring that would continue to attract and serve later travelers. The area between the mound and the river was a mangrove swamp until Melbourne residents filled it in. Two boys pause on their bikes at this famous meeting-place, but the stairs were named for their role as a rendezvous spot for courting couples. The Trysting Steps, originally wooden, have been rebuilt of concrete. They are the oldest landmark of Melbourne's riverfront days.

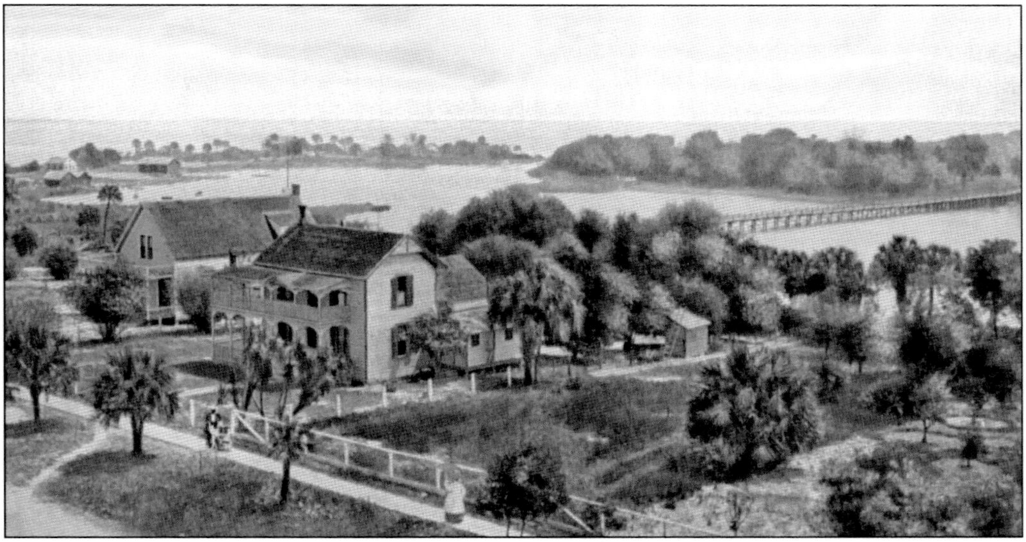

This early 20th-century view shows the first houses along Crane Creek and east of the Goode House/Bellevue Hotel. The photographer was looking east toward the mouth of the creek and the point of land where Front Street lay. The sidewalk in the foreground is parallel to New Haven Avenue. Today, a street runs between the backyards of these houses and the edge of the creek. To the right is the old highway bridge.

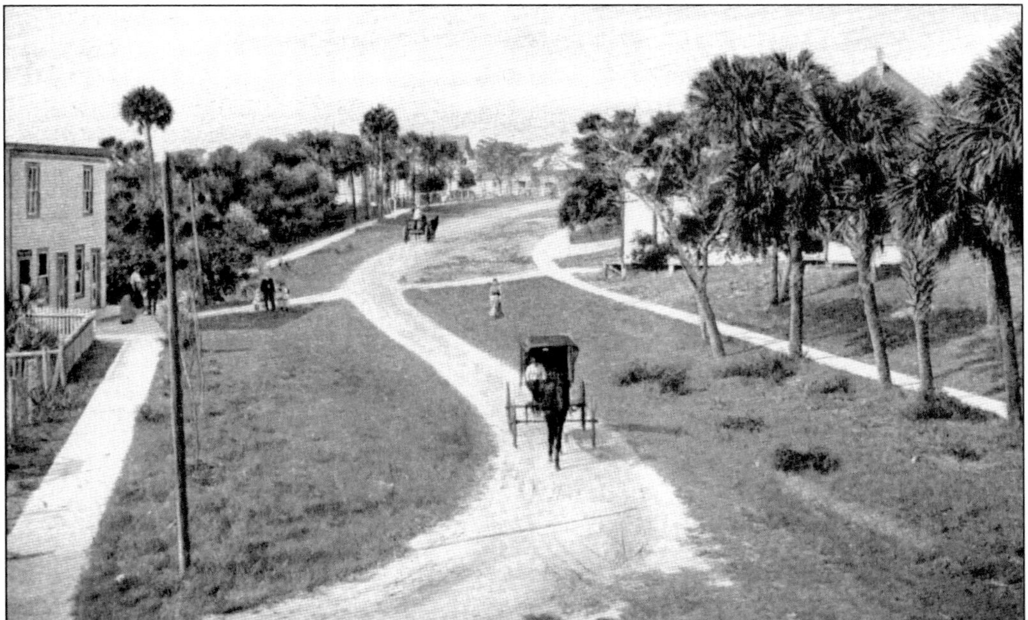

This quaint New Haven Avenue scene depicts the pace and quality of life in the early 20th century. A horse and buggy in the foreground and a wagon in the distance need only a narrow strip of road between the sidewalks. Up the slope to the west is the newer area of town where the railroad tracks have been laid. Mme. Campbell's Bazaar is on the right, and Goode's Real Estate is on the left. The curve in the foreground is the beginning of Front Street. Directly behind the photographer was the City Pier and, later, the approach to Melbourne's bridge across the Indian River. An artesian well located there was used to refresh draft animals.

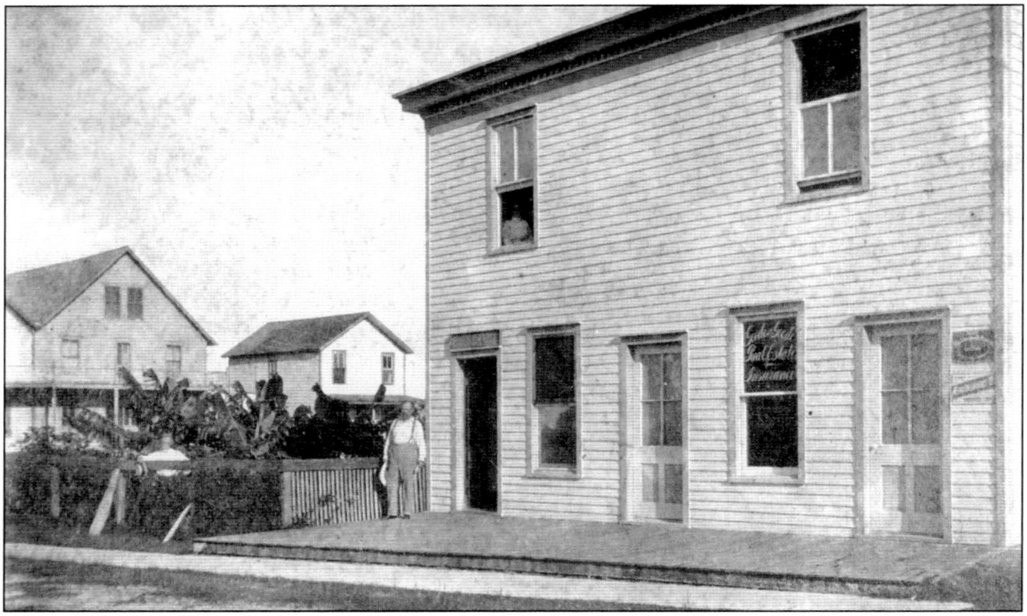

This is a closer view of Goode and Goode Real Estate and Post Office on New Haven, which still stands today. Richard Goode is seen in front. Stewart's and other businesses are visible around the corner. Front Street businesses went up in flames in 1919 and Melbourne's dependence on rail eliminated any need to rebuild at the riverfront. The new town was forming up the hill along the tracks. Below is a modern view of the rear of Holy Trinity Episcopal Church. The first services in Melbourne were held in 1884 in the Goode House. In 1886, the congregation built Holy Trinity on land purchased from Wright Brothers by Lucy Boardman. For a while, the Goodes, Campbells, McBrides, Nesbitts, Reverend Debose, and others rowed across to the south side of the creek to attend services. Later, they built a footbridge at the end of Grant Place. In 1897, Melbourne's harbormaster, Will Scott, helped move the church by barge to new grounds donated by Mr. and Mrs. William Wells at the corner of Fee and U.S. #1. The church was stuccoed in 1924 and moved to its present site on Strawbridge in 1963.

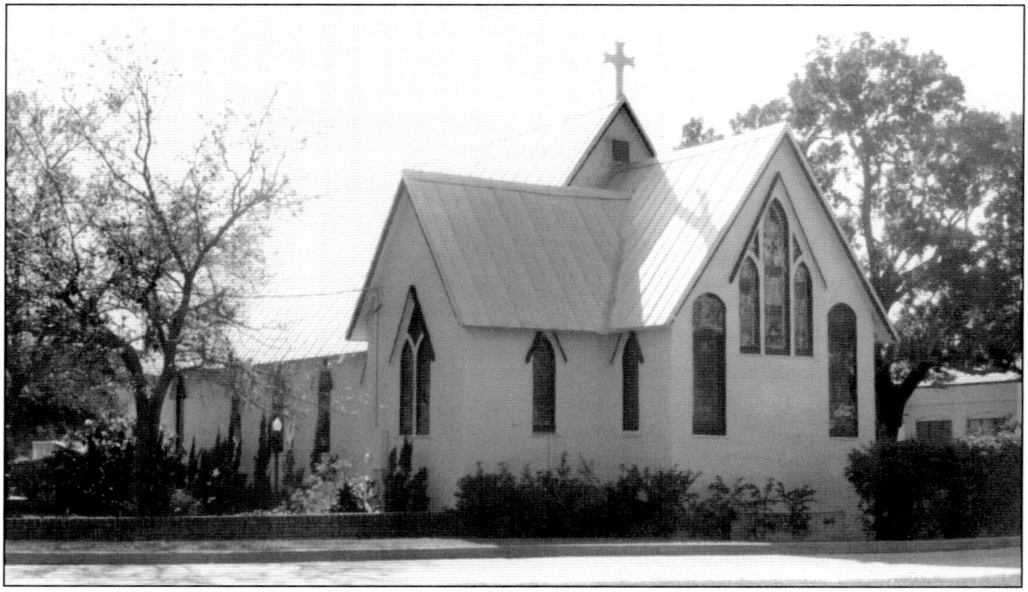

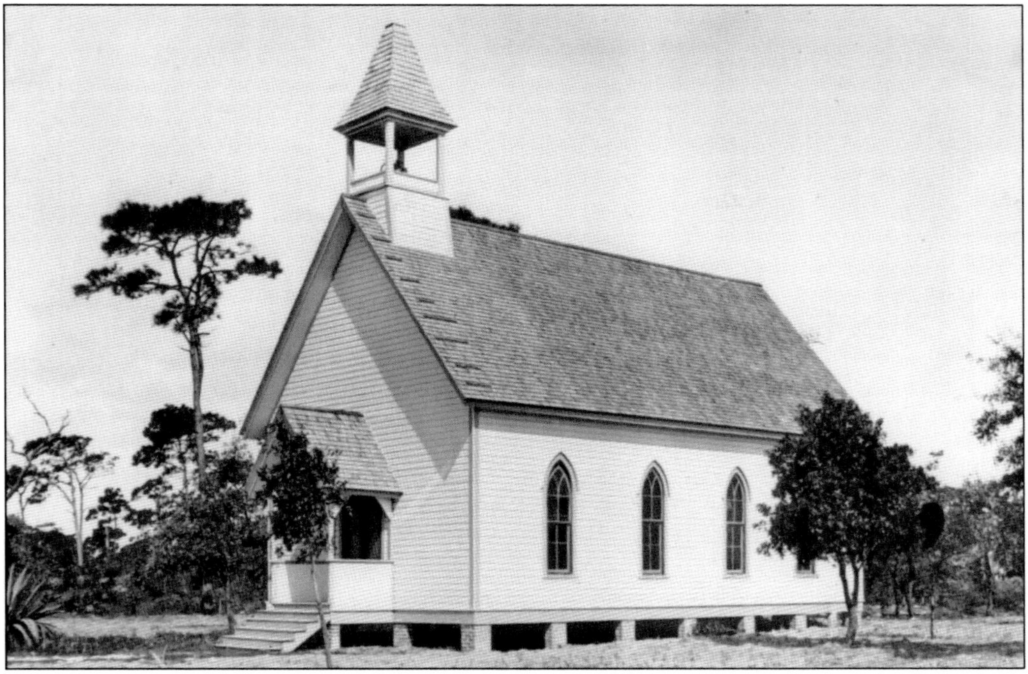

Melbourne's First Methodist Church was organized in 1887 by the Fee and Idner families. For a while, circuit-riding ministers served the congregation. In 1889, the church erected its building on New Haven Avenue, one block west of Washington Street (US #1). In 1904, the building was moved farther west to the corner of New Haven and Orange (Municipal Lane), where Meehan's is today. Since that time, the congregation has moved to new buildings twice. This old structure still exists as a portion of Grace Baptist Church on Palmetto Avenue.

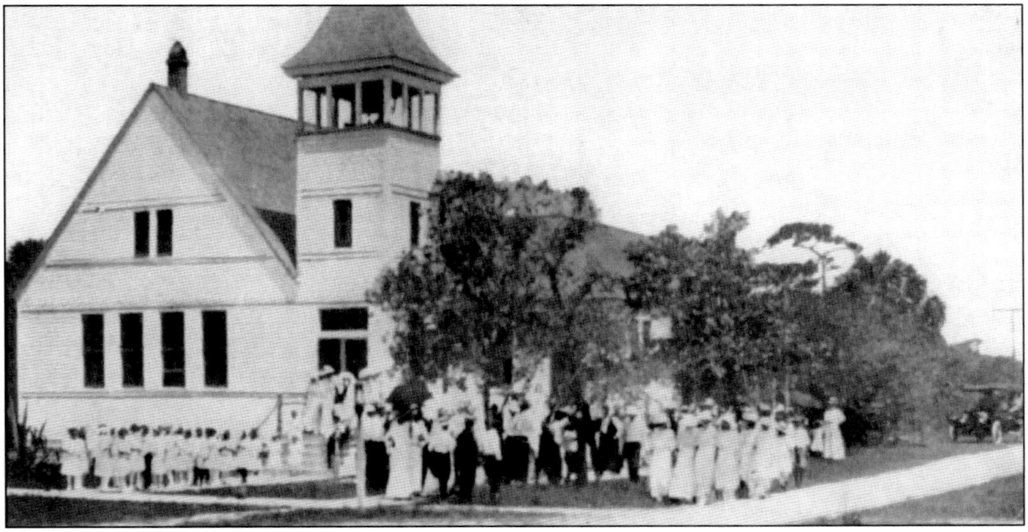

The First Congregational Church was organized by E.P. and Abbie Branch with the help of 10 others in 1889. In 1893, the church was built on land donated by W.H. Powell at the corner of Strawbridge and Washington Street (US #1). Union Cypress Mill donated the bell. The original structure, expanded and occupied until very recently by the congregation, still stands in its original location. E.P. Branch, an investor who came to Melbourne in 1886, negotiated with Henry Flagler to bring the F.E.C. railroad directly through Melbourne.

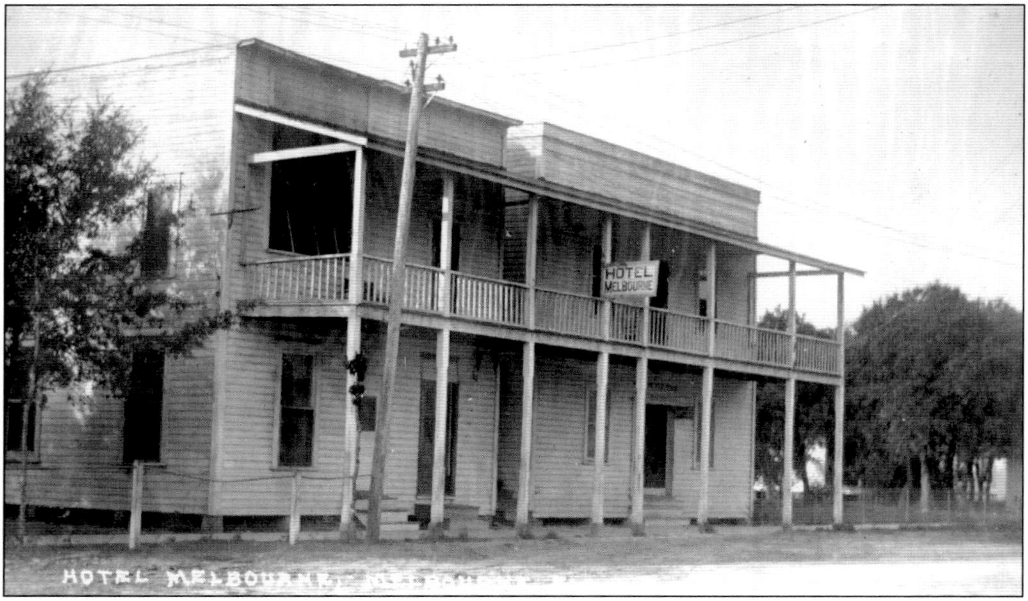

In the early 1920s, Hotel Melbourne was located in the Myles building on New Haven Avenue across the street from the Methodist Church. The two adjoining wooden structures, erected in 1913, opened with a pool hall and restaurant downstairs and the Midway Hotel upstairs. The Melbourne Times, founded in 1894 by David Oslin, was located here from 1914 to 1920. During 1916–1920, public school classes met here and across the street in the Methodist church. In 1930, the eastern half of the Myles Building became Shorty's Bar. The western half held Masch and Company, later Henderich's.

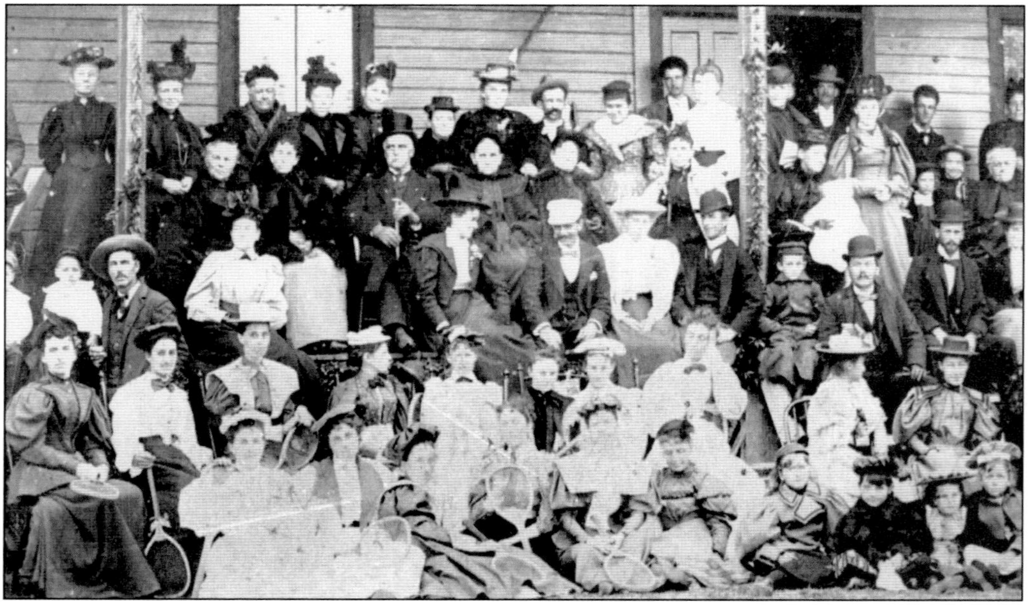

The railroad brought so much business to Melbourne that hotels prospered, especially in the winter. Madame Campbell added tennis courts and more rooms to the Bellevue Hotel. She also added a water wheel–powered freight elevator that was used to lift luggage to the second floor. Here is a scene on the front porch of the Bellevue in 1896 showing winter visitors at the Ladies Racquet Club Tennis Tournament.

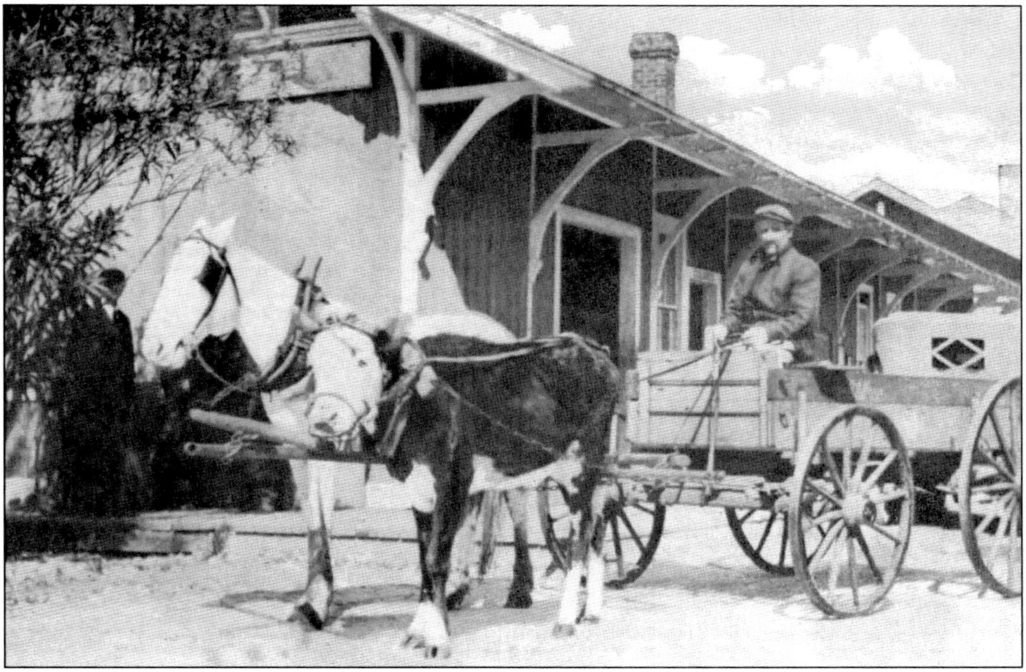

G. Davitt poses here with his freight wagon in front of the Melbourne railroad depot on Oleander Street. His team does the job—one horse with blinders and one cow!

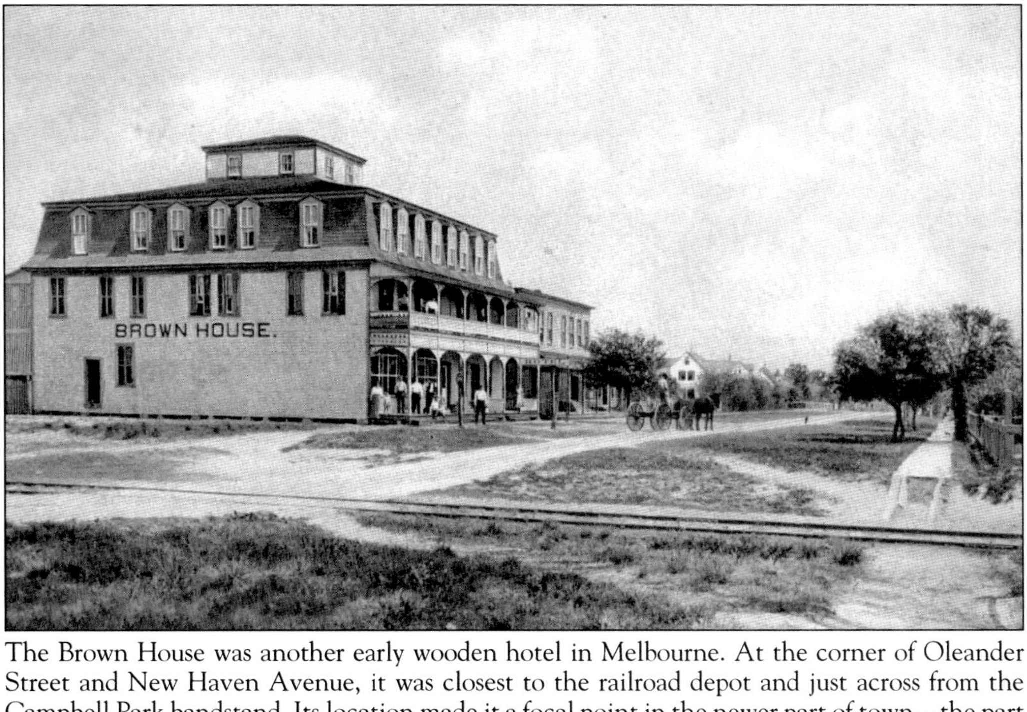

The Brown House was another early wooden hotel in Melbourne. At the corner of Oleander Street and New Haven Avenue, it was closest to the railroad depot and just across from the Campbell Park bandstand. Its location made it a focal point in the newer part of town—the part that was developing up the hill and away from the old Front Street district at the river's edge.

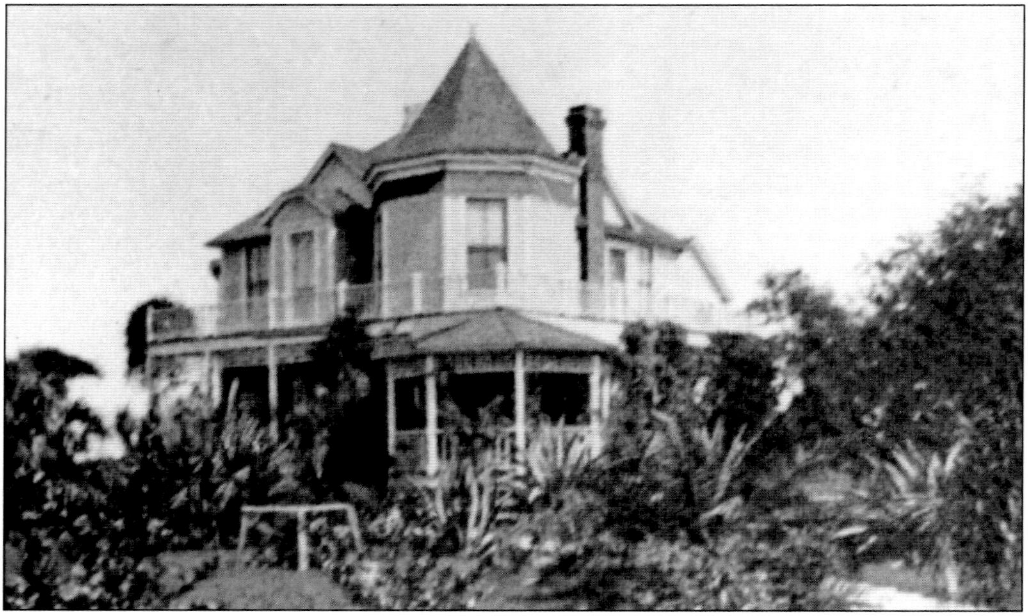

The large Queen Anne–style house, at the north end of the Bluff Walk, was Green Gables, the home of Mr. and Mrs. W.T. Wells. Built in 1896, Green Gables still stands, but it is in near ruins as of this writing. Near here, the Wells family donated a piece of land for the new site of Holy Trinity Church and several acres to the city to be kept in perpetuity as parklands. Wells also initiated the building of the first high school in Melbourne, which was located near the Florida Power and Light Company Ice Plant (not shown).

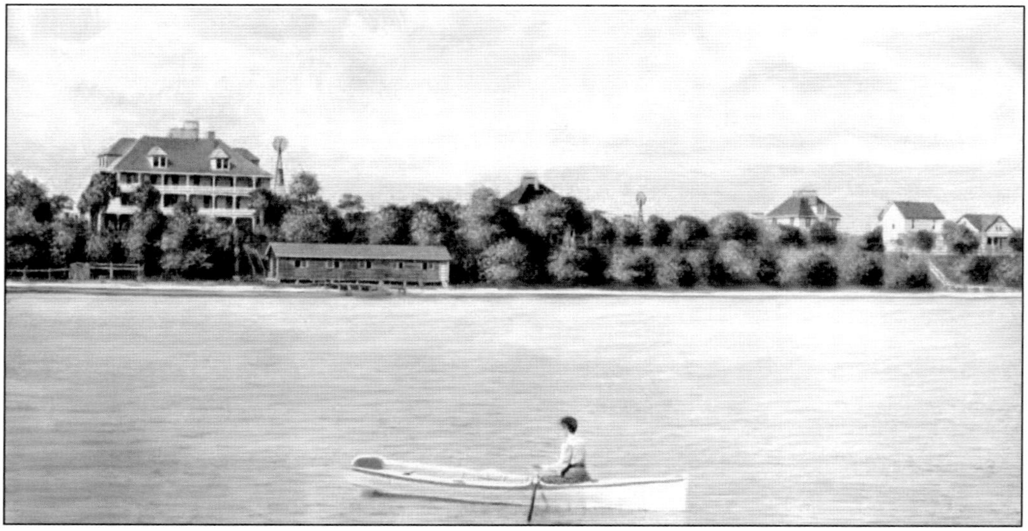

A woman in a rowboat pauses on the Indian River. The photographer stood at the end of Melbourne's City Pier to take this picture of the Carleton Hotel and boathouse. The hotel windmill is to its immediate right. Other homes on the shore face the river and back up to Riverview (Indian River) Drive north of Strawbridge. The area along the Bluff Walk, Peter Wright's home site, was originally a Florida hammock, an oasis of biological diversity dominated by huge oak trees. It became a fine residential district in the 1880s.

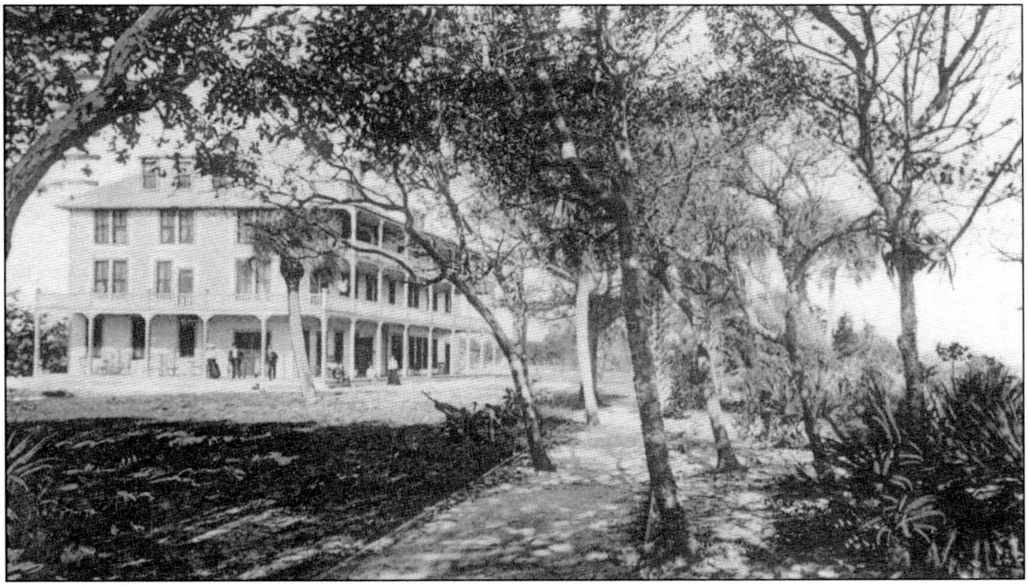

Jennie Strawbridge built the first Carleton Hotel in 1887, which burned in 1904. L.G. MacDowell rebuilt the Carleton and it burned again in 1925, catching fire from one of the nearby Bonter cottages. The gracious hotel catered to the well-off winter guests that came to Florida's east coast. Its dock and boathouse allowed direct river access and its grounds were known for their beauty. The hotel even had a sprinkling system to water the grass and plants.

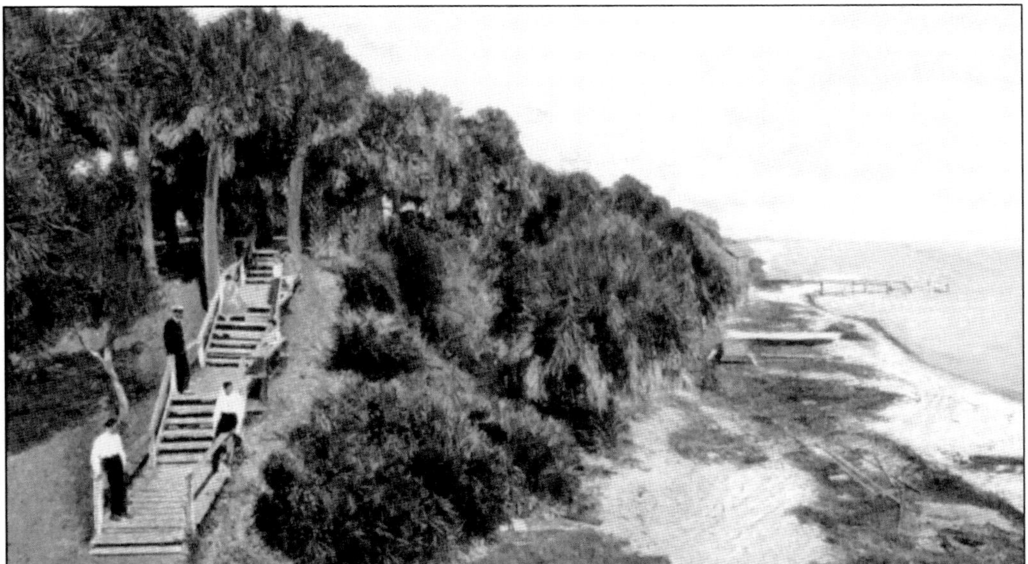

A walkway from the Carleton led to the lovely Bluff Walk, shown below. The Bluff Walk extended from the Trysting Steps at New Haven and Front Street, five blocks north to Green Gables. The best dressed ladies and gentlemen from the Carleton or other hotels and Melbourne's local society used the pleasantly breezy Bluff Walk as a promenade. Couples met and courted, businessmen and fine ladies impressed one another, and children grew up with wonderful memories of playing on the idyllic Bluff Walk. Mrs. Strawbridge deeded the right-of-way easement to the city with the stipulation that it remain open to the public in perpetuity.

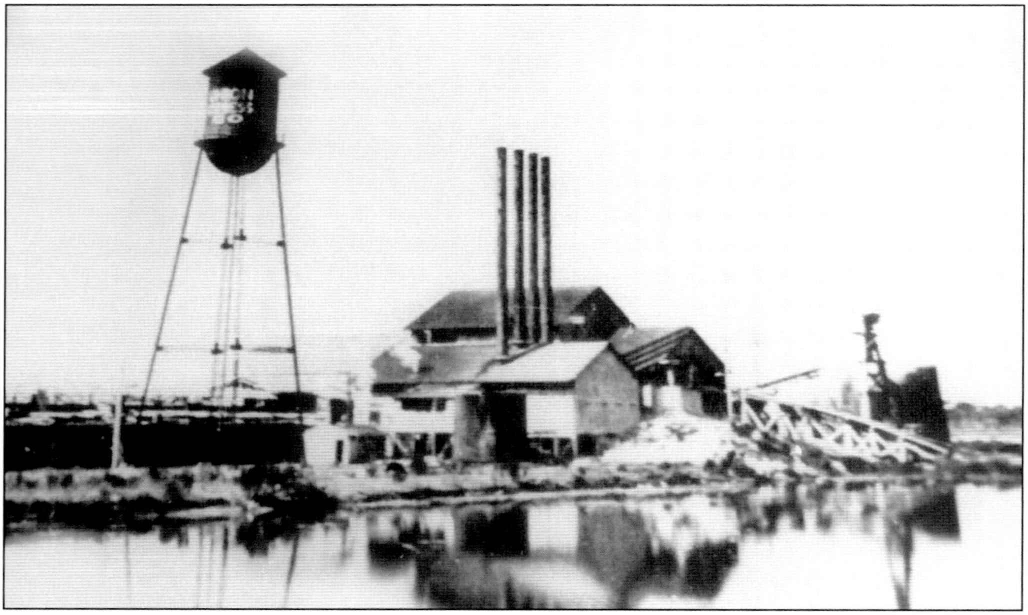

George Hopkins established the Union Cypress Mill in 1912 to process timber from his 104,000-acre holdings near the St. Johns River. From Deer Park, 18 miles west of town, Union Cypress brought logs by rail and deposited them in the millpond shown here. In addition to the pine and cypress sawmills, there was a turpentine still located in what is called Newtown today. A disastrous fire in 1920 caused the company to close temporarily. In 1924, Union Cypress got a contract to provide lumber for the Titusville Bridge. H.B. Foshee bought the mill, depleted what was left of the timber west of town, and went out of business as the Great Depression hit.

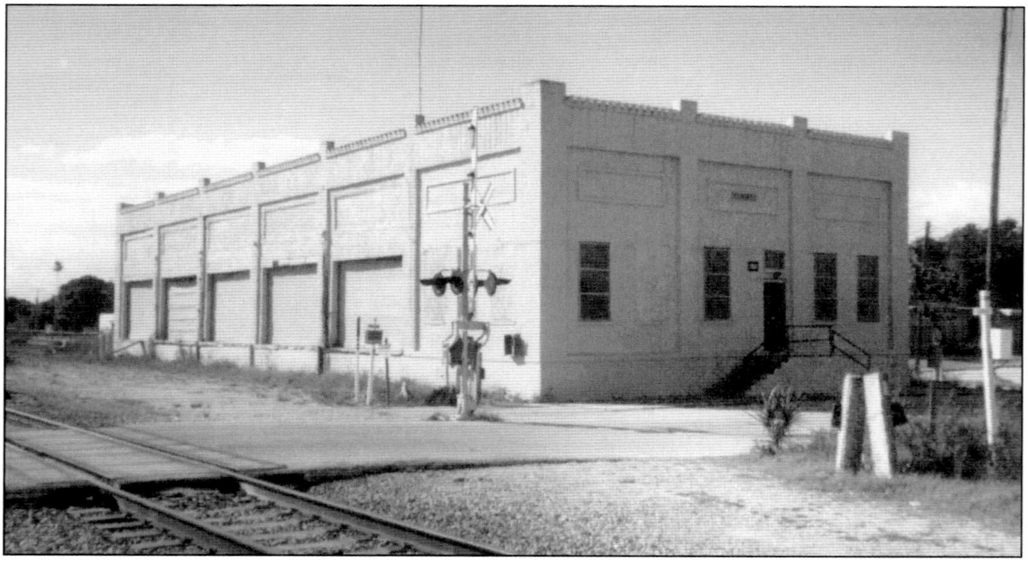

Hopkins, the mill town, had housing, stores, a non-denominational church, a school, doctor, and theater. The company was central to the economy of South Melbourne, employing more than 300 people at the mill and turpentine still, while another 200 worked in Deer Park. The Macedonia Baptist Church is located on the site of the former mill in South Melbourne. This historic church, organized in 1889, moved into its present sanctuary in 1975. The F.E.C. freight depot, shown above, was built in 1926 on the site of the former mill office.

John Stone and Mary Sears Stone, both children of freedmen, arrived in Melbourne in 1892. He opened a store and rooming house, while she became a midwife. Other midwives in South Melbourne were Louella Pittman, Lydia Duncan, Mandy Byrd, and Anneda Harris. Stone's general store was the second in the area owned by a black man. It was located at the corner of Brothers and Stone Streets. Line Street got its name because it divided the mill houses of Hopkins from Dr. Stone's subdivision, where order prevailed. Stone served as superintendent of the South Melbourne School. He donated land for Melbourne's first all-black school, erected on Line Street in 1906.

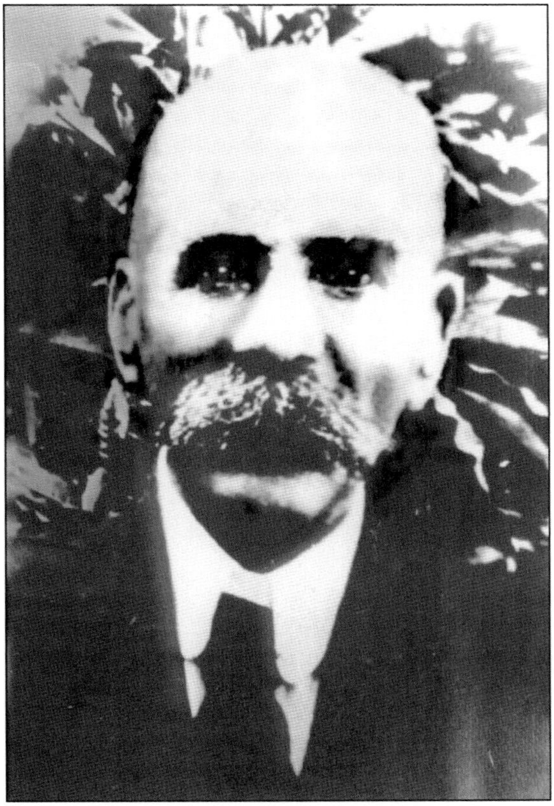

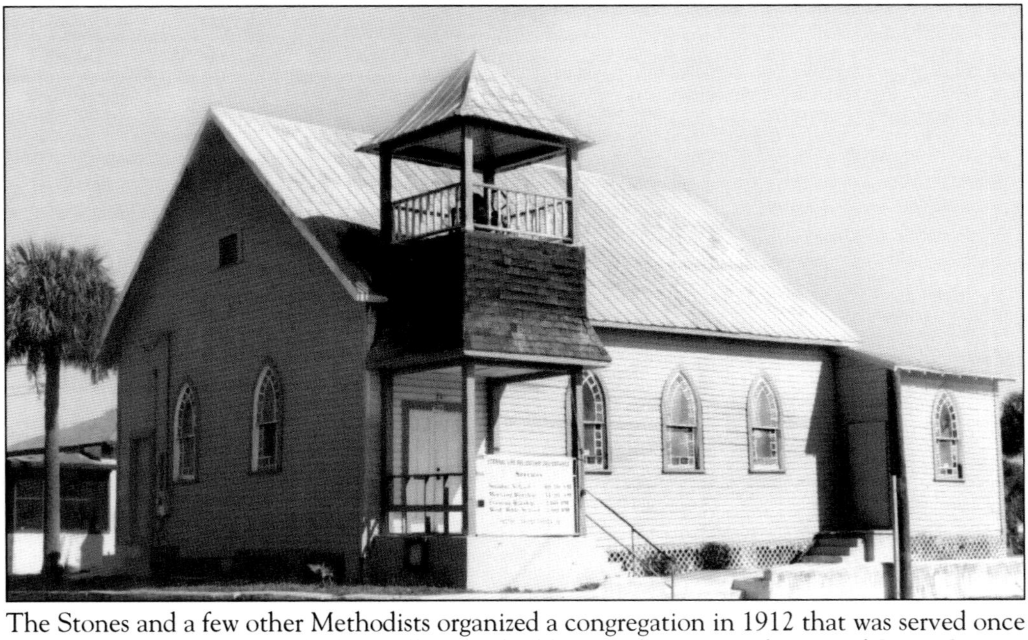

The Stones and a few other Methodists organized a congregation in 1912 that was served once a month by a minister from Jacksonville. This building, at the corner of Line and Stone Streets, was completed in 1914 under Stone's supervision and still stands. Stone also purchased land from the mill for a black cemetery. Some of South Melbourne's most historic figures are buried there, including Stone himself, who died in 1926.

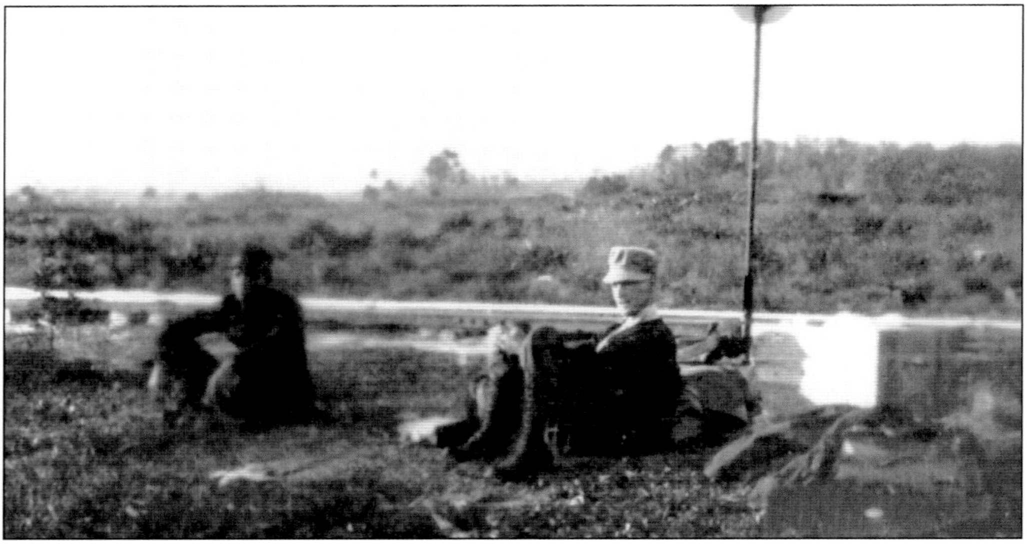

Turkey hunters Hiram Platt and John Rodes sit next to the tracks, waiting for the Union Cypress train to take them from Deer Park to Melbourne. The Platt family owned a great deal of land west of Melbourne. Before the Florida law against free-roaming cattle was passed in 1949, the Platts herded their cattle from Central to South Brevard west of the towns that hugged the river shores. Florida "cow hunters" (not cowboys) were so called because of the free-range practice. Cattle have been important in Florida agriculture since the Spanish imported them in the 1500s.

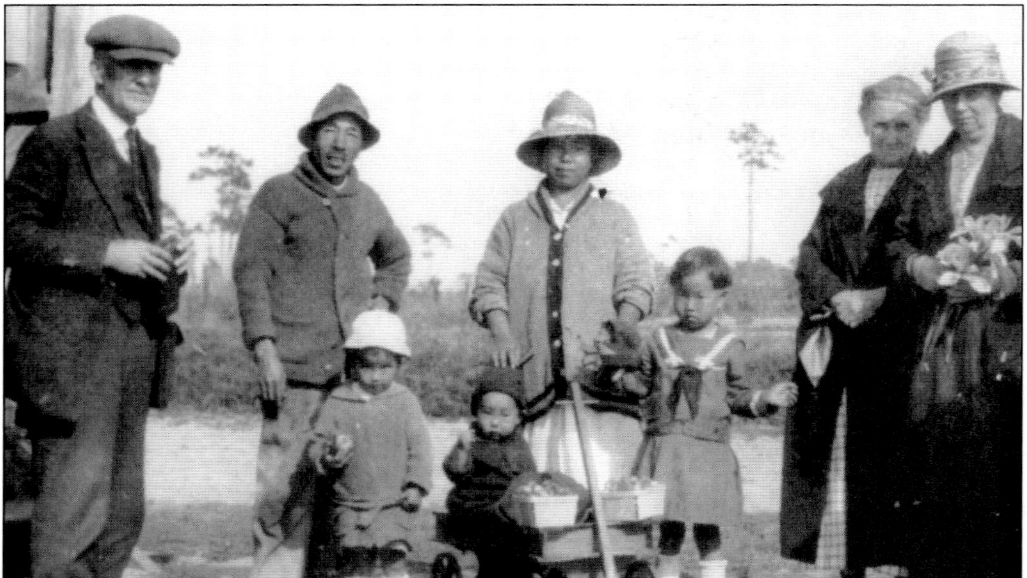

In 1908, a group of Japanese investor-farmers colonized an area of Eau Gallie near Aurora Road west of the railroad. E.M. Ohi was the leader of this group that included the Harada and Ozaki families. The Aurora farmers grew citrus, potatoes, and beans. They shipped by rail to out-of-state restaurants and sold vegetables to local stores and homes. The sons of the families attended St. Paul's Methodist Church and Eau Gallie schools. Many of them served in the United States military during World War II. Here, Ohi, his wife Torayo, and their children Louise, Eddie, and Florence receive a delegation of appreciative Eau Gallie residents.

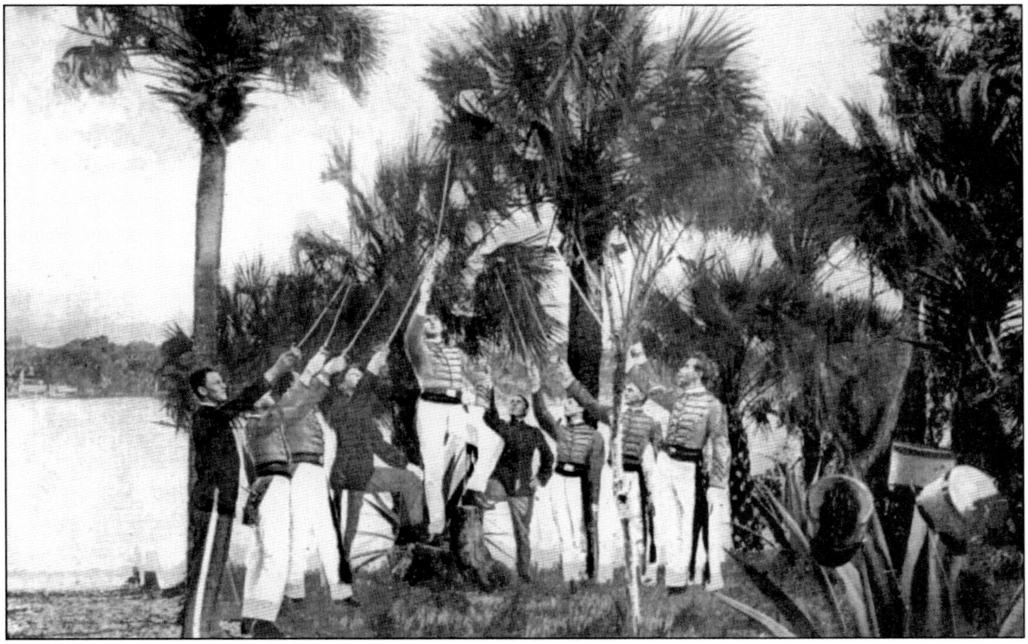

Entrepreneur John Green built a resort, the Hotel du Nil, on the south bank of the Eau Gallie River about 1890. Charles Verbeke, a partner, opened the Sarno post office there in 1895. The hotel failed and the post office closed. The hotel and grounds then became the winter home of the Kentucky Military Institute from 1906 to 1923. The school brought an increase in the population of Eau Gallie as students, teachers, and staff came south on the train each year. Above, KMI cadets raise their swords. Below is a view of the campus.

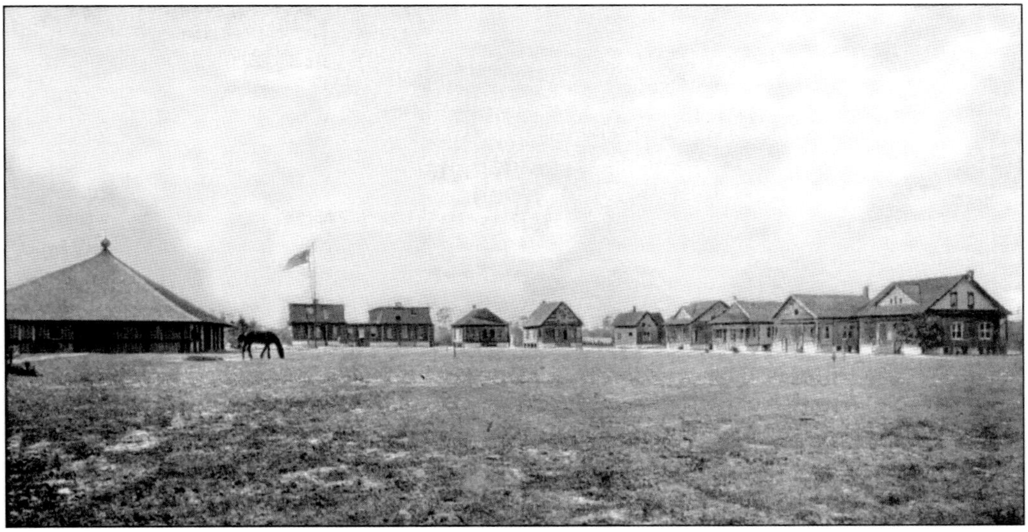

Eau Gallie grew under the Kentucky Military Institution's (K.M.I.) influence. Homes were built, sidewalks installed, and the older fish, citrus, and lumber industries prospered. Eau Gallie improved its streets and older structures. Col. C.W. Fowler, the commander of the institute, kept a beautiful boathouse on the Eau Gallie River as his winter home. He and his staff integrated fully with the townspeople and local activities. Eau Gallie was delighted to have the school. After three disastrous fires, the school moved to Venice, Florida.

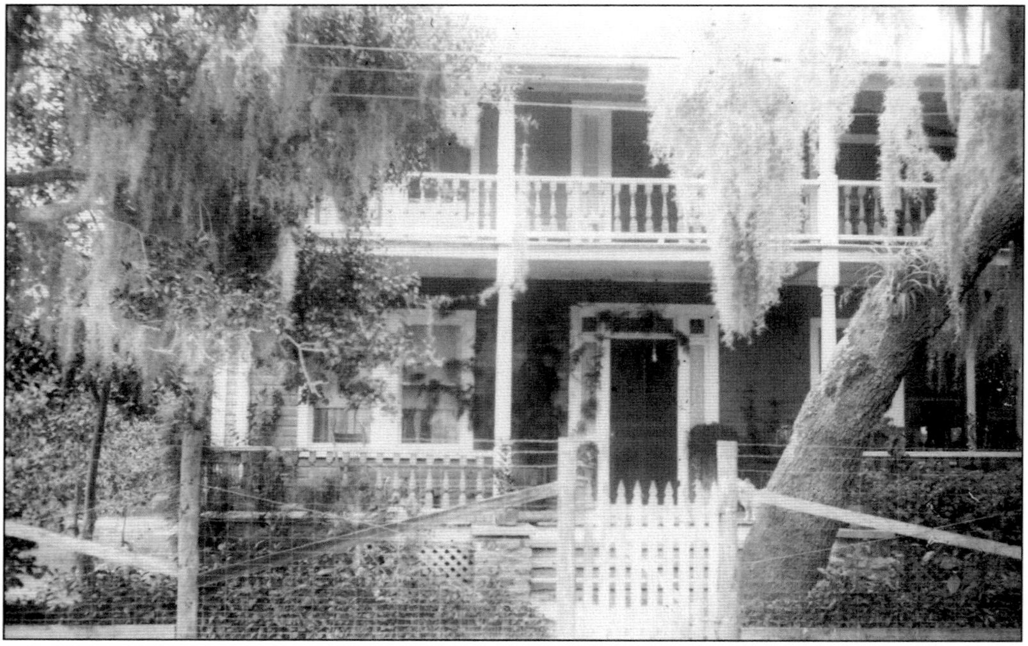

John Houston's slaves built the back portion of this house around 1859. James Rossetter came to Eau Gallie in 1902, purchased the property a year later, and enlarged the house. Rossetter operated a wholesale fish house and barrel factory until fish in the river became scarce. He then obtained the Standard Oil franchise, and his oldest daughter, Carrie, went to work for him. Rossetter died suddenly and Carrie—because she was a woman—had to get special permission to keep the franchise. She remained the area's Standard Oil agent for decades afterwards.

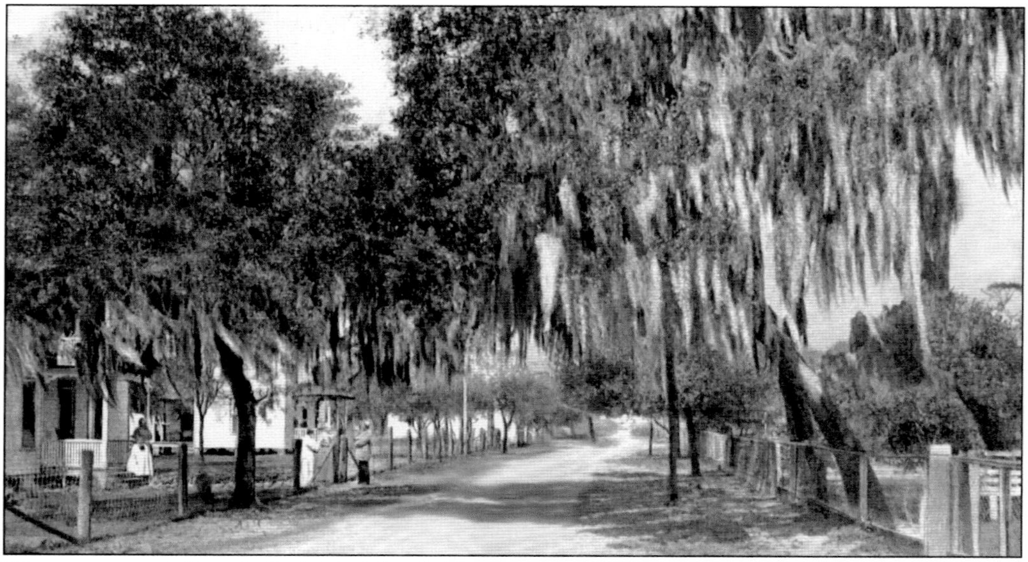

This scene is of Eau Gallie's Highland Avenue near Oak Street. Yards were typically fenced in to keep out wandering animals like pigs and other livestock that roamed the streets and fields. On the left is the home of early Eau Gallie mayor and publisher of the *Eau Gallie Record* William Roesch. The house beyond belonged to J.C. Carter. Both the Rossetter and Roesch houses, located across the street from each other, are now owned by the Florida Historical Society.

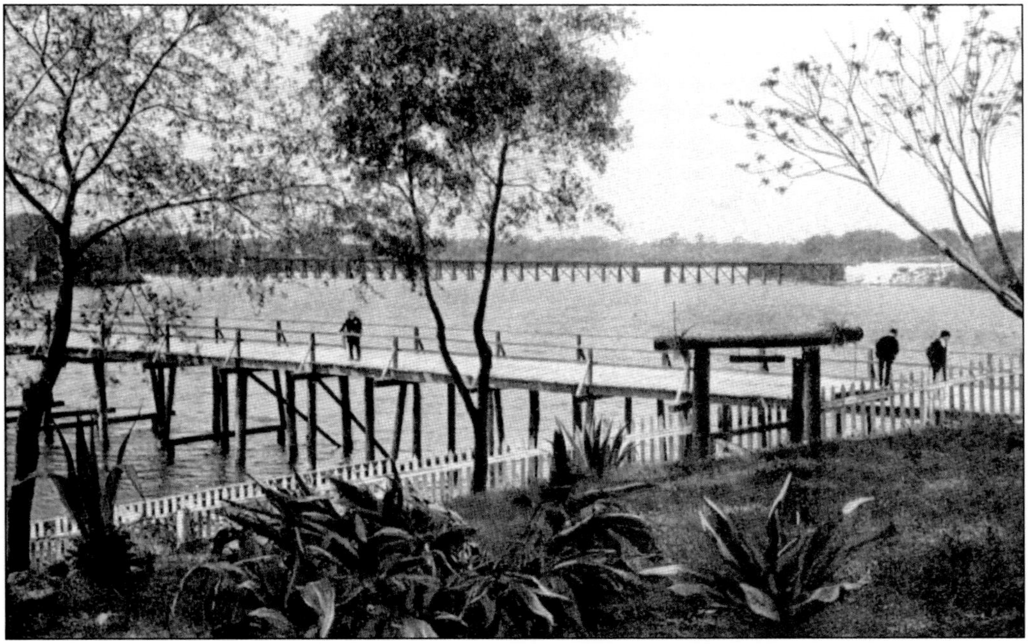

In the foreground is the site where US #1 crosses the river today. The more distant bridge is the Florida East Coast Railway trestle across the Eau Gallie River. It was built in 1893 when the railroad pushed south from Eau Gallie to Fort Pierce and then beyond.

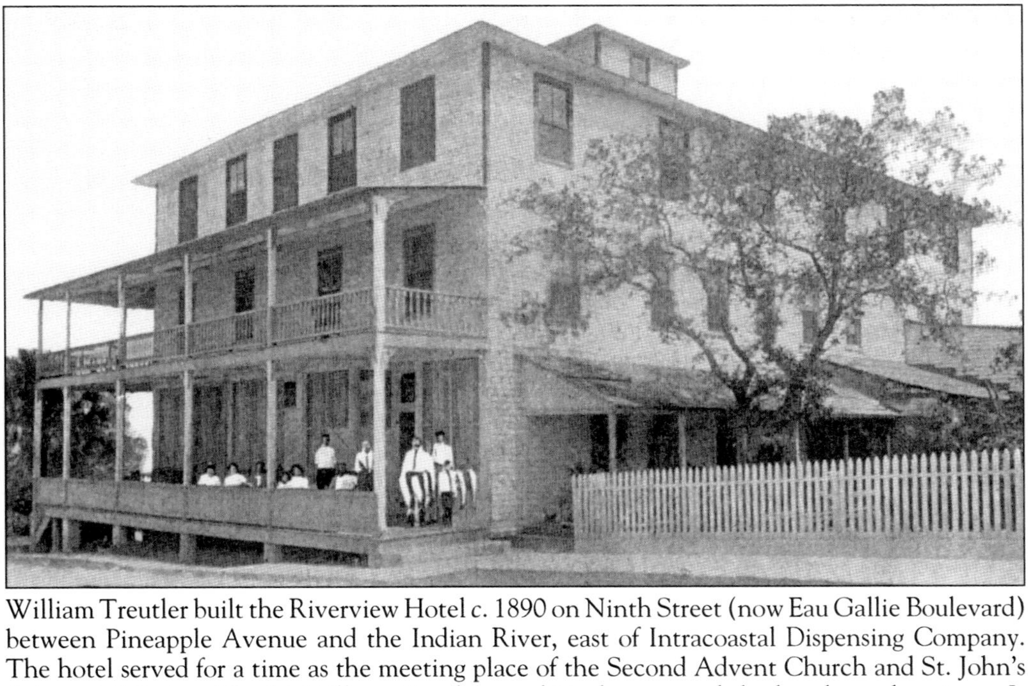

William Treutler built the Riverview Hotel c. 1890 on Ninth Street (now Eau Gallie Boulevard) between Pineapple Avenue and the Indian River, east of Intracoastal Dispensing Company. The hotel served for a time as the meeting place of the Second Advent Church and St. John's Episcopal Mission. The McMillans, Gosches, and Mathers owned the hotel at other times. It burned in 1923.

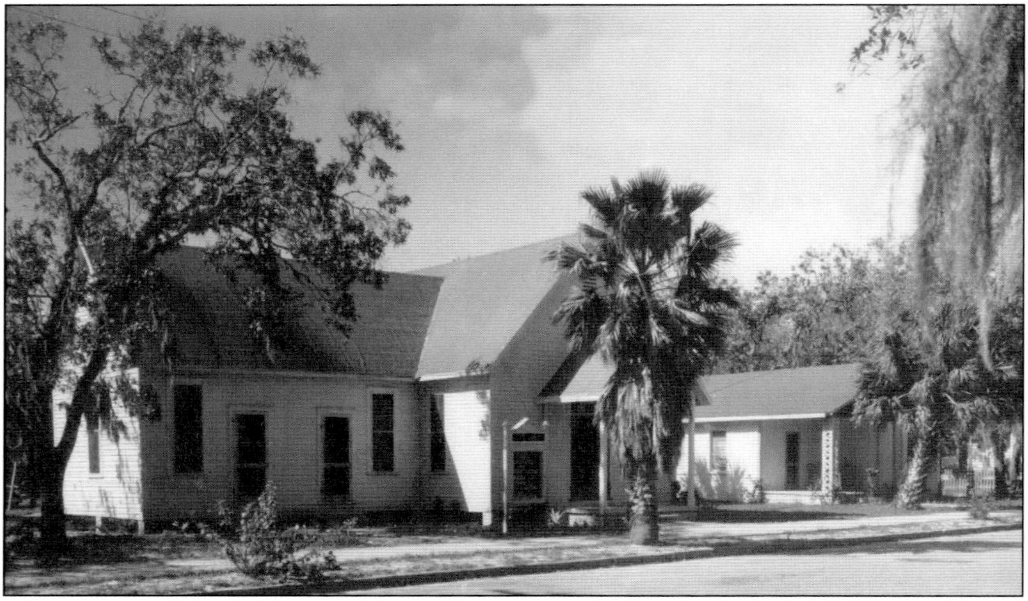

The First Baptist Church of Eau Gallie was organized in 1887. W.H. Gleason donated land, and the congregation erected this church in 1889. The town had established its first school in 1872 in a log cabin. After this church was built, classes were held there until 1894, when a new school was constructed at Highland and Creel.

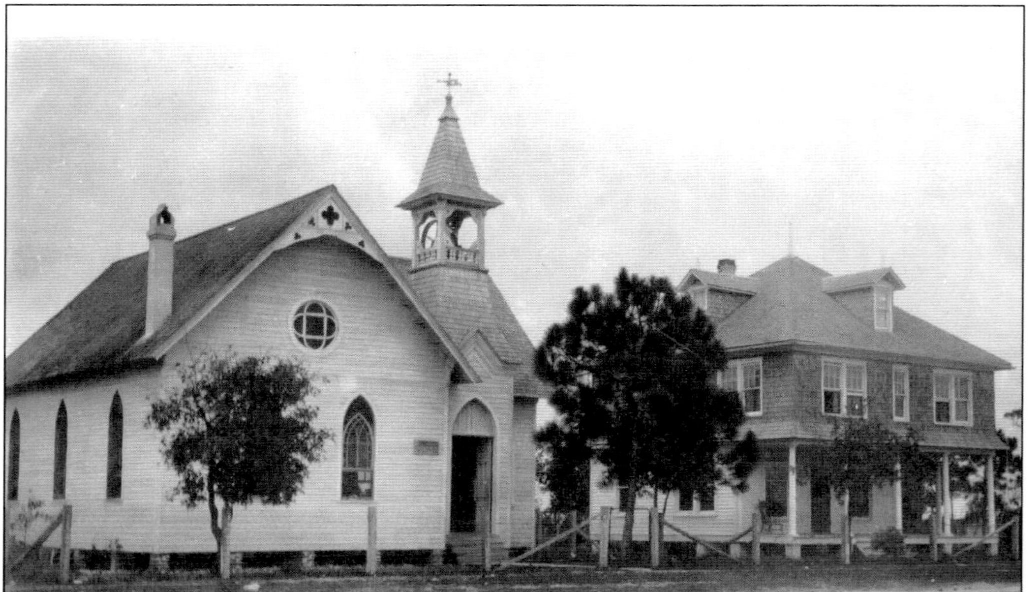

In 1900, William Roesch, Ada Houston Roesch, Hattie Houston, Isabelle Stewart, and others organized St. Paul's Methodist Church of Eau Gallie. Roesch was a citrus grower, a general store owner, and served as mayor of Eau Gallie in 1896. At first, the Methodist congregation arrived by boat to meet in a log building on Horse Creek north of Eau Gallie. Their church, seen above, was completed in 1903; high school classes met here as well. The house on the right is the parsonage.

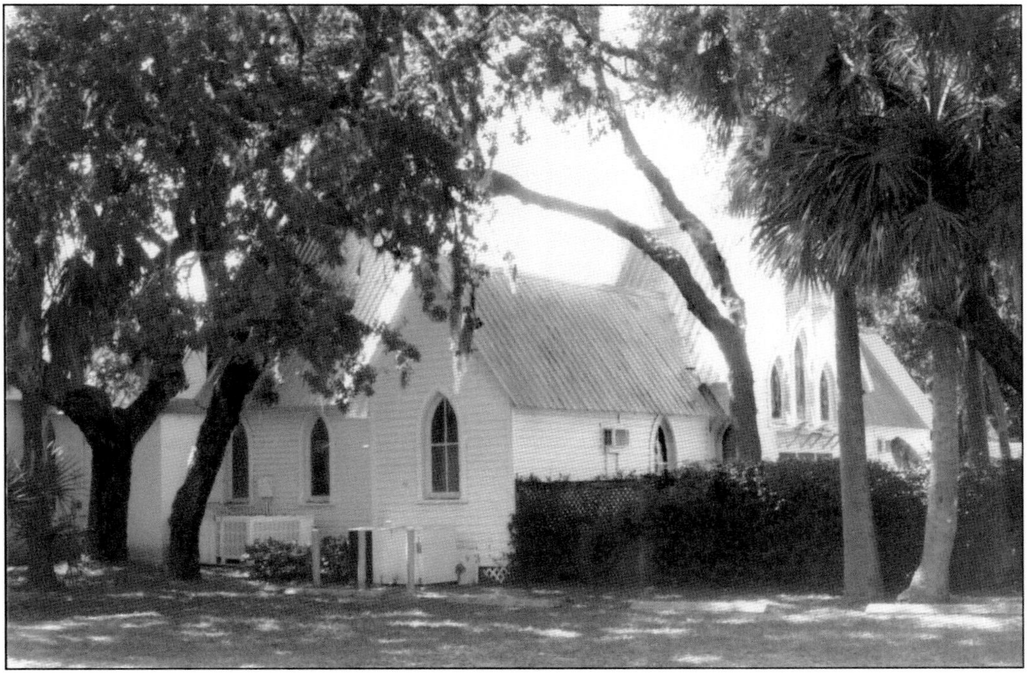

This is a current view of St. John's Episcopal Church in Eau Gallie. The original wooden structure has a large addition to the front, but the rear, seen here, remains unaltered. The church was organized in 1890 by a group of 29 people including the Hodgsons, the Nesbitts, the Aspinwalls, the Taylors, the Gilberts, the Harrises, the Randalls, Frank Turner, and others. W.H. Gleason donated the land. Some of the church collections went to help build the first bridge to the beach. St. John's also held special services for the K.M.I. cadets.

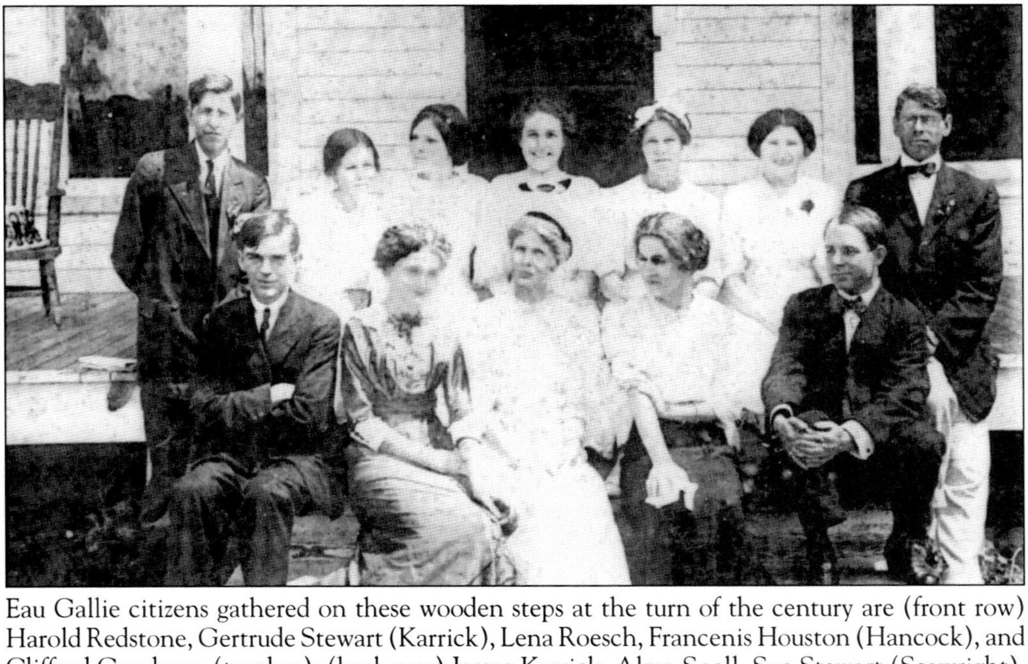

Eau Gallie citizens gathered on these wooden steps at the turn of the century are (front row) Harold Redstone, Gertrude Stewart (Karrick), Lena Roesch, Francenis Houston (Hancock), and Clifford Goodman (teacher); (back row) Jessee Karrick, Alma Snell, Sue Stewart (Seawright), Hilda, May Paddison (Osteen), Nell Stewart (Ginter), and Wilbur Karrick.

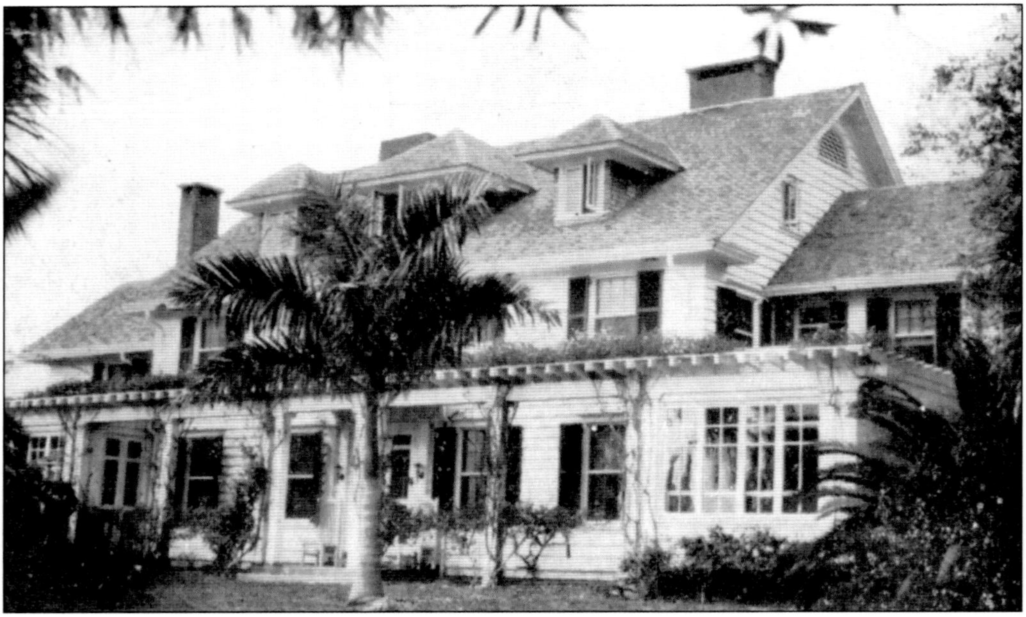

Built on land that had once been the location of John Houston's salt manufacturing operation, the home of S. Thruston Ballard was completed in 1915. Ballard (of Ballard-Obelisk Flour) had his own water tower and fire department on the property. Along with the Yacht Club, his home became the center of Eau Gallie social life. Ballard's widow sold the city the island in the middle of the Eau Gallie River after Ballard passed away. The city created Ballard Park by filling the area between the island and the southern shore of the river.

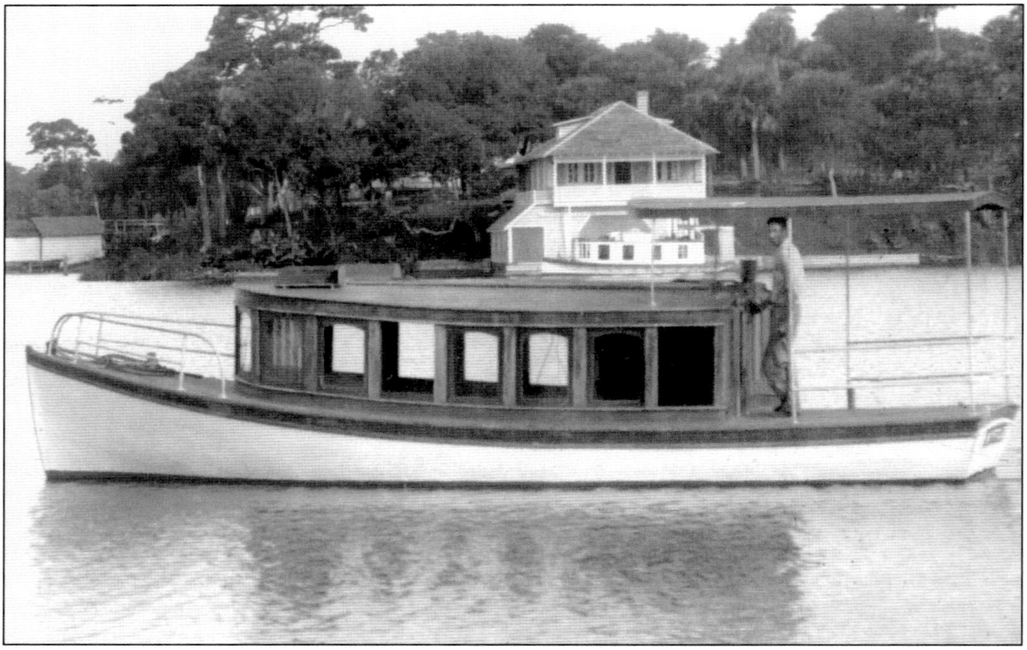

In the early part of the century, the charter boat *Myrtle* and her captain ease by the Rossetter boathouse on the Eau Gallie River.

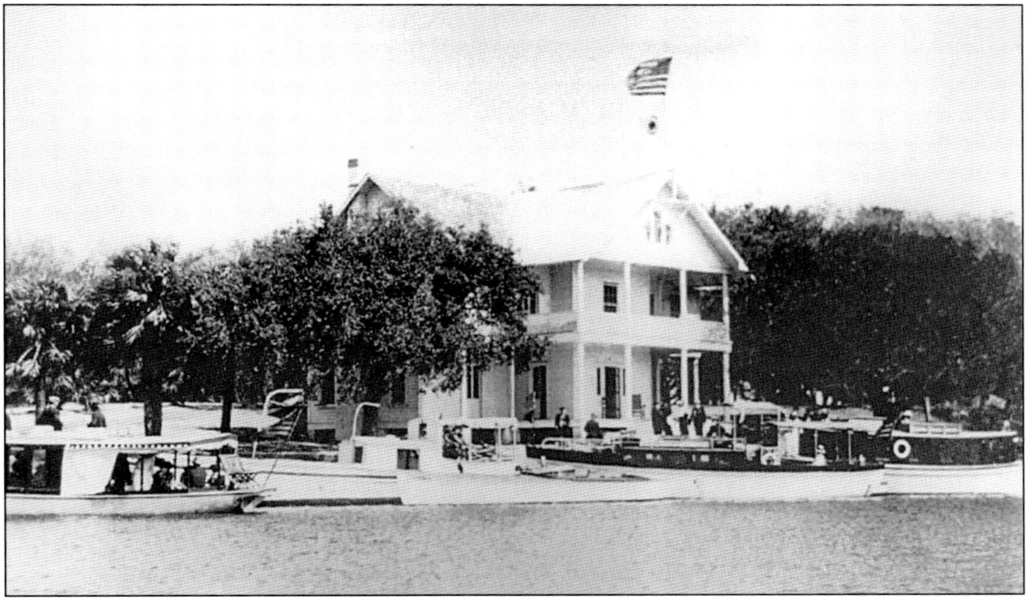

The Eau Gallie Yacht Club was organized in 1907, and the building was completed in 1911. George Paddison, owner of East Coast Lumber, donated the site and became the first commodore. Other founding members were the Gleasons, the Rossetters, the Castlemans, and Alexander Hodgson. One of the oldest yacht clubs in the state, it served as a social center for the local elites and winter visitors. Inside, there was a men's smoking room, a women's bridge room, a reception hall, and a large ballroom. The building is a private home today.

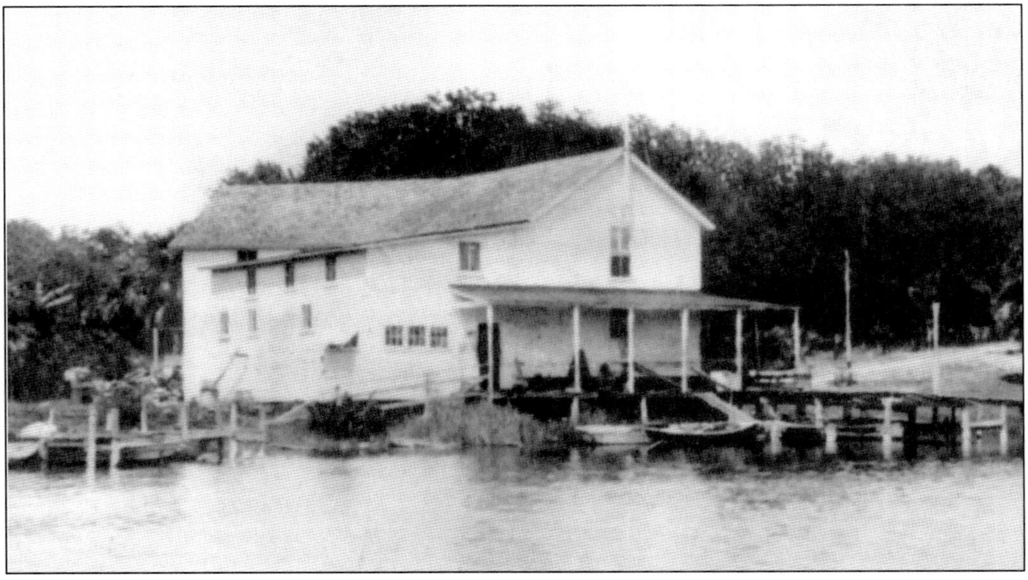

The Hodgson Brothers Boat Ways, Machine Shop, and General Store was located on the north shore of the Eau Gallie River directly to the west of the Yacht Club. The three Hodgson brothers moved to Eau Gallie from Canada in 1883–1884. They sold dry goods and groceries, and built, repaired, and chartered boats. They opened service on their steamer, the *Kathleen*, in 1888. Dr. Sarah Hodgson, wife of one of the brothers, opened a medical office and drugstore at the corner of Houston and Young. The structure was demolished around 1930.

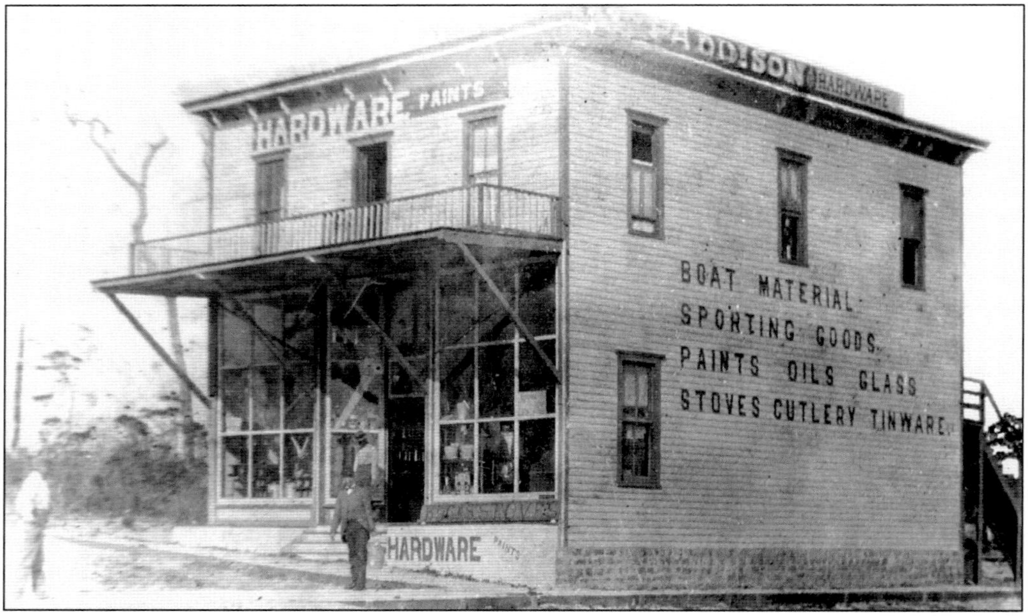

George Paddison opened a hardware business in 1889 where he sold general merchandise and building supplies. His store was located on Ninth Street (Eau Gallie Boulevard). Paddison's business grew, and he started East Coast Lumber and Supply in 1902. East Coast provided building material of various kinds, citrus packing supplies, and lumber. The plant was run on electricity powered by an artesian well. There was a large pier and a freight dock on the river. Later, Paddison expanded his business into Melbourne, Cocoa, Titusville, Stuart, and Fort Pierce. East Coast Lumber is still in business today.

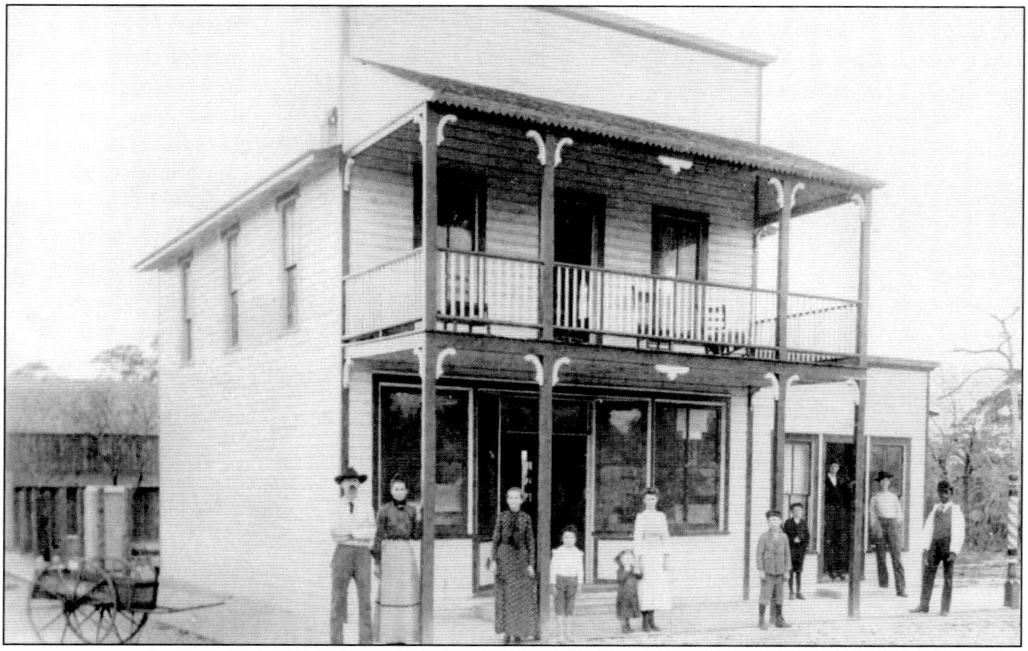

A block away from Paddison's, at the corner of Ninth and Highland, was the store shown above. Owner H. Bradford and family pose on the porch. Later this store would become G.W. Sullivan's Ice Cream Parlor. The barber next door poses in front of his shop, too.

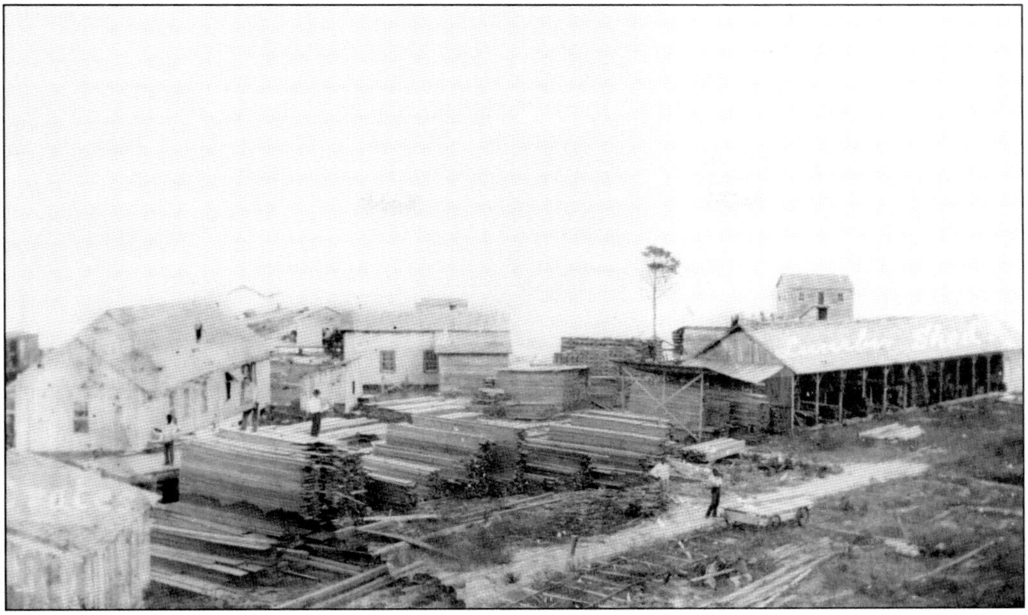

Eau Gallie's economic activity centered on the intersection of Pineapple Avenue, the Indian River, and Ninth Street. This is where the river-to-rail connections, Paddison's store and lumberyard, the Riverview Hotel, the Indian River Trading Company, and other businesses were located. The photo above shows East Coast Lumber. The one below shows the shore end of the railroad pier with East Coast's dock in the background.

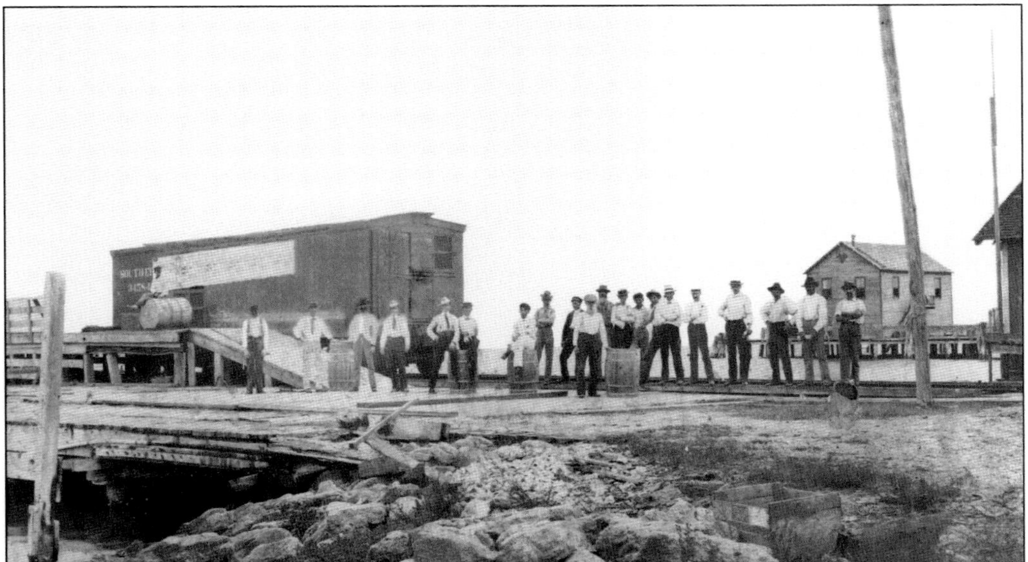

When the railroad came to Eau Gallie, economic activity increased. In 1893, when Eau Gallie was the southern terminus, the railroad created a "Y" so that trains could turn around. From the "Y" Henry Flagler ran a spur through town and down to the riverfront. A trestle carried the cars directly out over the river where freight could be transferred between boats and the train. For example, Rossetter's fish house received fish from the boats, packed them in ice, and loaded them into the rail cars for shipment north.

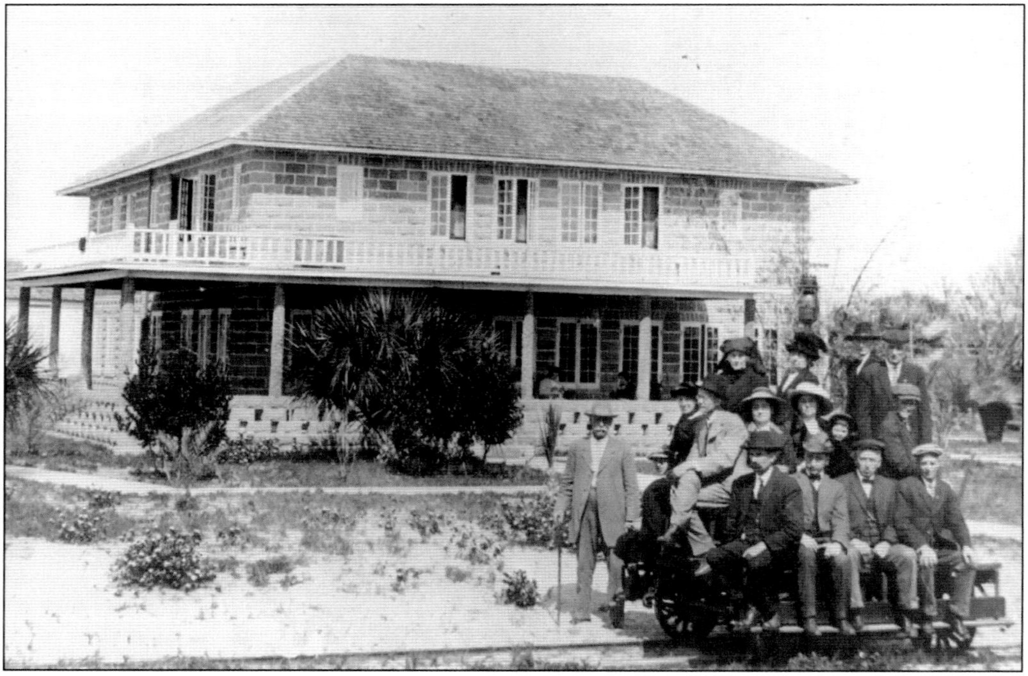

Capt. Rufus Beaujean was another successful entrepreneur of this era. In the picture above, taken in front of the Villa Marine Hotel, Beaujean stands to the left of a group of people riding the tramcar between the Melbourne Beach Pier and the Atlantic Ocean. As Melbourne and Eau Gallie grew and developed, the land across the river was used as farmland for pineapples. Later it became valuable as real estate for homes and hotels.

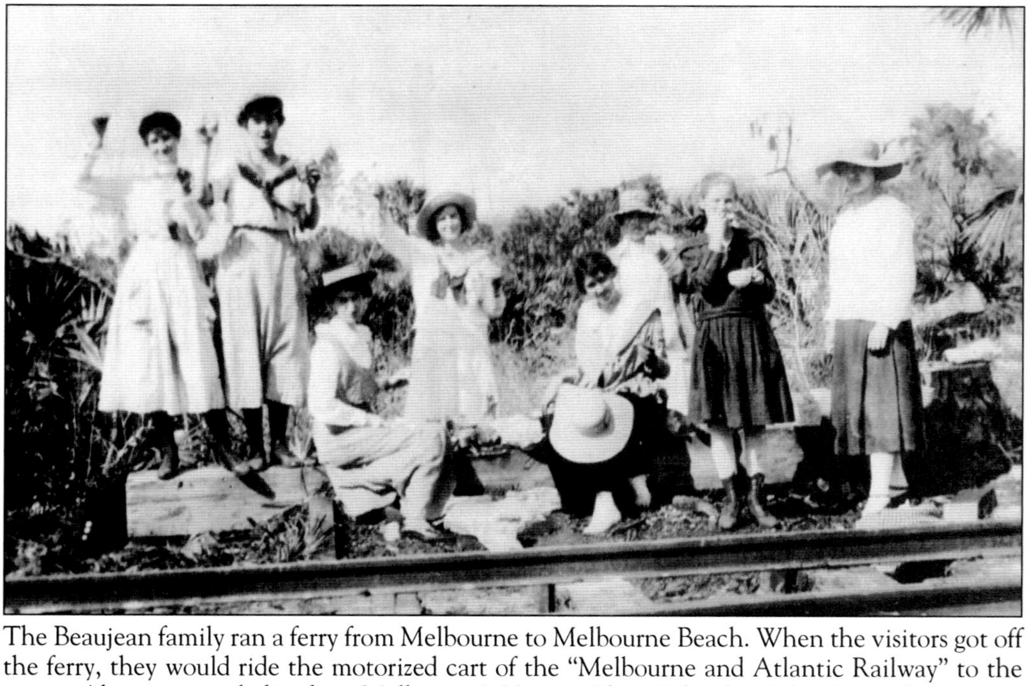

The Beaujean family ran a ferry from Melbourne to Melbourne Beach. When the visitors got off the ferry, they would ride the motorized cart of the "Melbourne and Atlantic Railway" to the ocean. Above, young ladies from Melbourne's Vernon Place School wait by the tracks on their day out at the beach in 1916.

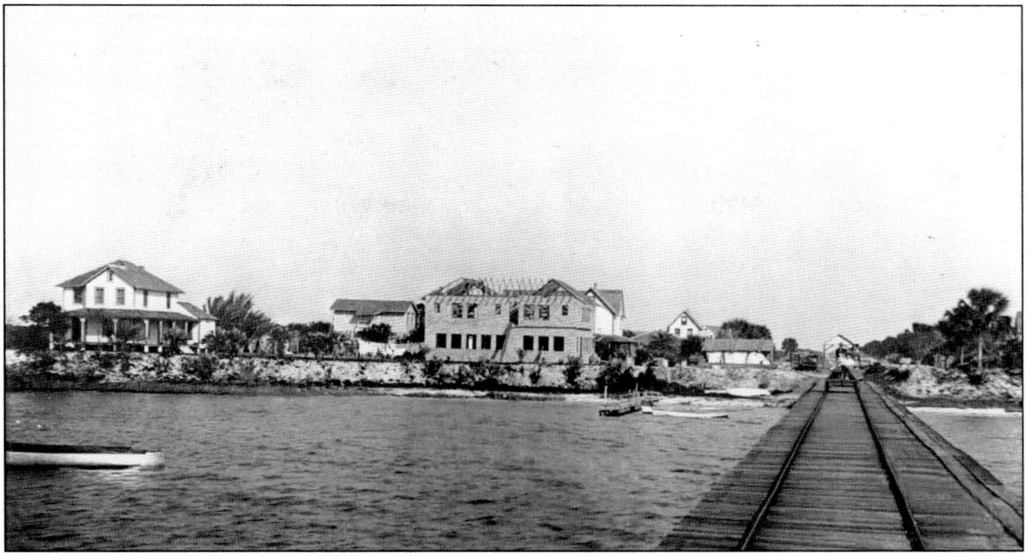

Alfred Wilcox built the Melbourne Beach Pier in 1889. In the scene above, the photographer stood at the end of the pier and looked east toward the community of Melbourne Beach. From the pier, the railroad extended to the beach. The Villa Marine, under construction here, was completed in 1912.

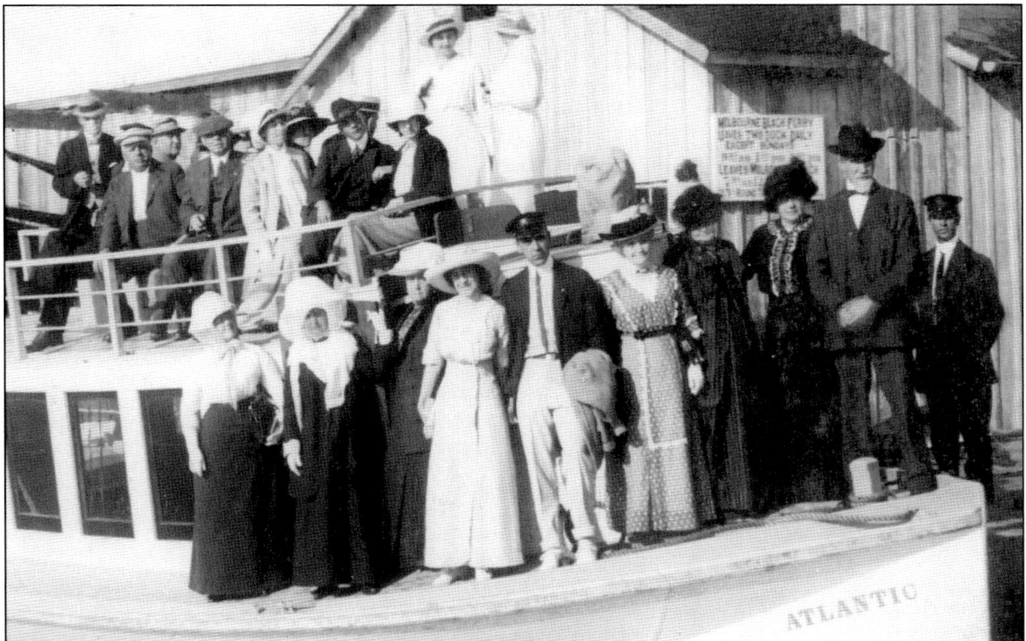

In 1916, visitors and locals board the ferry *Atlantic* for their trip from the Beaujean dock on Crane Creek to the Melbourne Beach Pier. According to the sign, the ferry left and returned three times daily except on Sunday. The fare was 25¢ for a round trip. When Melbourne Beach residents rode the ferry into Melbourne to get groceries, they could buy fresh vegetables from the Harada, Ozaki, and Ohi family members who sold their produce at the dock.

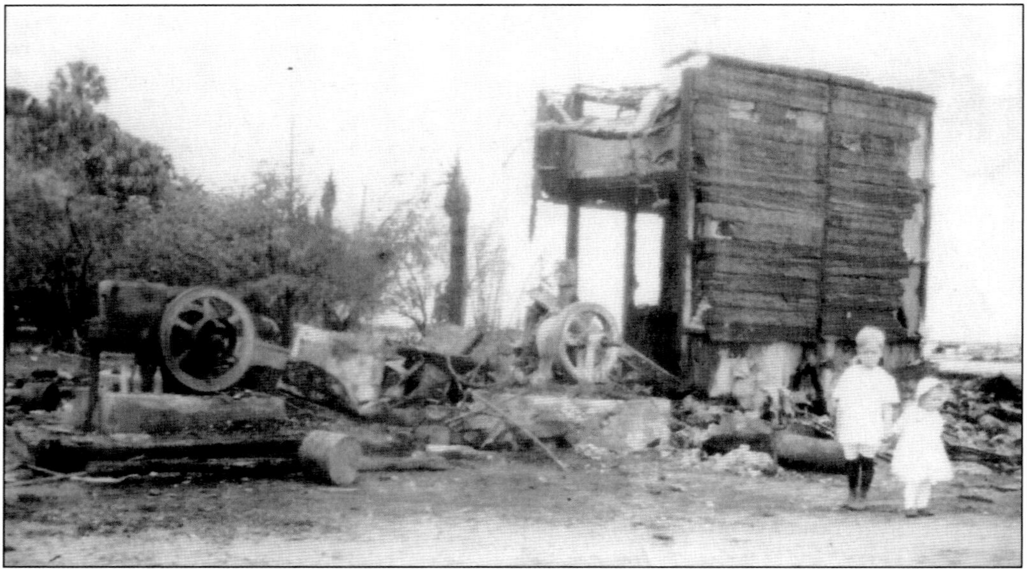

The end of an era for Melbourne is shown in this picture of the remains of the Claude Edge building on Front Street. The business district of Melbourne was quickly reduced to ashes after someone threw a malfunctioning stove out a second-story window. The stove lit the wooden sidewalk and the fire quickly spread. This was the death knell for the old riverfront business district, and although Edge rebuilt at the corner of Front and New Haven, others did not. Stewart's new location was up the hill and next to the Brown House and the railroad tracks. Christmas Cottage occupies that building today.

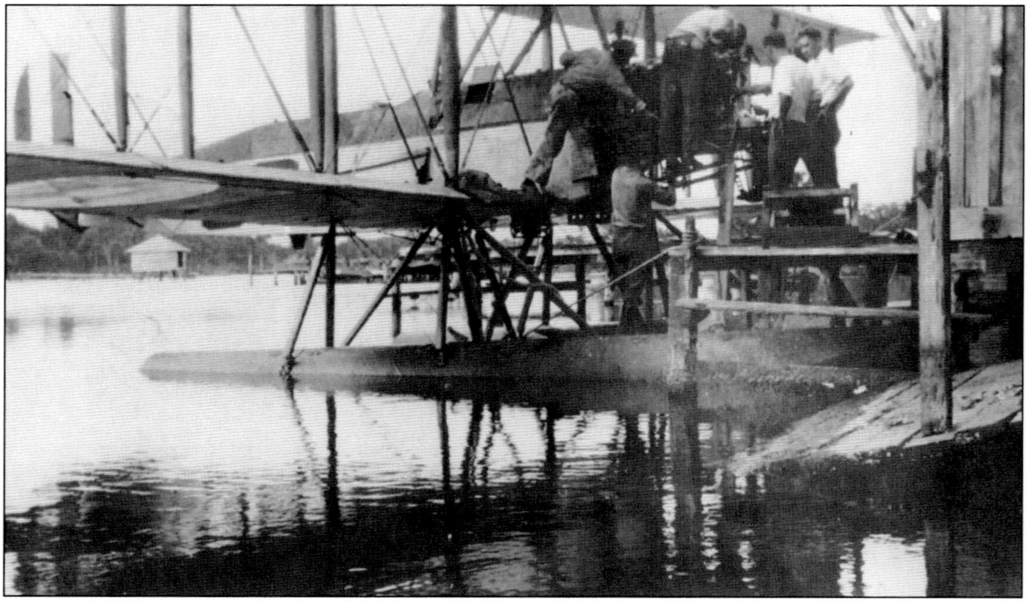

Another new era of transportation was in the wings, so to speak, as the gasoline combustion engine gave rise to a more versatile form of mobility than the railroad. The age of the automobile was on, and beyond that, air transportation would have its day. Here a floatplane has landed in Crane Creek in 1920. From 1910 to 1912, there were demonstration landings of Wright Brothers' airplanes on some Florida beaches and, by 1928, a Flying Circus was making its way around the state.

Three

The Dixie Highway

After World War I, tourism in Florida increased sharply. Railroads brought in a prosperous class of visitors, but "tin can tourists," who tented by the side of the road and fished for their dinners, came in camping vehicles. Other automobile travelers stayed in tourist homes, motels, or trailer parks. The state helped fund the Dixie Highway, which was cut through with draft animals and scrape pans by 1915 and paved in 1926. Main roads became ribbons of real estate promotion. Melbourne and Eau Gallie experienced a building and housing boom as population increased and more "snowbirds" chose the area for their winter homes. Vacationers and part-time residents lived in cabins, swam in community pools, and played horseshoes or shuffleboard.

While the tourist trade became more democratic, the large hotels with their golf courses and tennis courts also enjoyed a boom. Many durable structures of Mediterranean Revival architecture remain today as testimony to the Florida Land Boom. Drainage and road projects that began during the early 1920s have also left a lasting mark. Decline set in by 1926, and big hotels like the Oleanders, the Lincoln, the Melbourne, and the Indialantic suffered. Platted lots and streets went undeveloped as land values tumbled and banks failed. The Great Crash of 1929 dealt a final blow to the national economy and, during the Great Depression of the 1930s, people struggled to get by.

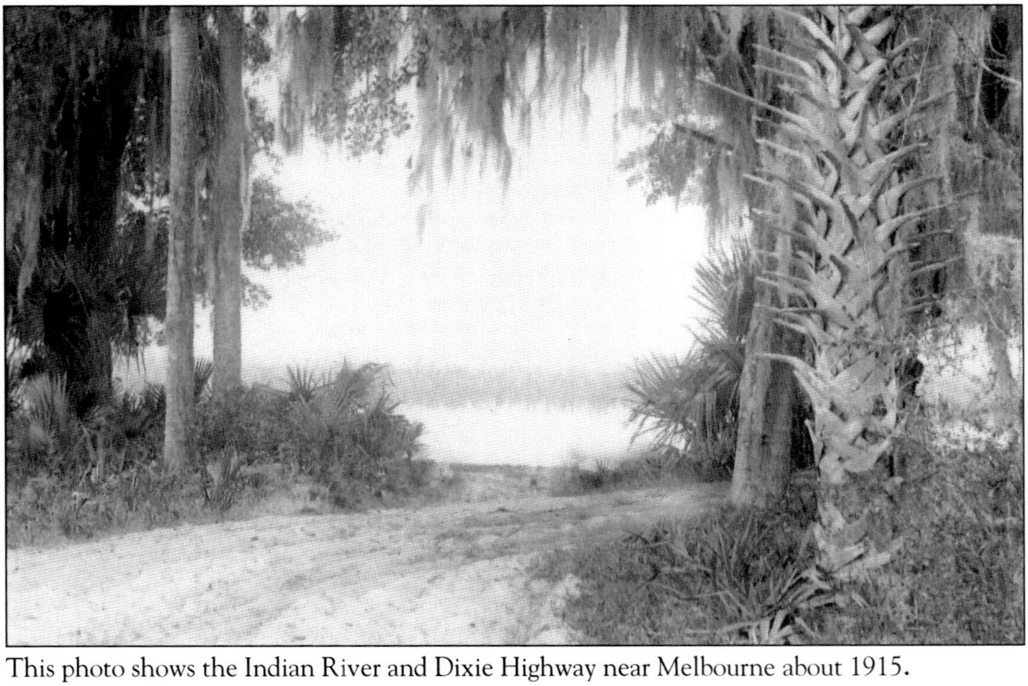

This photo shows the Indian River and Dixie Highway near Melbourne about 1915.

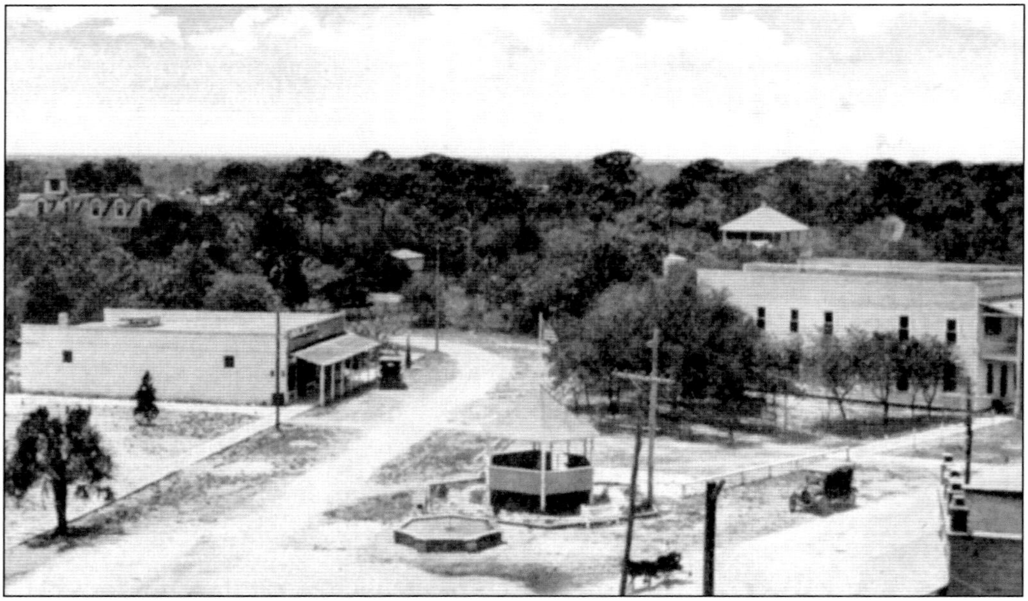

Scenes like the one above, in which autos and horse-drawn wagons share New Haven Avenue, were over quickly as mass production of cars and the innovation of consumer credit brought on a new era for the United States. In the view above is Campbell Park and bandstand. The Myles Building is visible on the right. In 1925, the Flat Iron Building would occupy the space between the park and the Myles.

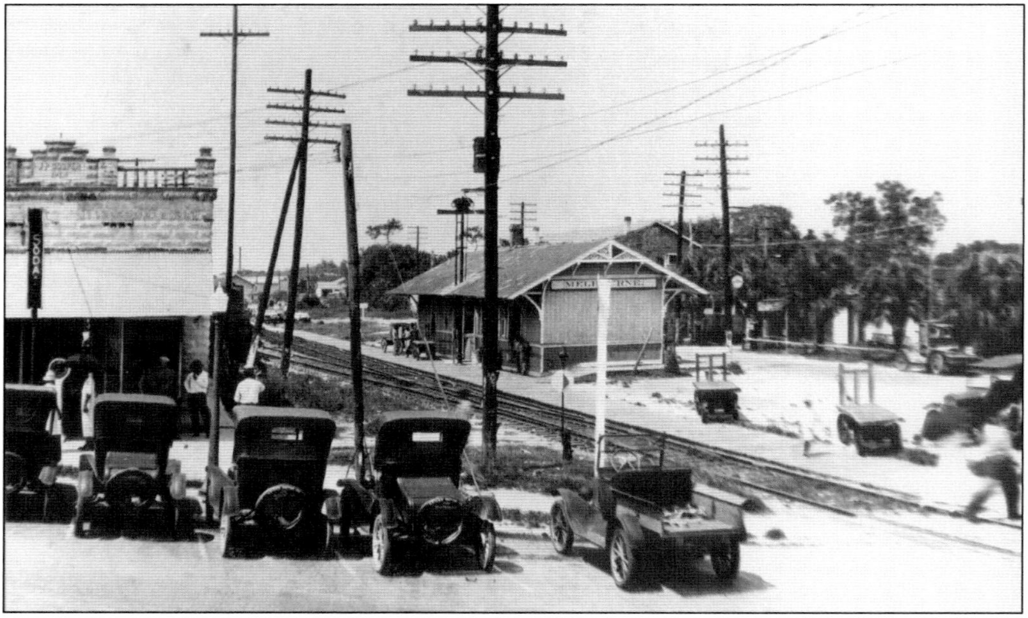

The center of Melbourne's transportation had shifted from the river to the depot on Oleander Drive. A bus service connected the hotels and the railroad and Melbourne's new downtown area grew rapidly. As railroads spread across the country, telegraph lines went with them. Next came telephone and electrical wires in the same rights-of-way. This photo was taken in 1925. The 1920s were the years of the greatest growth in the automobile industry and the decade when telephone service became widespread in cities across the country.

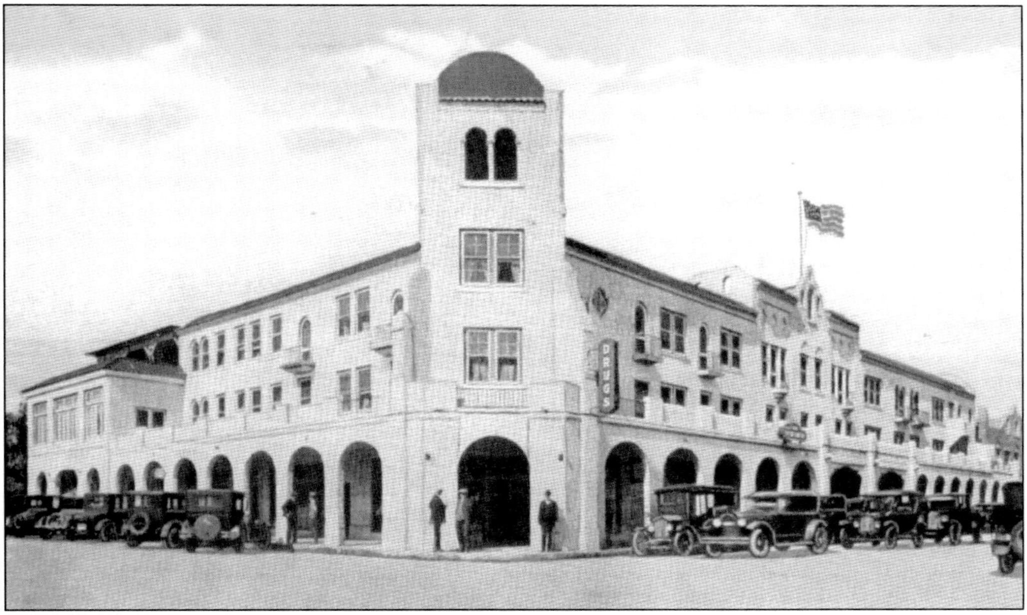

Melbourne's monument to the automotive age was built in 1924 during the land boom years. Located at the intersection of the Dixie Highway and New Haven Avenue, its corner faced Melbourne's first traffic light. The Mediterranean Revival structure had 100 rooms, office space, a bar, a restaurant, and the telegraph office. For a while, it served as the police dispatch office. The hotel's signal characteristic, its dome, could be seen from the river. The Melbourne Hotel has been remodeled, but still dominates the busy intersection.

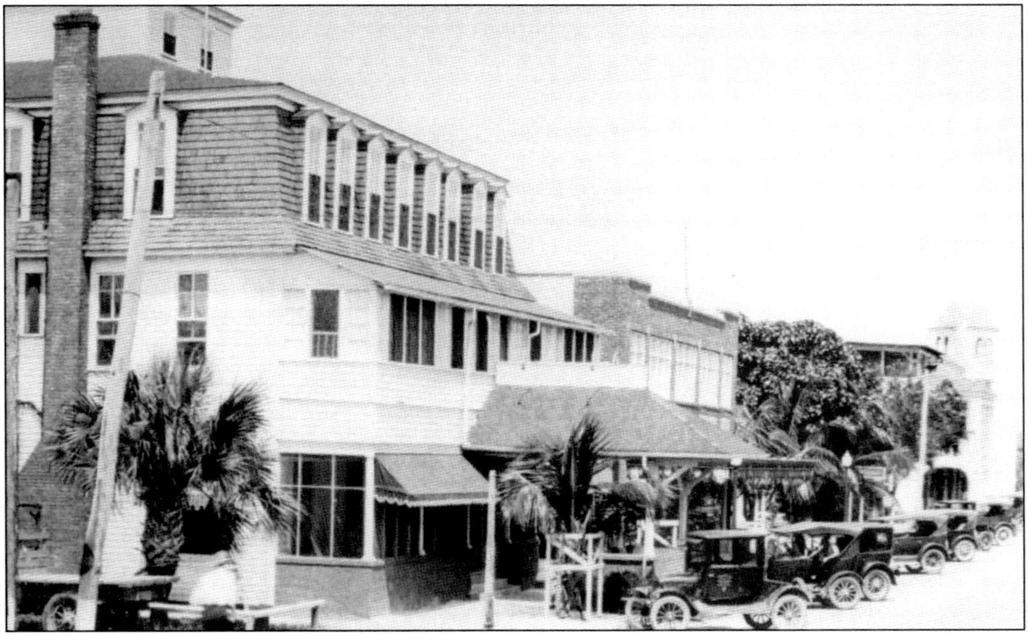

The Brown House stood at the northeast corner of New Haven and Depot Drive. It was remodeled and its upstairs porch enclosed to create more rooms during the boom years. To the right of the hotel is Stewart's Hardware, now Christmas Cottage, and farther down the block is the Melbourne Hotel, now the 1900 Building.

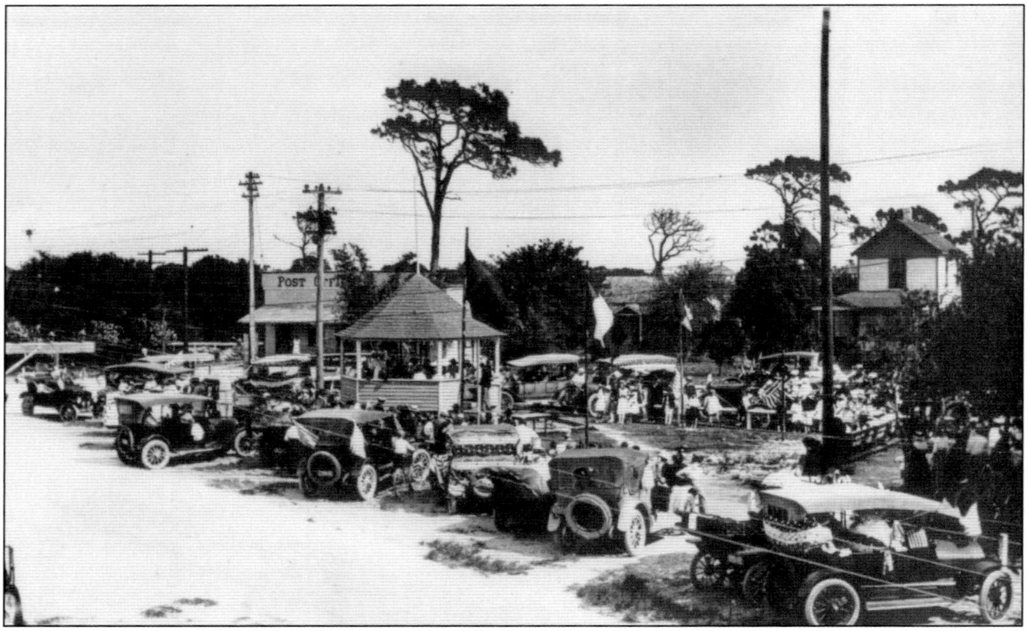

In April of 1918, the city held a Liberty Bond fundraiser at Campbell Park. Even at this early date, the presence of the automobile is overwhelming. The building to the left and rear of the bandstand is the Post Office and Land Office. The historic structure is now Betty's Antiques. The bandstand has been removed to enlarge the intersection, but the park remains.

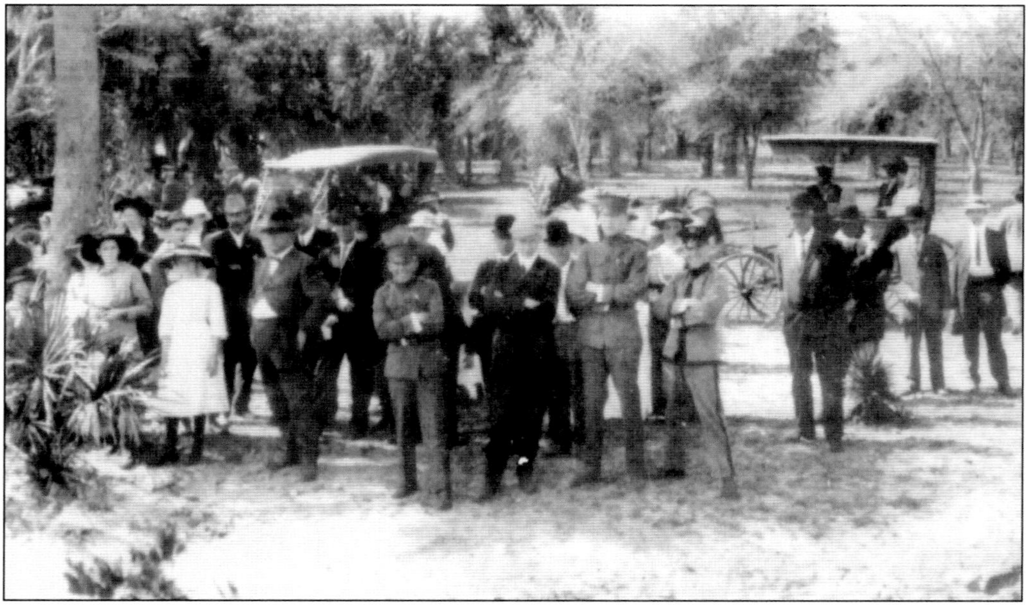

A crowd celebrates Washington's Birthday in Pineapple Park on the riverfront in Eau Gallie. To the left are cadets from K.M.I. Taken in 1914, this photo gives a glimpse of the brief era that was on the cusp between the horse and the automobile. Notice the early cars on the right and the horse-drawn surrey behind the crowd on the left.

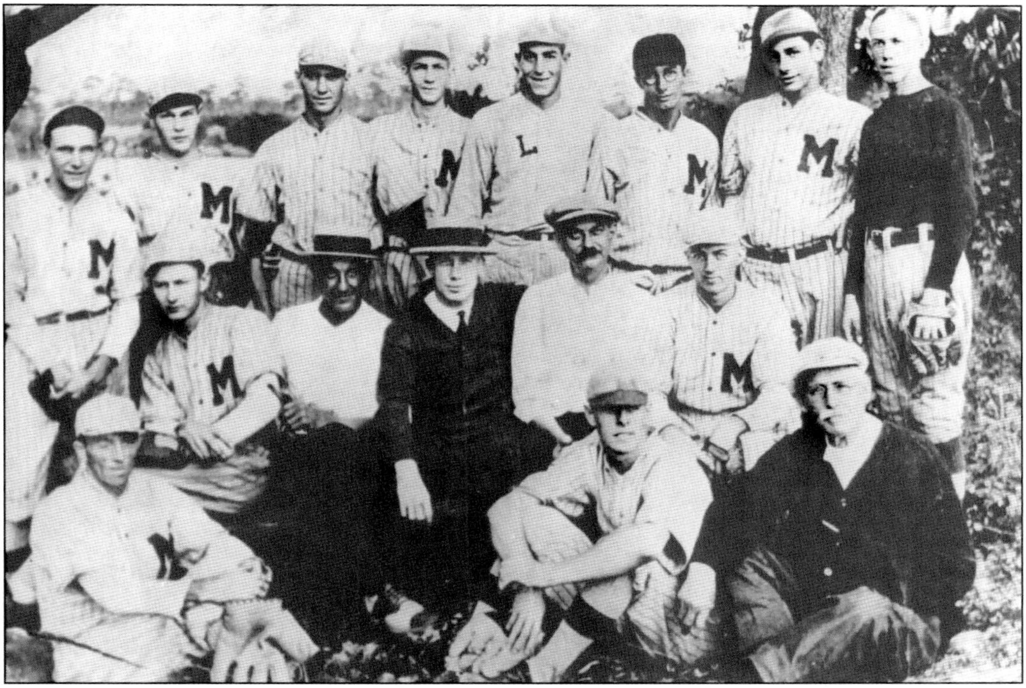

During the boom of the 1920s, Melbourne's baseball team, the Melbourne Magnolias, was organized. In the 1924 photo above are (first row) Dad Callahan, Emmet Hedges, and E.P. Simpson; (second row) Ferdinand W. Schaap, E.G. Sweetland, Thomas Horne, Fred Fisher, and Bion E. Hewett; (third row) James Pollard, Cecil Powell, John Perry, Max K. Rodes, Warren Miles, Harvey Huggins, John Scott, and J.W. Strange.

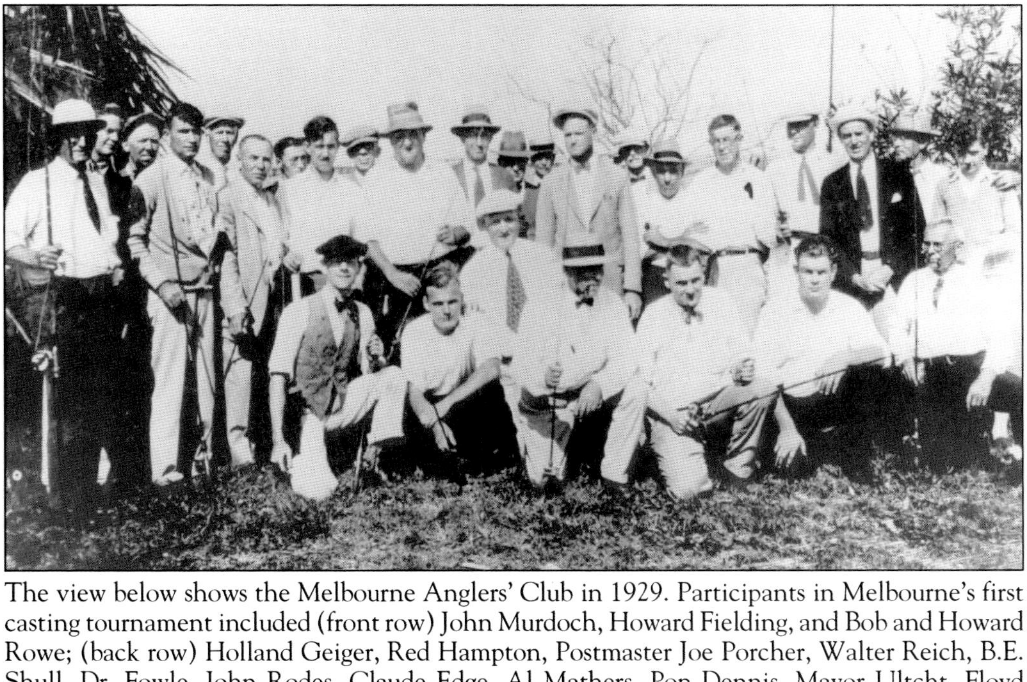

The view below shows the Melbourne Anglers' Club in 1929. Participants in Melbourne's first casting tournament included (front row) John Murdoch, Howard Fielding, and Bob and Howard Rowe; (back row) Holland Geiger, Red Hampton, Postmaster Joe Porcher, Walter Reich, B.E. Shull, Dr. Fowle, John Rodes, Claude Edge, Al Mathers, Pop Dennis, Mayor Ultcht, Floyd Ultcht, and V.C. Brownlie.

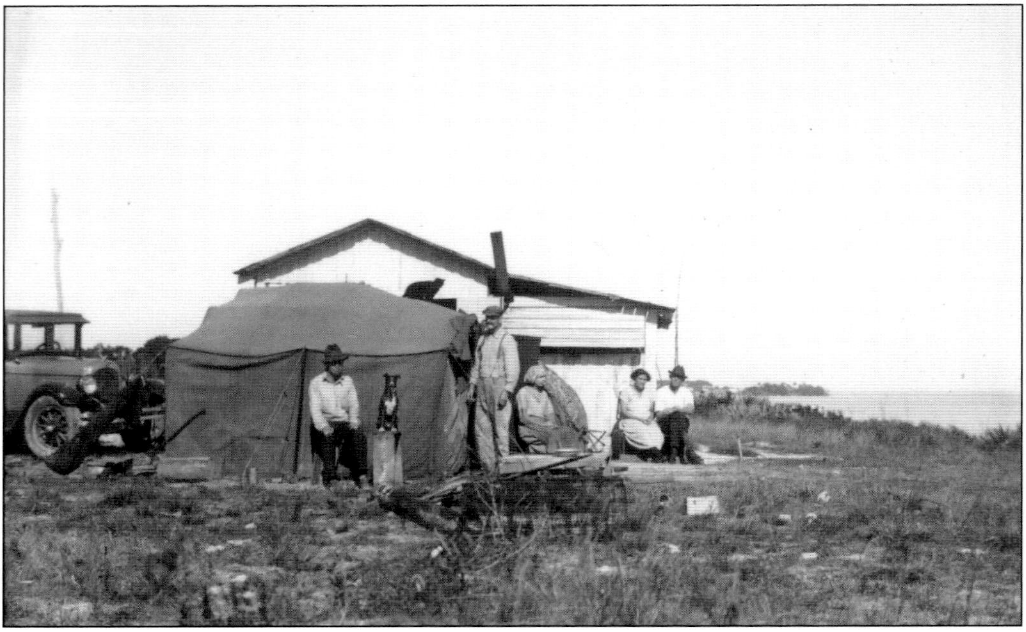

The automotive camper movement began just after World War I with surplus tents and vehicles from the war. In 1919, the Tin Can Tourists of the World organized in Tampa, Florida. Municipalities and private investors opened Tin Can campgrounds across the state, beginning in the 1920s. Florida began paving highways under its "good roads" program. Tin Canners Ernest and Jenny Myer stopped by the side of the Dixie Highway south of Melbourne at the "Barnacle Camp" in the photo above.

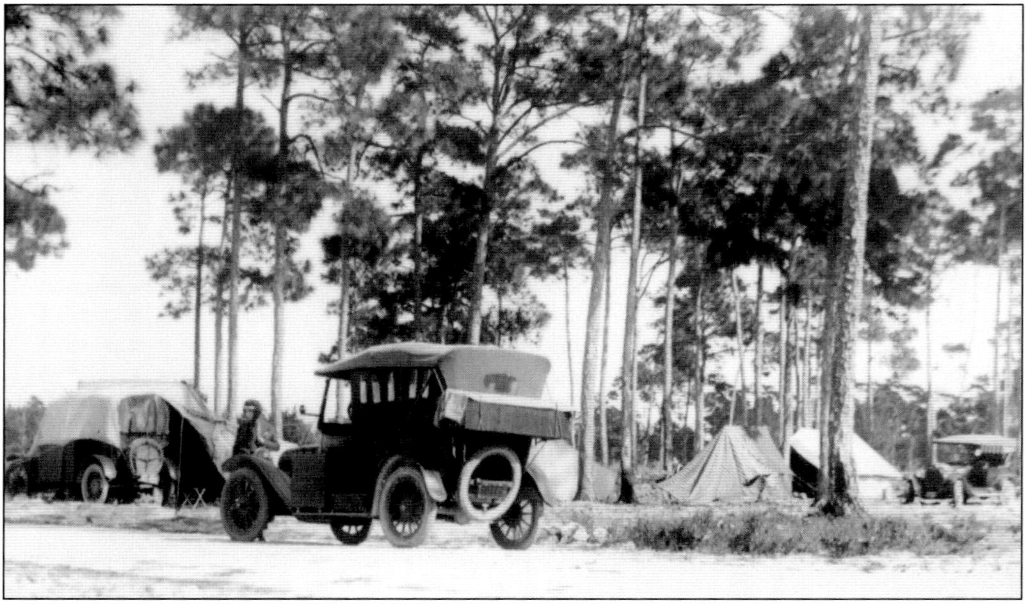

Tin Can Tourists stopped at campgrounds like this one on the Florida East Coast. Tents were pitched on the ground or as attachments to cars. Campers carried gear strapped to the running boards and on the trunks of their vehicles. The Melbourne Campground operated in the early 1920s and was located on the north side of New Haven Avenue between Grant and Waverly. The campground had outhouses and a water pump.

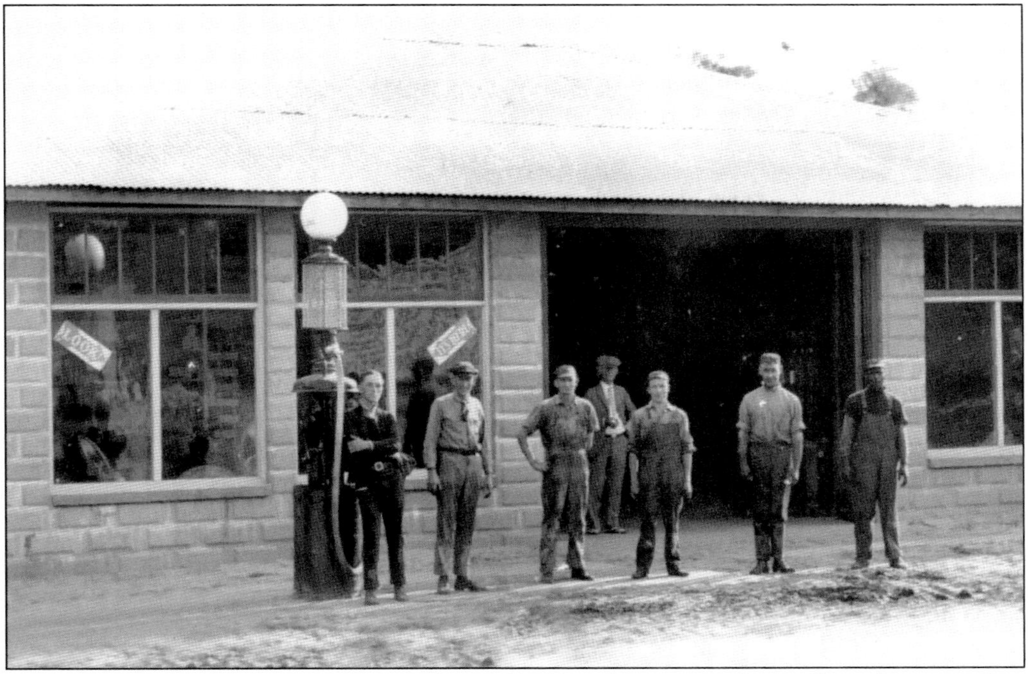

Because Melbourne and Eau Gallie are located halfway between Jacksonville and Miami, they were ideal places for highway traffic to stop, buy gas, take an overnight break, or just eat a meal. During the 1920s, the Tin Can Tourist movement, the Florida Land Boom, and the Automobile Decade converged, and the little midway towns became stopover points on the popular Dixie Highway. W.S. Maxwell opened a gas station in Melbourne in 1913. By 1931, there were 15 gas stations in town. Above, John Raymond and his mechanics stand outside his new station in 1922.

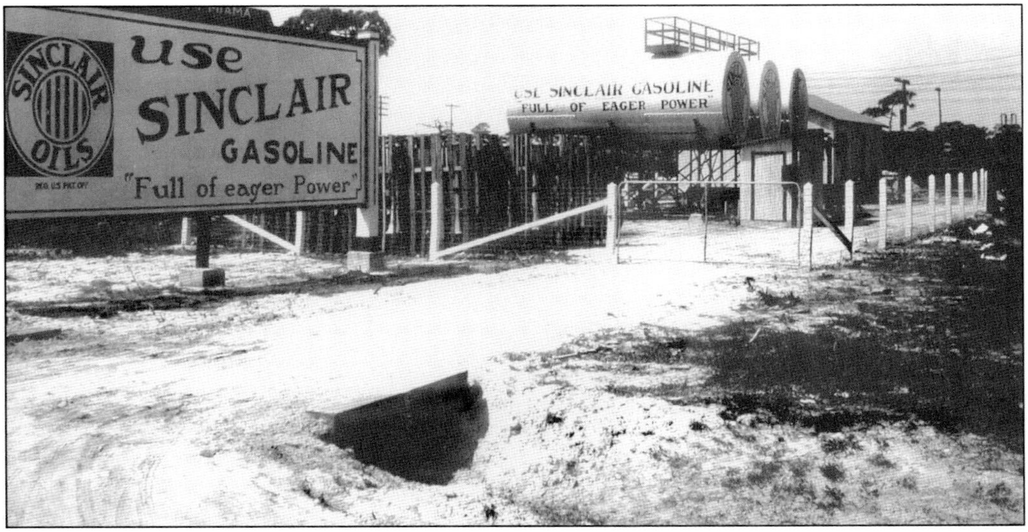

In the early 1920s in Eau Gallie, an auto sales and service business stood at the corner of Pineapple and Ninth Streets. The Rossetters owned service stations next to the railroad spur on Pineapple and in north Melbourne on the Dixie Highway. In 1926, Sinclair Oil built the tank facility shown below on South Dixie Highway in Hopkins next to the railroad. That facility remains in business today as Glover Oil.

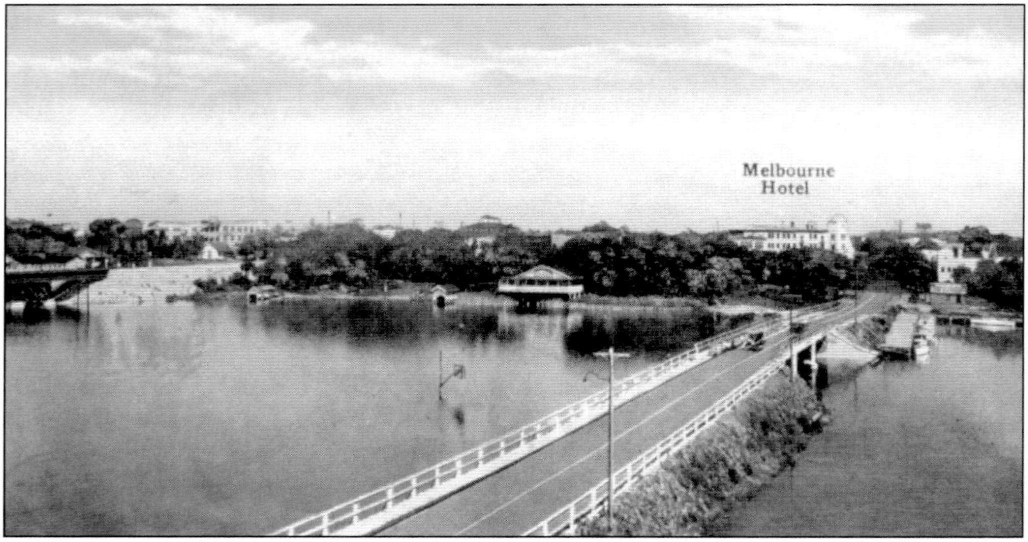

This mid-1920s view, looking north across Crane Creek into Melbourne, shows the Dixie Highway Bridge over the creek and the Melbourne Hotel one block into Melbourne on the road. On the left is the railroad bridge. The road dips at the end of the bridge and rises up a slope into town. When the second bridge was built across the creek in 1958, it was higher and the dip was removed.

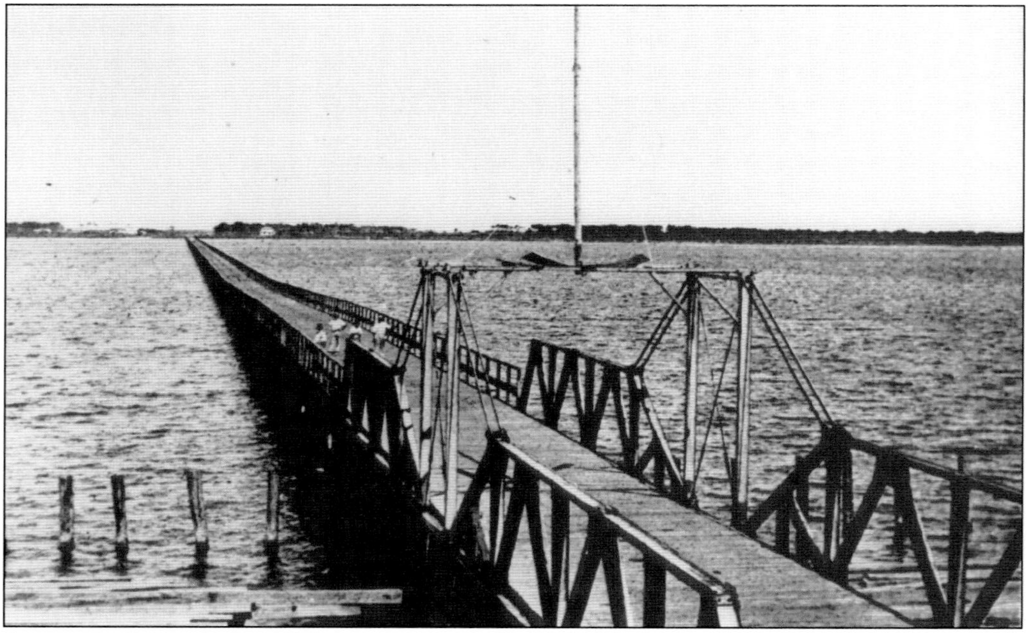

Ernest Kouwen-Hoven, developer of Indialantic-by-the-Sea, built the first bridge from Melbourne across the river. Work began in 1919 and partially financed through the sale of private bonds. Bondholders could buy lots in Kouwen-Hoven's Indialantic for $20 each. Its opening in 1921 motivated city fathers to pave New Haven between the bridge and the railroad tracks. "Old Shaky," as it was later known, was 9,706 feet long and rattled fearsomely. Kouwen-Hoven set up sawmills in the Melbourne Village area and Merritt Island to provide the lumber. The bridge charged a toll until 1933. This view shows the original hand-operated draw.

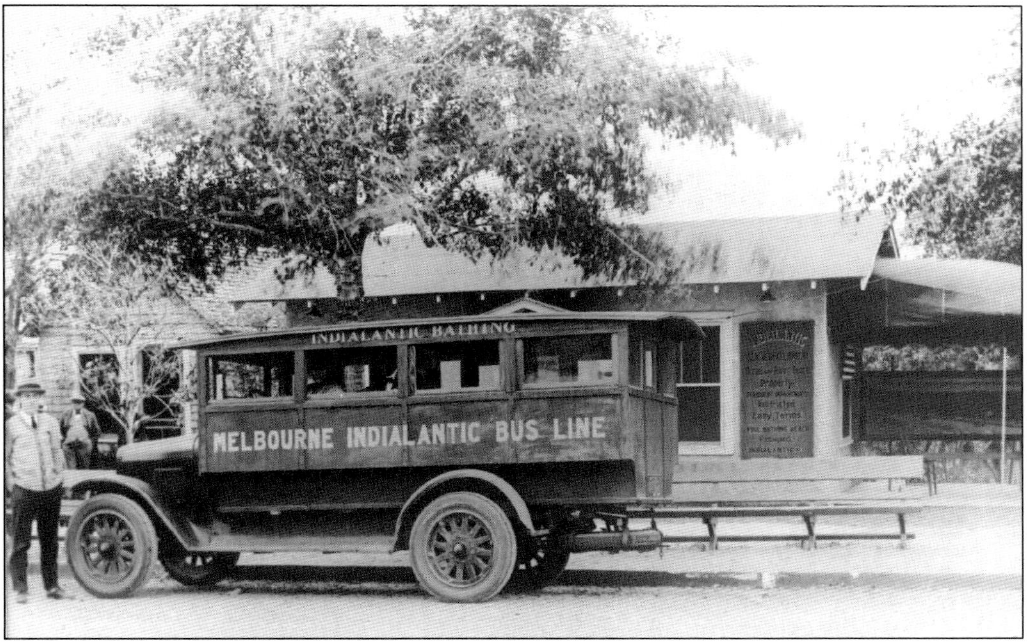

Once the bridge was built, a bus line operated between Melbourne and Indialantic. The bus advertised "Indialantic Bathing" and took interested buyers from Kouven-Hoven's office on New Haven and the Dixie Highway to the beach and his properties. The Beaujeans still operated their ferry to Melbourne Beach since there was no road between there and Indialantic.

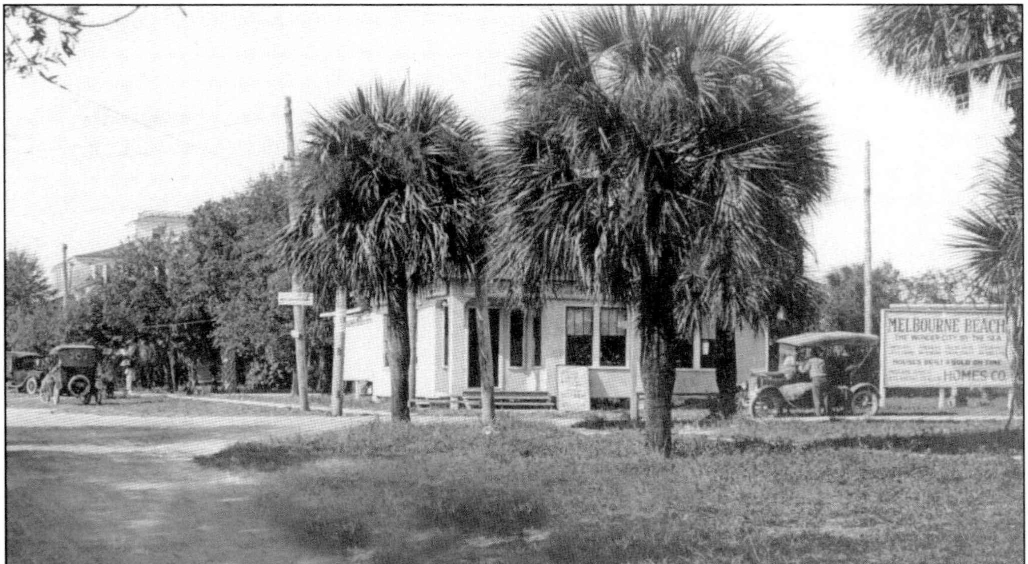

The boom was on in earnest in the early 1920s. The sign on this New Haven Avenue building advertised properties in Melbourne Beach. Another sign on New Haven touted lots in Hiawatha Gardens. North of Eau Gallie, investors promoted Coquina Ridge. The depot in Eau Gallie burned *c.* 1925, compounding rail problems so much that local businessmen decided to buy a steamer, *The City of Eau Gallie*, to haul lumber and other building supplies into the town directly from Jacksonville. At the peak of the boom, Eau Gallie's population had grown to 1,200.

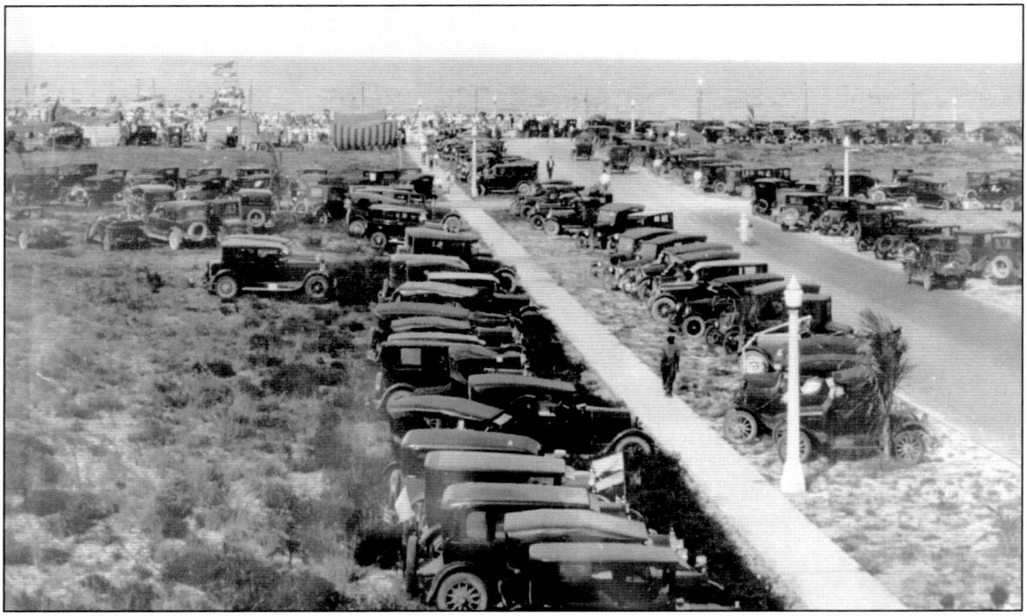

Indialantic and Melbourne Beach were very popular with vacationers. In this Fourth of July gathering in Indialantic, it is clear that beach development was tied to the automobile. In 1924, the area on the left at the end of Fifth Avenue would become the site of the Indialantic Casino. The Melbourne Beach Casino was built that year, too, and both offered bathing in artesian-water pools.

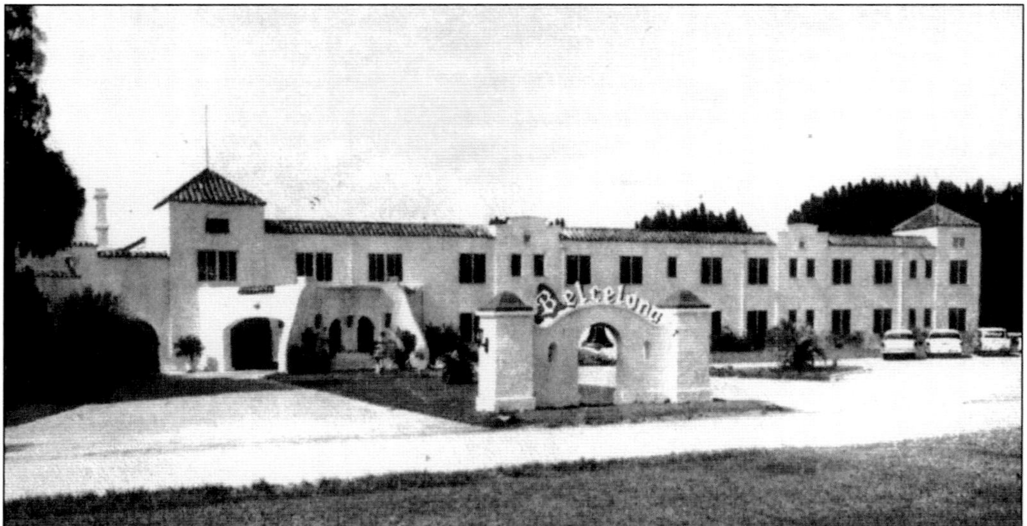

In 1923, Ernest Kouwen-Hoven built a Mediterranean Revival home on New Haven Avenue west of town and across the street from the new golf course. Advertising Magnolia Park as an exclusive subdivision with access to golfing, hunting, and fishing, he built a few impressive Mediterranean Revival homes and platted lots for more modest development in the future. In 1926, Robert Widrig bought the house, added two wings, and opened it as the Lincoln Hotel. It failed during the Depression but rose again as the Belcelona in 1957. The property was sold to Florida Air Academy in 1963. Magnolia Park was never finished but the land became the Magnolia Manor subdivision in the 1950s.

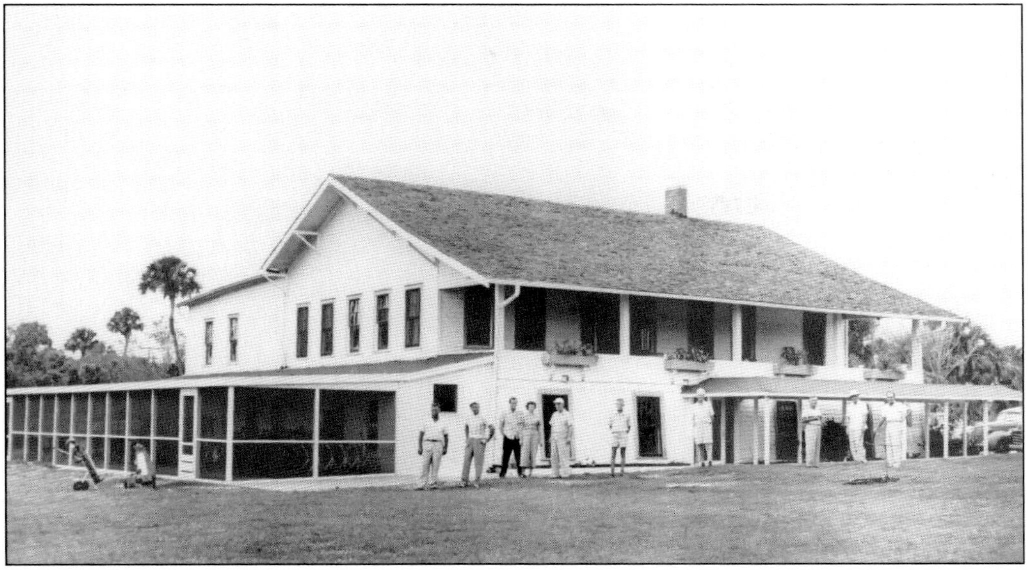

Kouven-Hoven, Charles Stewart, Claude Edge, L.G. McDowell, F.C. Powell, Ernest Every, and other Melbourne boosters established the Melbourne Golf and Country Club in 1920, hoping to increase Melbourne's appeal to buyers. Since so many land deals were made on golf courses, it was a logical step. The picture above shows the clubhouse at Melbourne. In 1926, the course expanded from 9 to 18 holes and, in 1929, an airstrip was added. Melbourne's little airport at that time was a few miles farther west. In 1924–1925, Charles Singleton uncovered the fossilized bones of a mastodon and the "Melbourne Man" at a bend in Crane Creek on the Melbourne golf course.

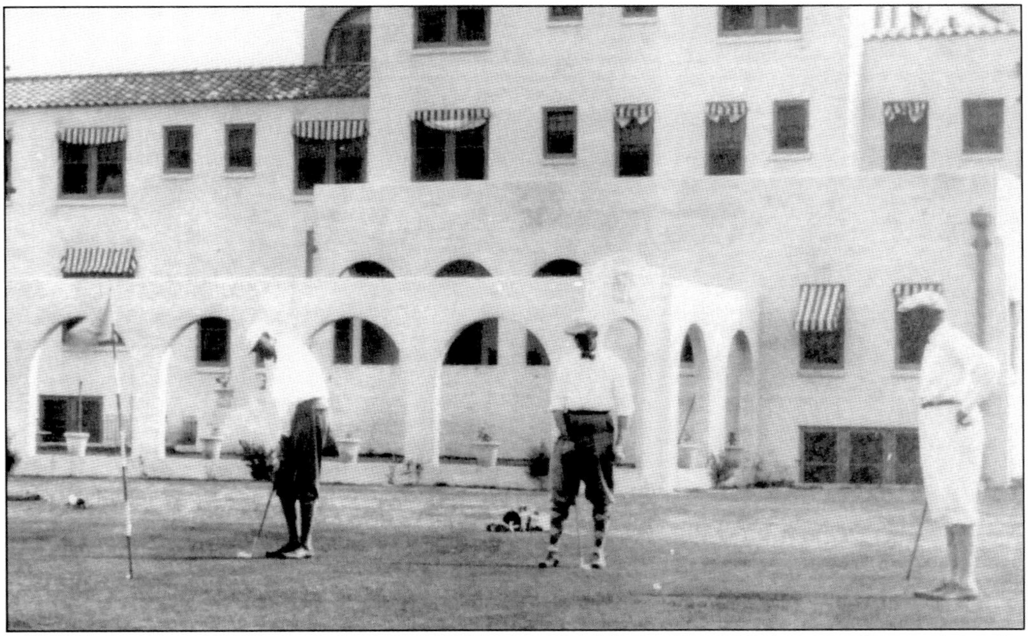

Golfers putt a round at the Indialantic Hotel course in the 1920s. The hotel suffered when the boom ended but revived under the ownership of Karl Abbott as the Tradewinds Hotel during the 1950s. Tom Doherty owned the hotel in the 1960s, after which it was sold to Florida Air Academy. It was demolished in the early 1980s and then replaced by several private homes.

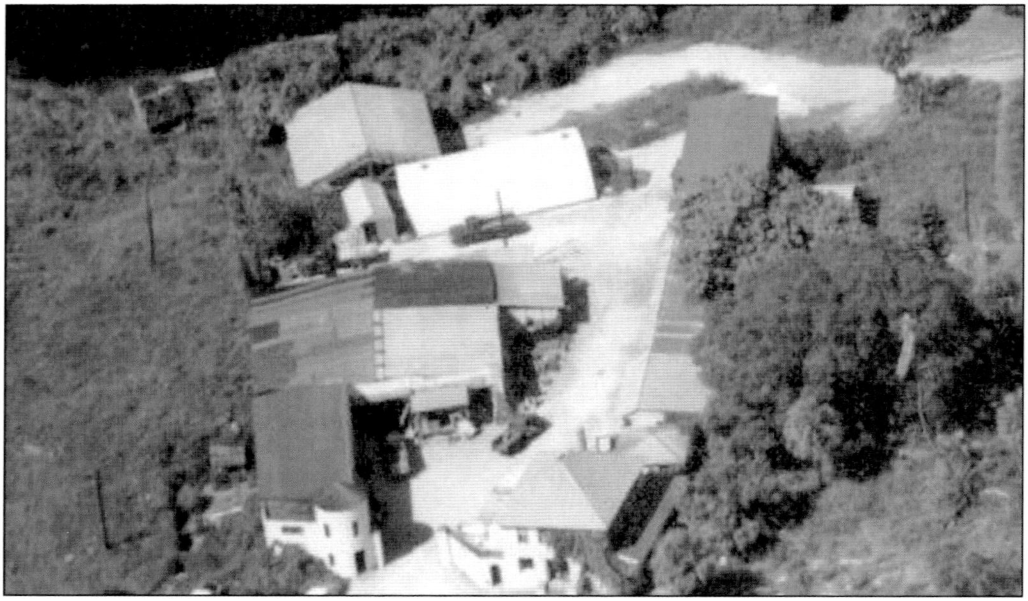

The aerial photo above shows Guerin Lumber and Construction Company on the south shore of Crane Creek between the railroad and Dixie Highway. Hal Guerin opened his business in 1923 when the boom was on the rise. When lumber and other supplies grew short, he opened a concrete block factory and sawmill on the site. A railroad spur led directly into the lumberyard. Building homes and sailboats, Guerin expanded the business to five locations from Cocoa to Vero Beach. When the boom died, he lost all of them excepting the Melbourne location. The business remained open until the 1970s, operated by Fred Guerin and Charles Dare.

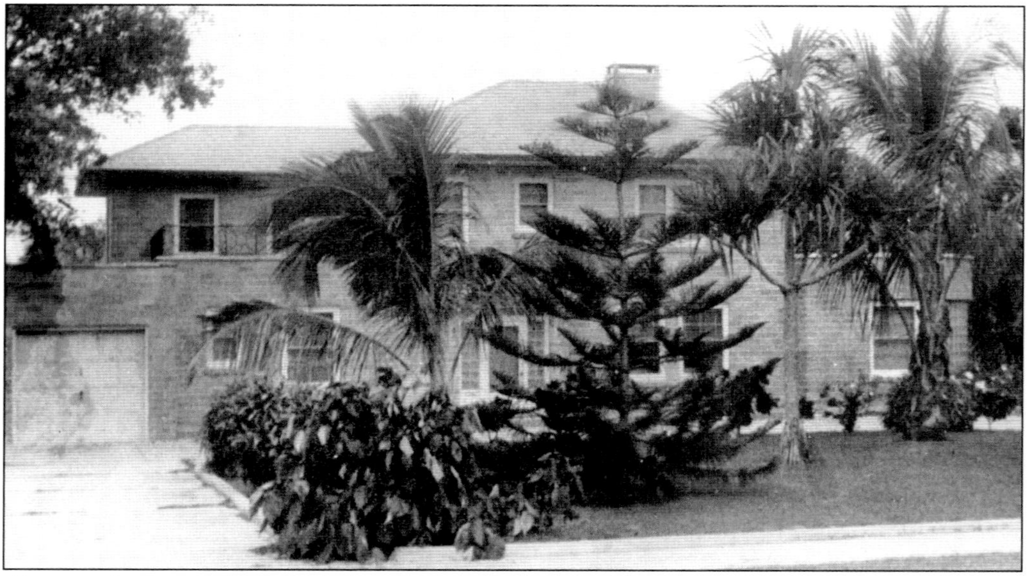

Above is the home of Roy and Florence Couch on Riverview Drive, south of the creek. Couch, inventor and pump manufacturer, was responsible for the successful Sebastian Inlet plan. The inlet was dredged and a rock barrier and 500 feet of jetty were built to create a current that would prevent the inlet from closing. The inlet refreshed the salt water content of the river, improving fishing and helping to balance the fresh water runoff from mainland drainage projects. The opening of the inlet has also deepened the Indian River slightly.

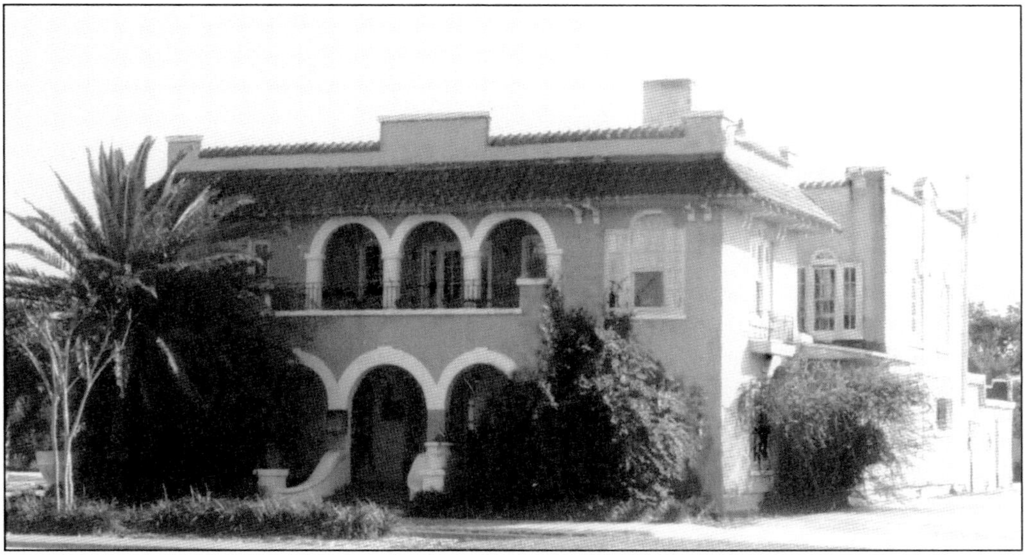

Typical of the boom is this 1926 Spanish or Mediterranean Revival mansion by local builder George Fowler. It was the home of William P. "Doc" Sloan, a citrus grove owner and bootlegger in the Roaring Twenties. During World War II and the housing crisis it created, the building was converted to apartments for servicemen. It was later used as a private health care facility. Today it is Miguel's Restaurant.

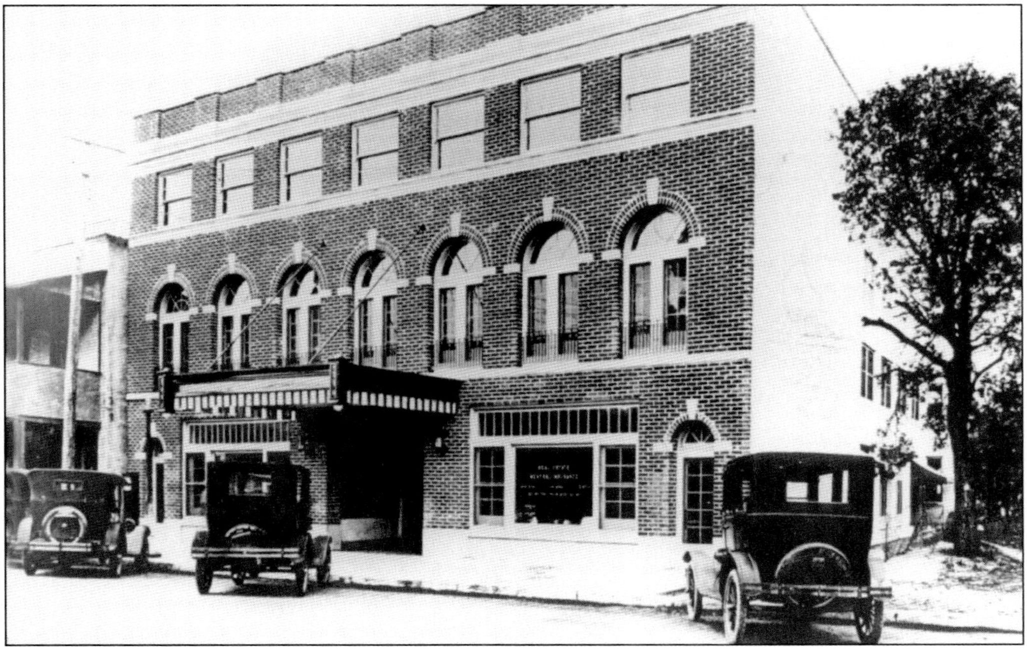

Local architect W.C. Christen designed the Melbourne Arcade Building to reflect the arcades of West Palm Beach and Miami. Built in 1925, it and the Flat Iron Building, completed in 1926, added storefront and office space to downtown Melbourne. Lock Davidson, realtor, promoter, and president and treasurer of the Melbourne Tillman Drainage District, had his office here. Development west of Melbourne progressed with Davidson's Melbourne Farms, Kouven-Hoven's Magnolia Park, and Frazier Campbell's June Park Speculation. Development pushed south as well, and the town of Palm Bay was chartered at Tillman on Turkey Creek.

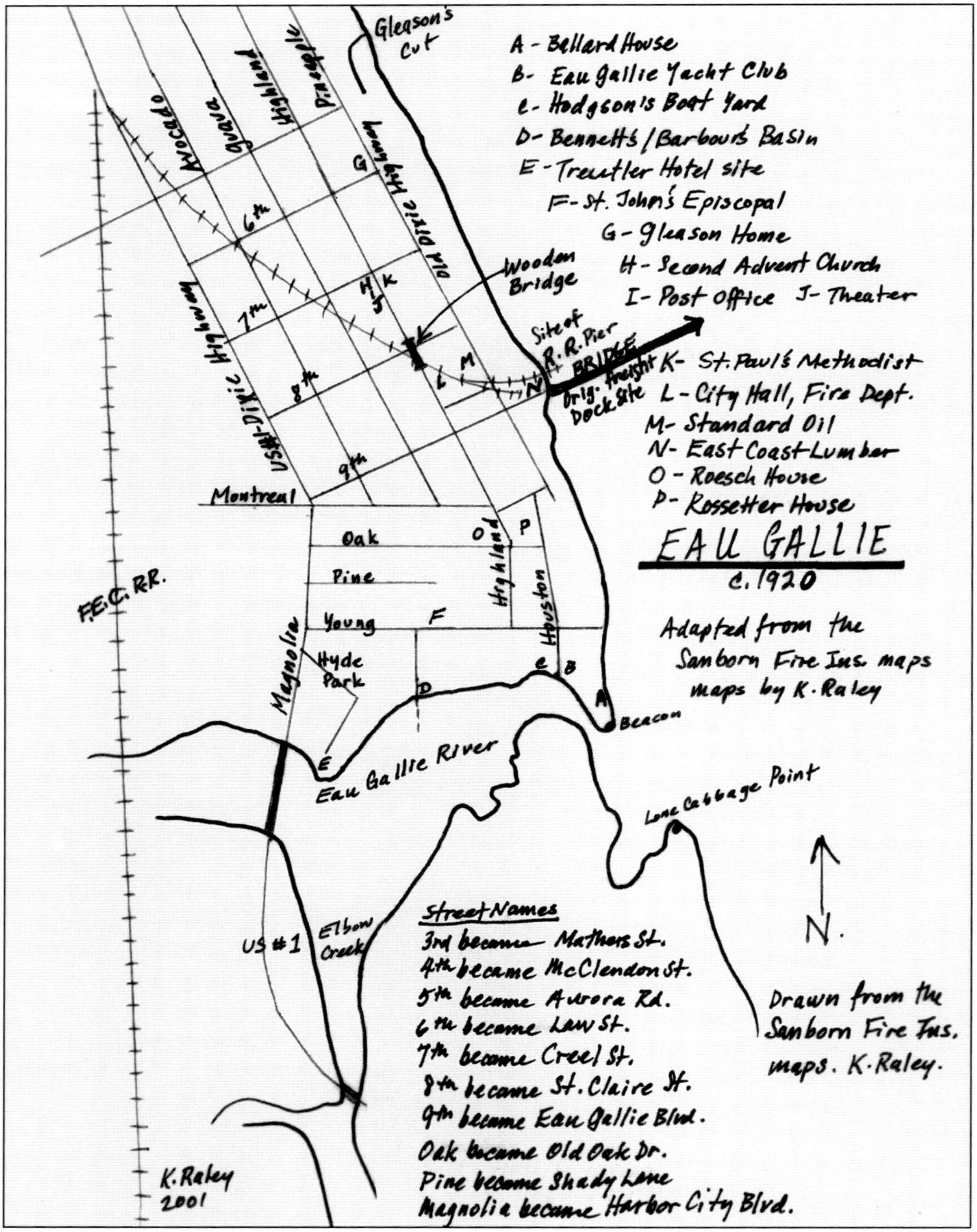

This map depicts Eau Gallie, Florida, *c.* 1920.

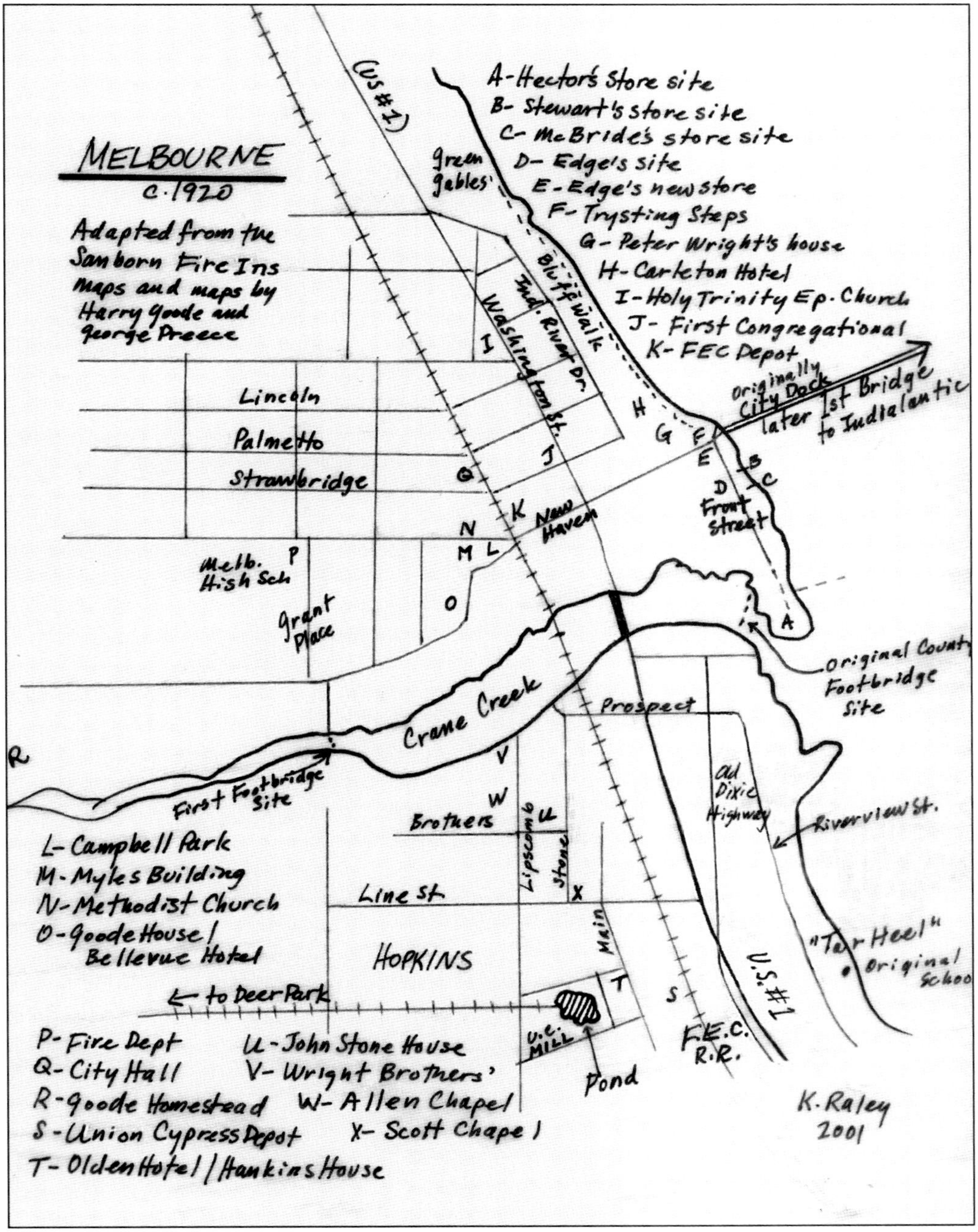

This map depicts Melbourne, Florida, *c.* 1920.

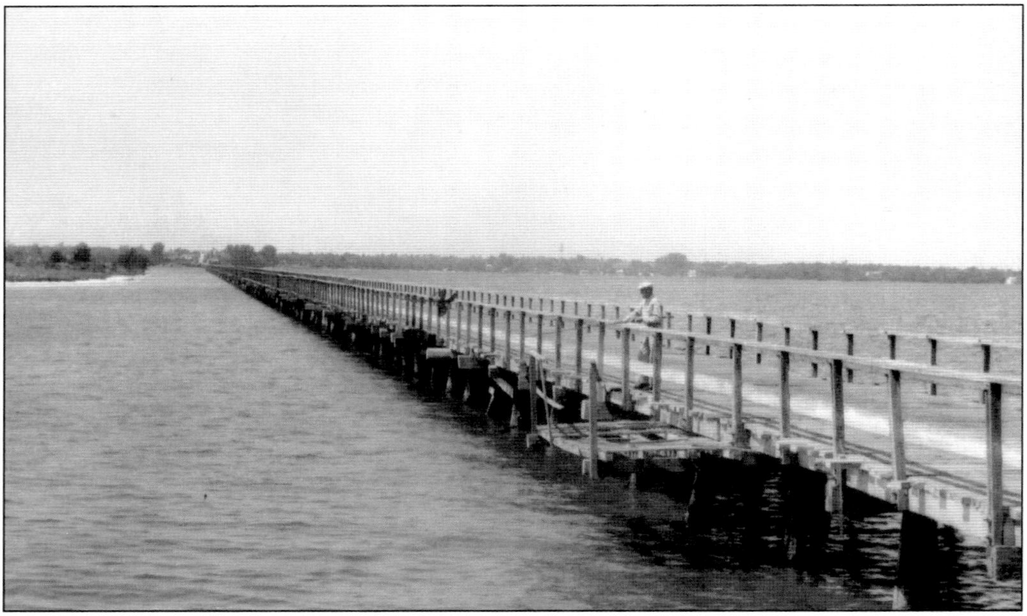

The first bridge across the Indian River from Eau Gallie originated at the foot of Ninth Street, passed just south of the tip of Merritt Island, and ended at the sandy path to Canova Beach. The bridge formally opened in 1926 on Eau Gallie's favorite civic holiday, George Washington's birthday. John Mathers completed his wooden drawbridge between the Barrier Island and Merritt Island the next year. The Eau Gallie Bridge had a hand-operated draw. The toll was 25¢ per car, plus #10¢ per passenger. During the Great Depression, the toll was discontinued and the State Road Commission took charge of the bridge.

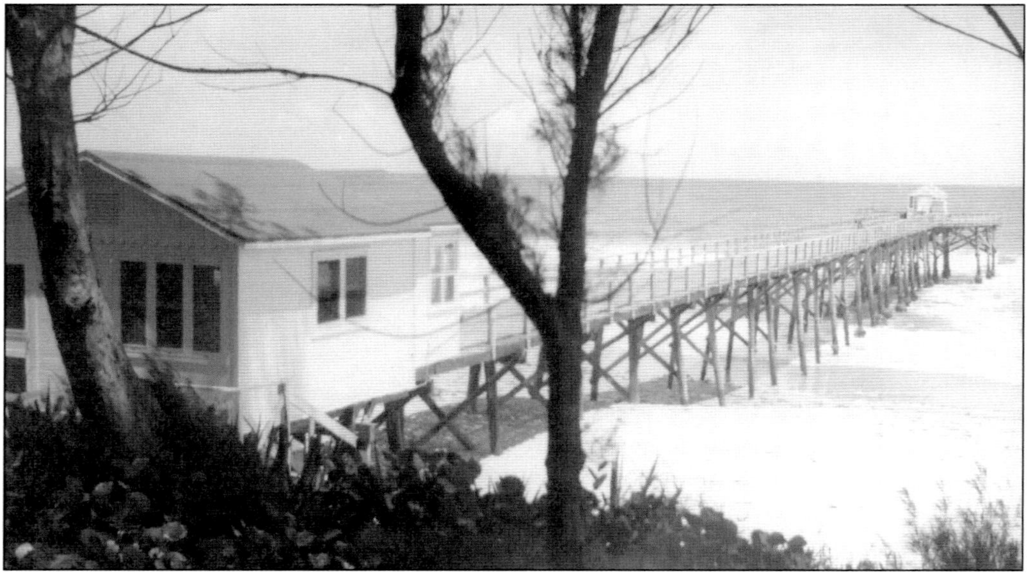

Carlos Canova's 160-acre homesite lay at the end of the new Eau Gallie Bridge. The sandy path that led to Canova Beach and Pier is now Eau Gallie Boulevard. Canova lived in the structure shown here until the bridge was built. He was then able to get the supplies he needed to construct the 400-foot fishing pier and the Casino, which was an apartment house and ballroom. The Casino burned in the 1970s.

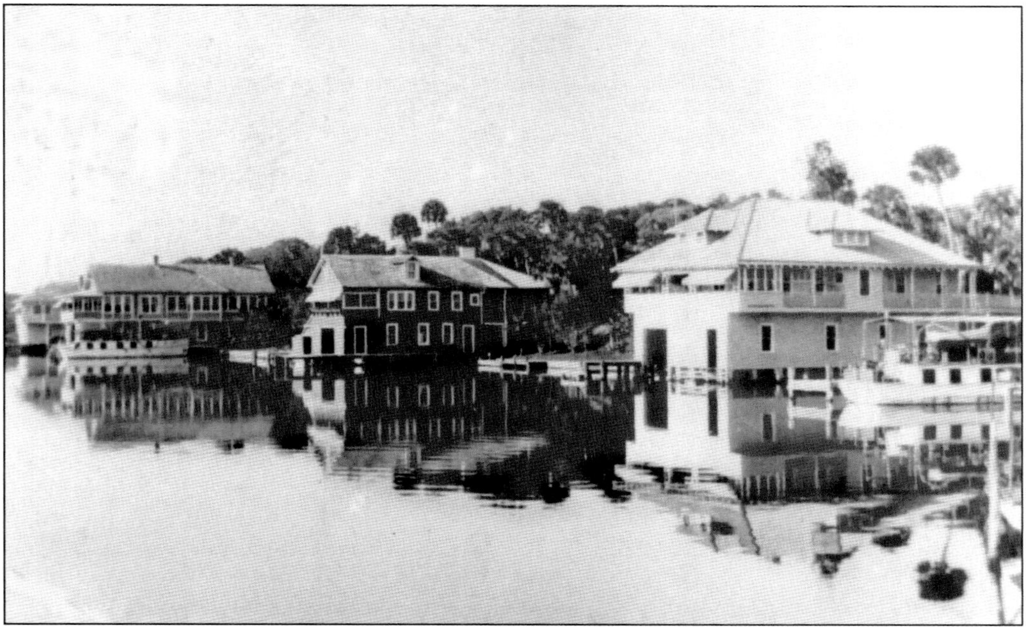

Boathouses on the Eau Gallie River date from the 19th and early 20th centuries. Col. and Mrs. C.W. Fowler wintered in the center building here. Others who lived along the water's edge were the Aulds, the Stackpoles, the Redingtons, and the Moores. These historic structures remain today.

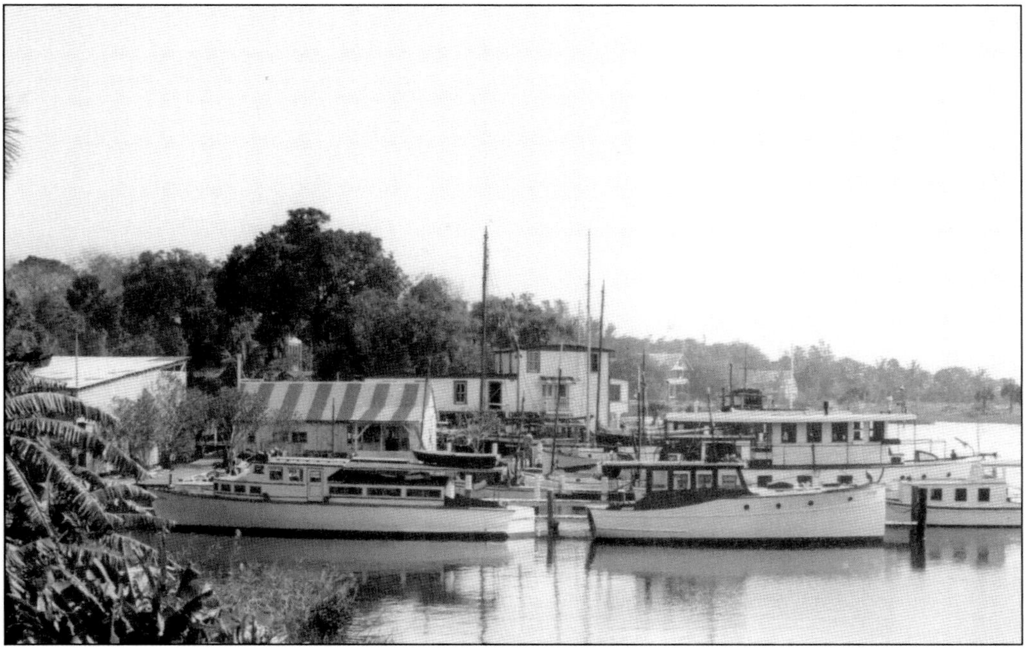

P.D. Barbour bought Captain Bennett's Storm Proof Basin and built the structure in the center of this photo in about 1920. This photo was taken in the 1930s. Later owners of Barbour's Basin have been Tom Whitehead, Homer Denius, E.J. Threadgill, Tim Davids, and Chuck Baird. Today, it remains in business as the Eau Gallie Yacht Basin. The three-story structure was ruined beyond repair after Hurricanes Floyd and Irene, but parts of it have been salvaged.

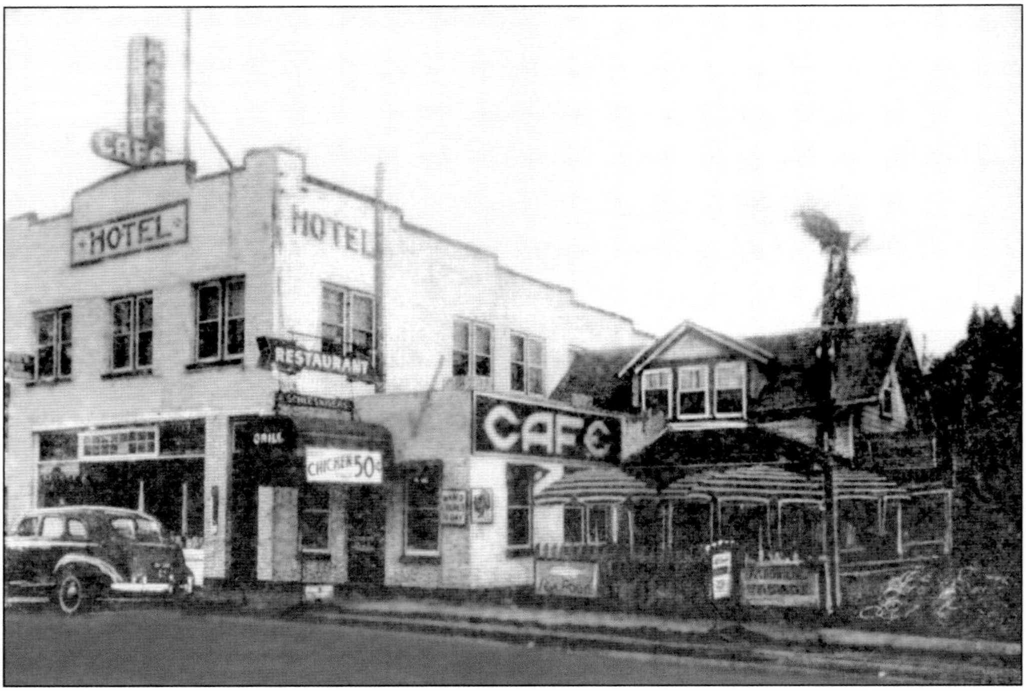

After the boom years, small hotels and cafes like Schlesinger's on US #1 in Eau Gallie, hung on. The view above is from 1938. Unable to pay their bills, the big hotels closed. The finest hotel in Eau Gallie was the Oleanders. Built in 1925, the hotel occupied the former site of the East Coast Lumber Supply at the corner of Pineapple and Ninth Street. The lobby, dining rooms, and guest rooms were spacious and elegant. The hotel provided office space as well. Shown below is the dining room in the 1940s, after the country had recovered from the Depression.

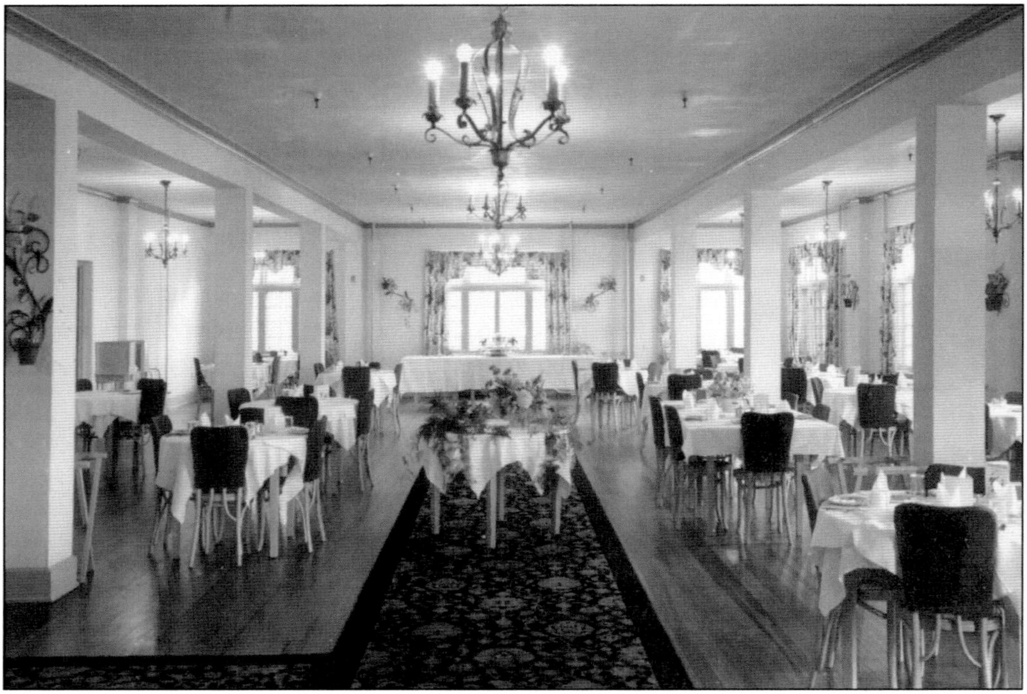

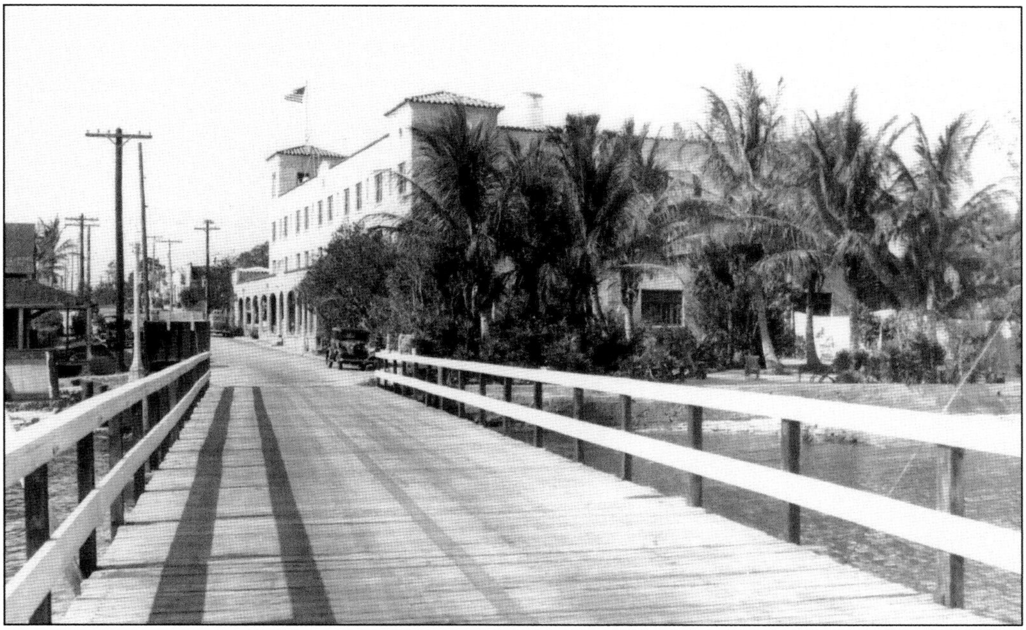

When it opened in the peak of the Florida Land Boom, the Oleanders (originally named the Harbor City Hotel) was typical of the impressive style of the day. It was Eau Gallie's biggest and finest business and it dominated the town's central intersection. As seen in the photo above, the Eau Gallie Bridge to the beach was adjacent to the hotel. The view below shows the front entrance of the hotel on the Dixie Highway. The signs indicate mileage to various probable and improbable destinations. As Eau Gallie grew, US #1 moved a few blocks west to Magnolia, and Pineapple Avenue retained its mid-century character. The bust hit Eau Gallie in 1926. The big hotel and other businesses in town faltered. In 1928, the State Bank of Eau Gallie failed. The town's population had declined by a third when, in 1938, the City of Eau Gallie declared bankruptcy. The Oleanders revived during the 1940s when these photos were taken. The building was torn down in 1990, and portions of it were used to build Conchy Joe's Restaurant, on the site today.

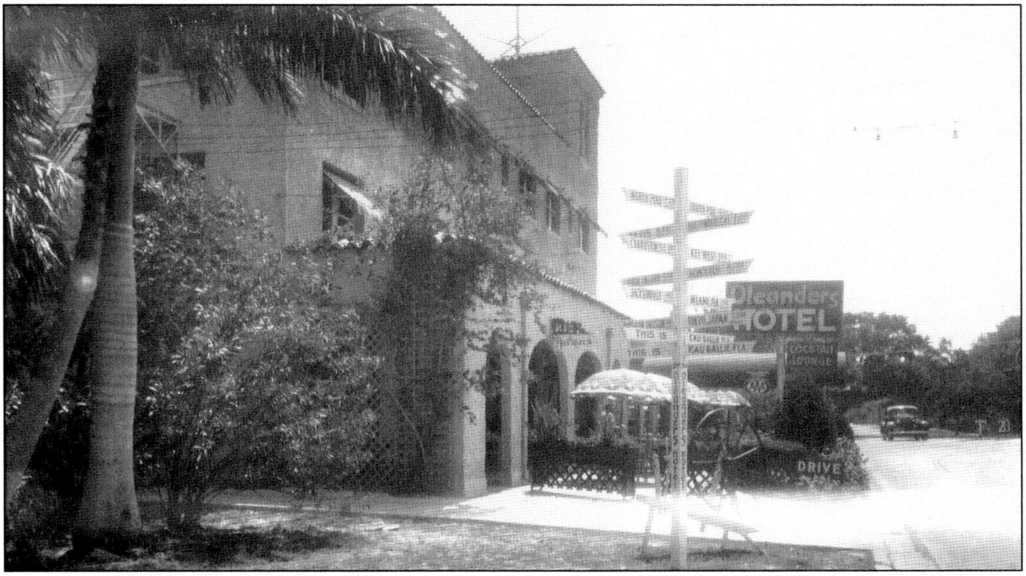

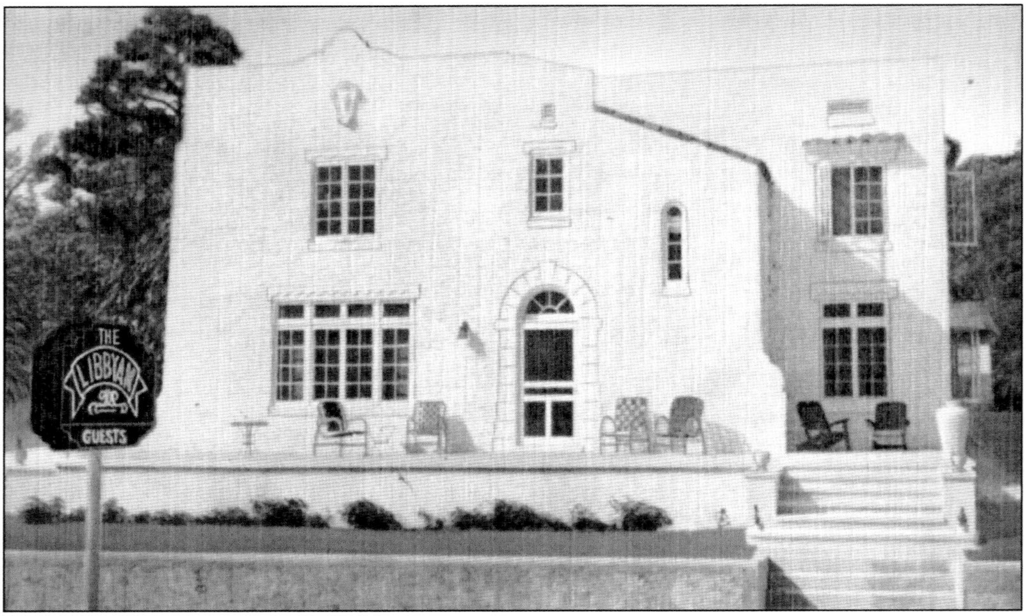

The Libbyan, a small guesthouse on Pineapple Avenue, opened in the 1920s. The owner, Mrs. E.O. Hembree, rented rooms and apartments. Another example of the typical Mediterranean Revival style, it housed the quickly expanding population of boom time Eau Gallie. During World War II, Eau Gallie's population swelled again and apartments like this were in great demand. The building remains in its original use today.

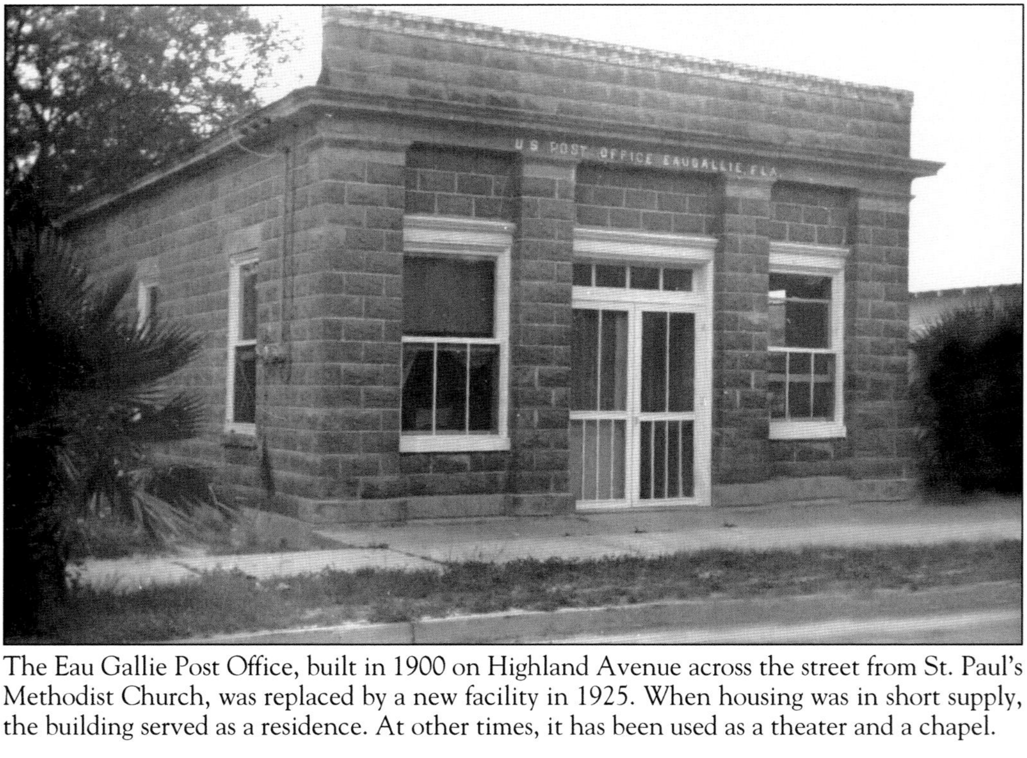

The Eau Gallie Post Office, built in 1900 on Highland Avenue across the street from St. Paul's Methodist Church, was replaced by a new facility in 1925. When housing was in short supply, the building served as a residence. At other times, it has been used as a theater and a chapel.

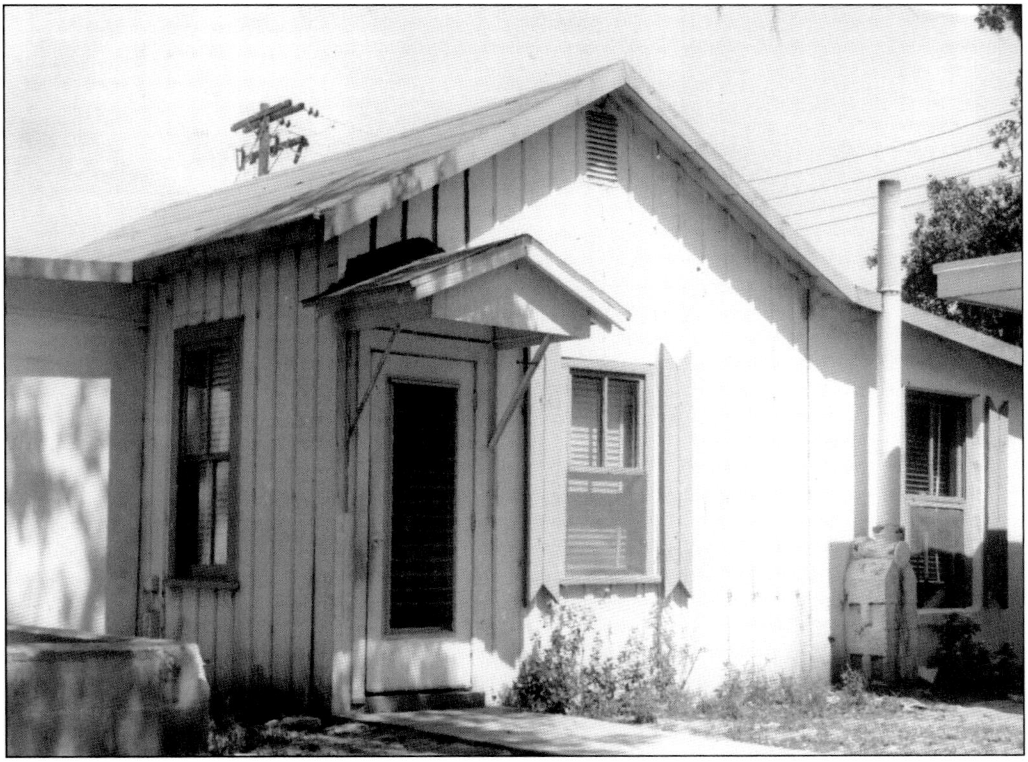

The building above, located behind the old jail on Highland Avenue, was Eau Gallie's first city hall. The lean-to rooms on each side are additions to the original. In 1925, the Mediterranean Revival city hall on Highland Avenue, shown to the right, replaced the wooden structure. The Fire Department was on the left and the Police Department on the right side with offices upstairs. The city kept the old wooden building and, during the 1940s and 1950s, it served as a temporary residence for the families of policemen and firemen.

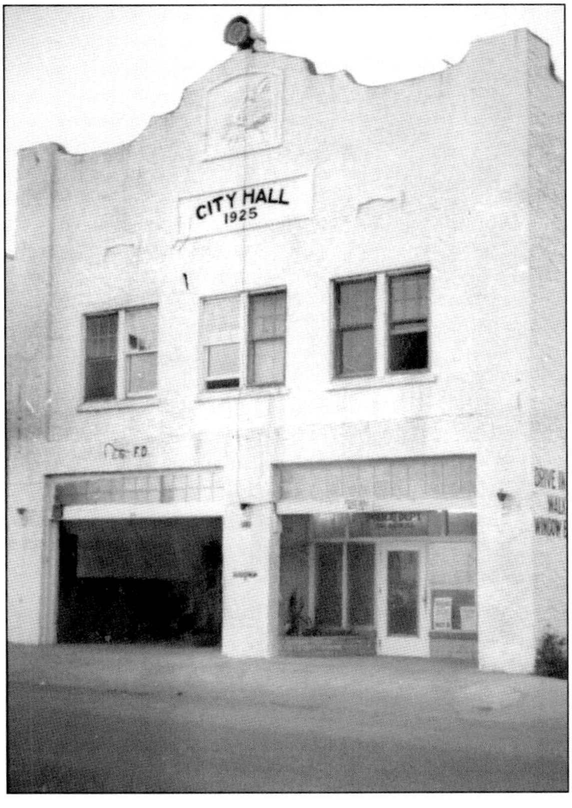

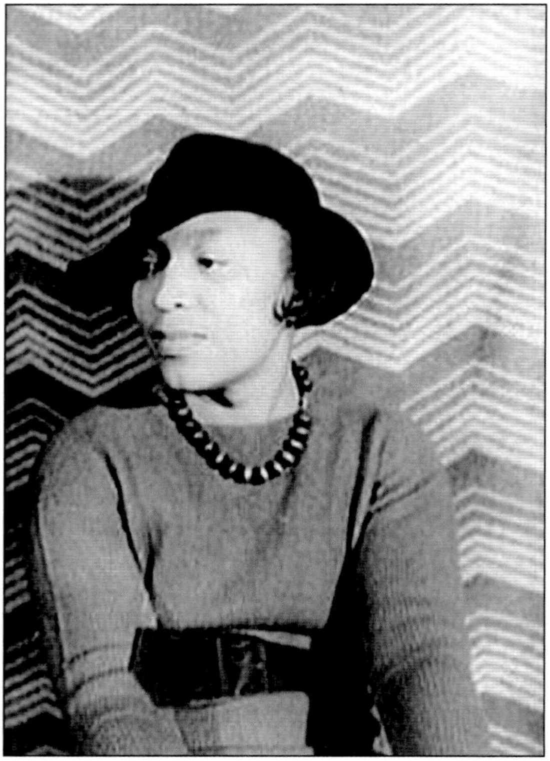

One of Eau Gallie's most famous residents was writer Zora Neale Hurston (1899–1960). Hurston was a member of the Harlem Renaissance movement who studied anthropology and folklore under Franz Boas. She traveled throughout the South collecting and researching black folklore. She lived in Eau Gallie in the early 1930s and wrote *Mules and Men* during this time. Hurston returned in the 1950s and taught school. Later, she worked at Patrick Air Force Base as a librarian and in Fort Pierce for the local newspaper. Hurston lived in a house, now torn down, near the intersection of Guava Avenue and Fifth Street (Aurora Road). She occasionally lectured at Stone School in South Melbourne.

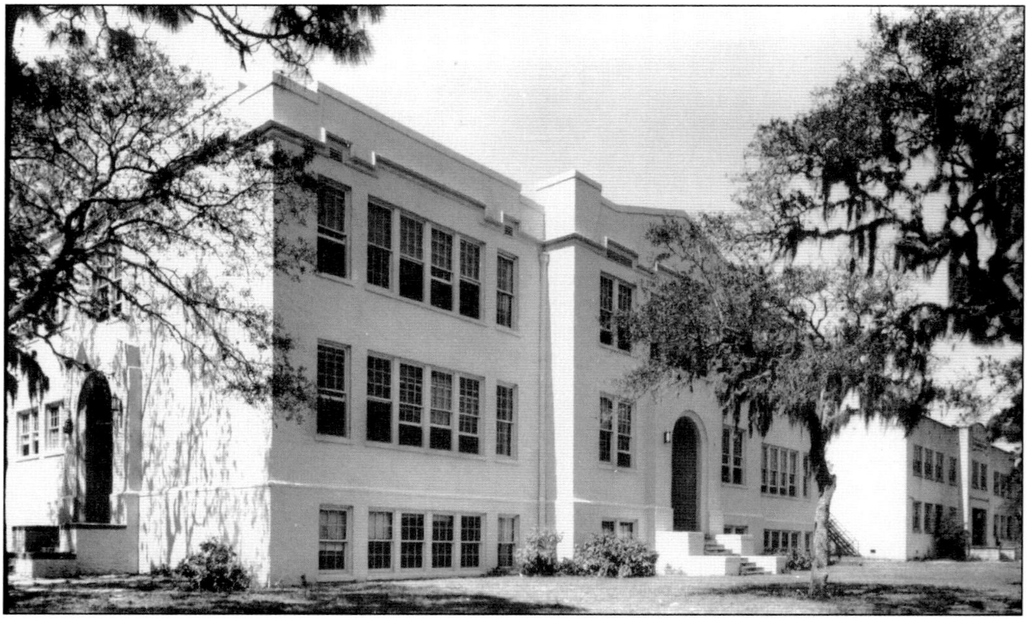

The Eau Gallie School, on the right, was built in 1923. Eau Gallie High School, in the foreground, was built in 1929. W.H.H. Gleason and Dr. W.J. Creel were trustees at the time. In 1949, Eau Gallie High School combined with Melbourne High School, and the building on the left became Creel Elementary. The Brevard County School Board still owns these buildings. Creel Elementary, used as office space, has been restored and modernized, and the older building is currently utilized for storage.

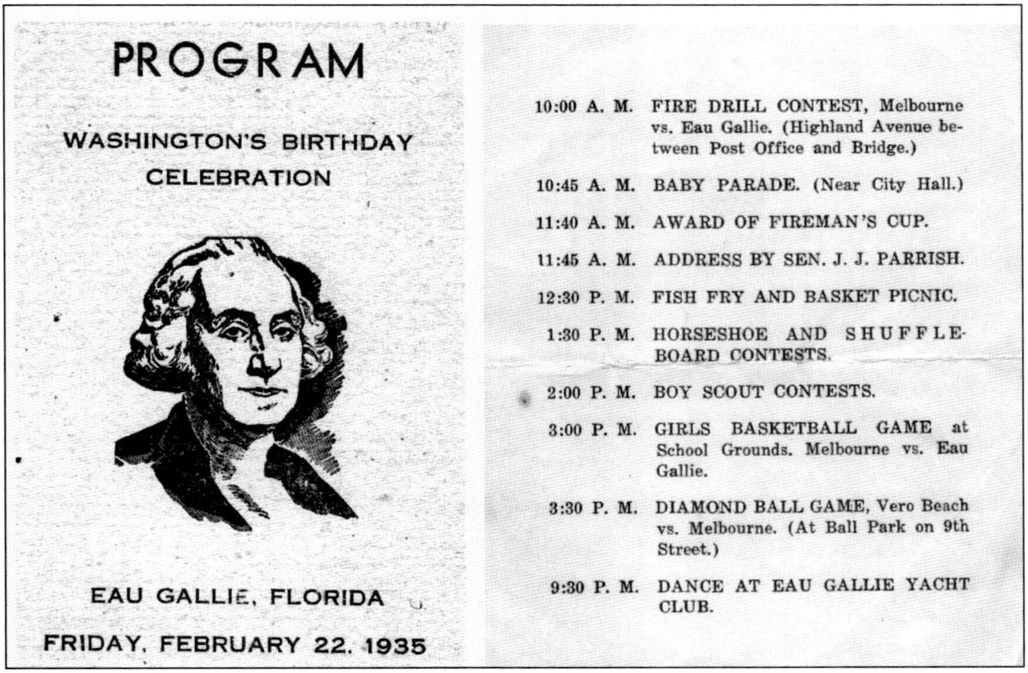

PROGRAM

WASHINGTON'S BIRTHDAY CELEBRATION

EAU GALLIE, FLORIDA

FRIDAY, FEBRUARY 22, 1935

10:00 A. M.	FIRE DRILL CONTEST, Melbourne vs. Eau Gallie. (Highland Avenue between Post Office and Bridge.)
10:45 A. M.	BABY PARADE. (Near City Hall.)
11:40 A. M.	AWARD OF FIREMAN'S CUP.
11:45 A. M.	ADDRESS BY SEN. J. J. PARRISH.
12:30 P. M.	FISH FRY AND BASKET PICNIC.
1:30 P. M.	HORSESHOE AND SHUFFLEBOARD CONTESTS.
2:00 P. M.	BOY SCOUT CONTESTS.
3:00 P. M.	GIRLS BASKETBALL GAME at School Grounds. Melbourne vs. Eau Gallie.
3:30 P. M.	DIAMOND BALL GAME, Vero Beach vs. Melbourne. (At Ball Park on 9th Street.)
9:30 P. M.	DANCE AT EAU GALLIE YACHT CLUB.

Eau Gallie loved to celebrate Washington's Birthday with a fish fry at Pineapple and Ninth Streets (Eau Gallie Boulevard), just opposite the Oleanders and in the heart of the business district. Eau Gallie citizens' participation reflected the community identity and structure that held small-town life together during this period.

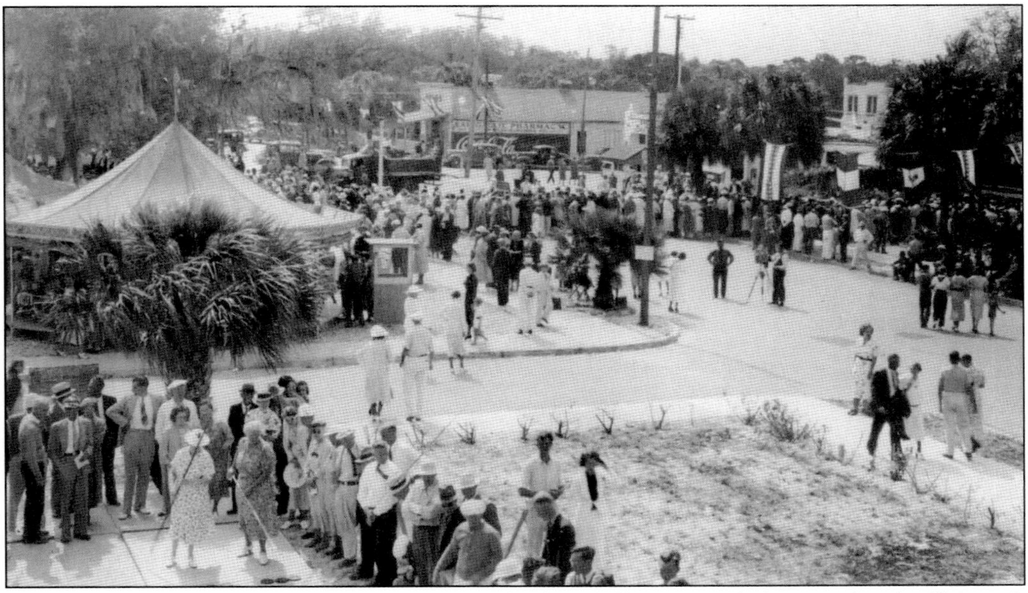

Programs would include an automobile parade, fire drill contest, baby parade, shuffleboard, horseshoe contest, moth boat race, basketball and baseball games, casting contest, bike races, roller skate races, and the like. In 1935, residents of the Midway Camp put on a special program. A fancy dinner and dance at the Eau Gallie Yacht Club or the Oleanders followed the fish fry in the street. Local businesses donated supplies for the street party and the toll for the bridge was cancelled for the day!

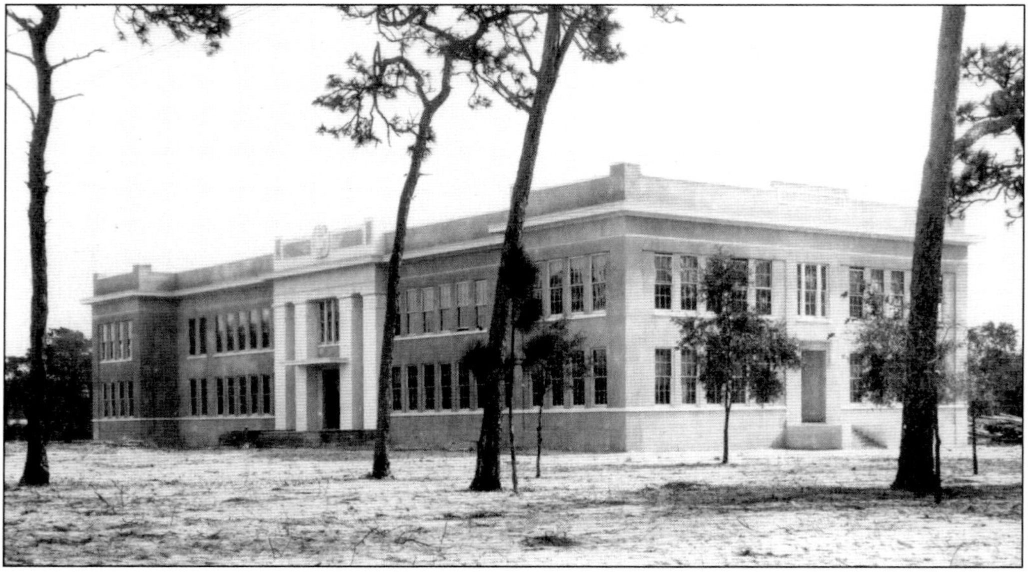

The Melbourne School was built in 1918–1920, the first of three adjacent buildings. When W. Christen designed it, there were objections that the school could never be filled. Others were reluctant because they felt that the site was too far west of town. Only eight years later, there was not enough classroom space, and Melbourne had expanded far west of this site. In 1940, a proposal that the buildings be torn down was stymied by the discovery that the walls were 13 inches thick. Today, the building above has been renovated by the city and is in use. The high school building, erected in 1926 and directly to the east, is maintained on the outside and has been used as a hurricane shelter.

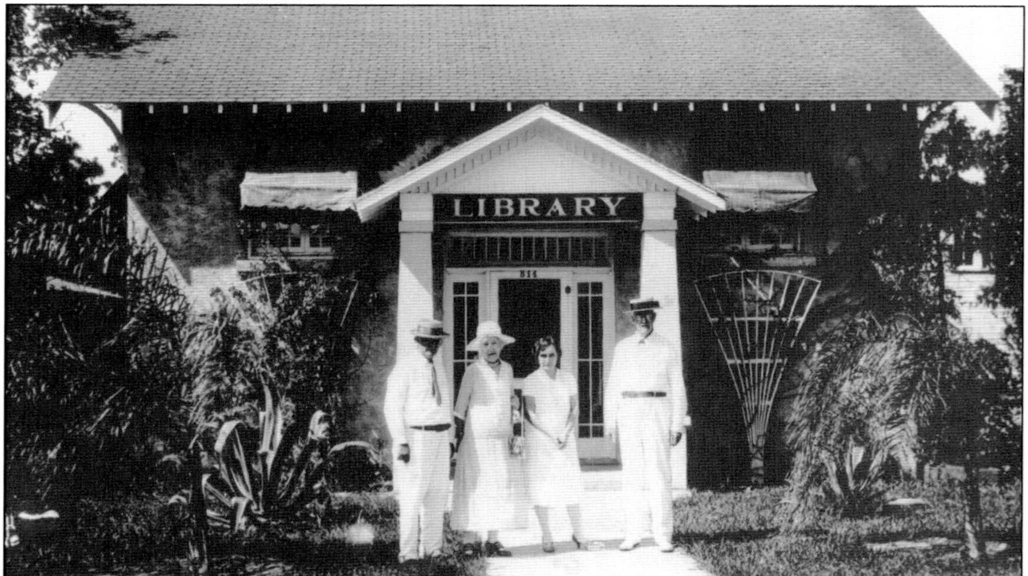

Melbourne's library has had several locations. It opened in 1918 in Mme. Campbell's Bazaar, moved to Vernon Place Girl's School, and was then located upstairs in the Fouchee Building. In 1922, Mrs. Stanford Wells headed a library association. With the support of the Chamber of Commerce, she spearheaded a drive to build the library shown above on Strawbridge Avenue at Waverly Place. Above are Mr. and Mrs. Wells and City Manager Seitz and wife.

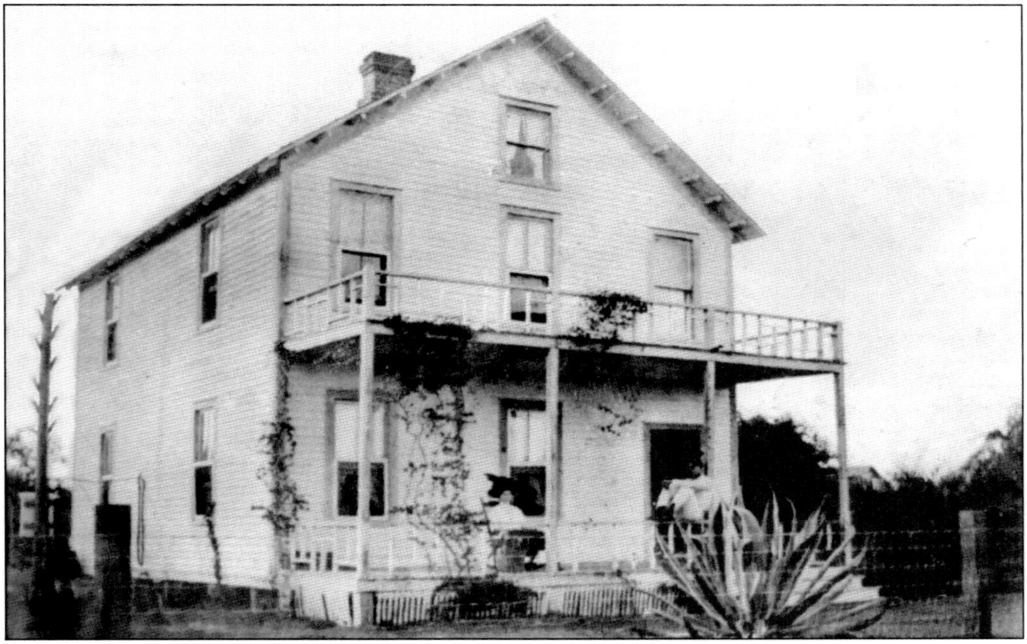

Mazie Goode became Melbourne's first telephone operator when the switchboard was opened in her house, shown above, in 1906. Later operators were Mattie Mae Peek and Olive Coe, who lived with her children upstairs in the Southern Bell building on Palmetto Avenue.

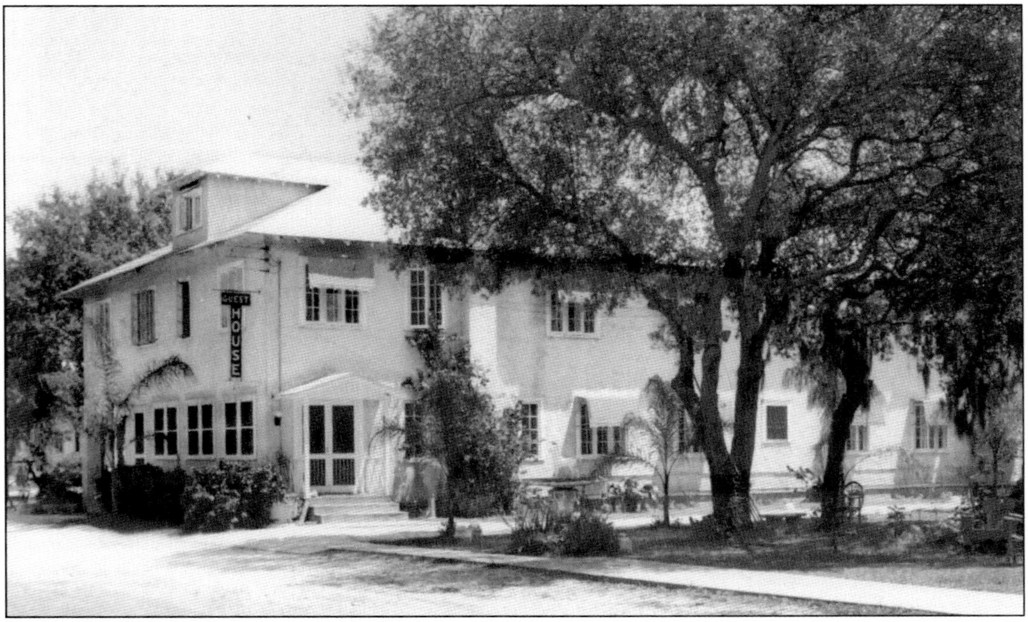

The area was without a hospital until Dr. Isaac M. Hay bought the Crenshaw Hotel at River Drive and US #1 and opened it as a 20-bed private facility in 1928. Miss Valentine and Mrs. Kibbe worked as nurses and Mrs. Hay prepared the meals. Doctors I.F. Bean, W.J. Creel, and I.K. Hicks also treated their patients at the hospital. The Hays barely made ends meet in the Great Depression. In 1937, Harry Crenshaw re-opened the hotel. It has been extensively remodeled and is currently an apartment building.

Southern Bell Telephone and Telegraph Co.

Incorporated

MELBOURNE, FLA.

O. E. PENNINGTON, Manager.

T. J. ROEBUCK, Group Mgr., Daytona Beach, Fla. J. A. MOONEYHAM, Dist. Mgr., Orlando, Fla.

VERNON BAIRD, Fla Mgr., Jacksonville, Fla.

Employes of this Company are forbidden to accept either oral or written telephone messages to be transmitted by an employe of this Company over the lines of this Company. In case of trouble with your telephone call REPAIR SERVICE.

(By arrangement with the Postal Telegraph-Cable Company and the Western Union Telegraph Company, any telephone subscriber of this exchange may have charges for messages received or sent by Postal Telegraph-Cable Company or Western Union Telegraph Company charged to his telephone and collected with his telephone bill.)

Corrected through DECEMBER 5, 1931

Amco Service Stores 45 S Dixie hgwy 8
Aspinwall Hazel Mrs r Telephone bl 9085
Austin Harriet L Miss 40 Grande pl 220-W

B

Bean I F Dr ofc Arcade bl **17**
  Res 133 New Haven av 11
Beaujean C M r 130 New Haven av 223-J
Beaujean Don R Melbourne Beach .... call L D
Beck T G r 115 Lincoln av 121
Berg R H r Indian River Bluff 132-W
Bernitts Garage 54 Front 9130
Blumer G E Dr r 138 New Haven av 113
Boggess King r 406 Palmetto av 147
Boritz R A plbg & htg contr 207 Ind Riv av 194
Brevard Steam Laundry Oak 269
Brother Hood Farms 454 Pine 148-W
Brownlie V C r 26 Magnolia Ind Bch 226-J
Burgess Clare H Mrs r 513 Melbourne av 126-W
Bus Station of Fla Motor Lines Inc
  Melbourne Hotel 66
BUTLER F W
  Atty Arcade bl **5**
Butler and Hogan attys Arcade bl 5

C

CADIEU J V
  Funrl Dir S Dixie Highway 53
CADIEU AND GEIGER
  S Dixie hwy 53
Callahan M r Country Club Colony 268-R
City—See Melbourne City of
Cofield S V Rev r 14 Livingston av 129-J
Coleman Percy L r Lincoln av 215-J
Cooper Leroy W r 540 Strawbridge av 255-W
Couch Mfg Co Grant Fla .... Call L D
Country Club Country Club Colony 9199

D

Daniels Charles E Dr r 6 Prospect av 260
Davis J C r 145-J
DeLoe Earl F Mrs r Country Club Colony 151-J
Deputy Sheriff S Dixie 101
Dick J Bruce Hyde Park Way 117-J
Ditchendorf C L r 526 Lincoln av 84-J
Dorman D C Palm Bay Fla .... Call L D
Dorset F W B Rev 317 Washington av 163

E

EAST COAST LUMBER & SUPPLY CO
  Ofc 218 Fee av 40

East Coast Transfer & Storage Co 72
Edge Claude gen mdse 101 New Haven av 22
Edwards A r 143 Stone 248-W
Edwards Clyde V Dr r New Haven av 181-J
Edwards Drug Store 300 New Haven av 96
EDWARDS PHARMACY
  200 New Haven av 9198
Elliott Oscar E r Indian River Bluff 202-J
Eschbach G F r 101 Palmetto av 213
Evans John H Jr r 434 N Washington av 208-W
Every E H r 100 Lincoln av 245
Ewing H L r Palmetto av 262-W

F

F E C Ry Co freight depot 191-W
F E C Ry Co passgr depot 225-J
Fire Department City Hall bl 15
Florida Motor Lines Inc Melbourne Hotel 66
FLORIDA POWER & LIGHT CO
  Ofc 414 New Haven 3
  Trouble Dept 317 N Seminole av 2
  Ice Plant 317 N Seminole av 2
Foshee H B r Hopkins Fla 149

G

Garvey Emma Mrs r Indian River Bluff 252-M
Gilbert & Given 23 Melbourne av 97-J
Goode A R r 300 Melbourne av 218-W
Green Beauty Shop Flat Iron Hotel bl 186
Groves R L r 618 Lincoln av 255-J
Guerin Henry H r Indialantic Beach Fla 226-M
GUERIN LUMBER CO INC
  216 Prospect av 217
Guest Thomas r Strawbridge av 268-W
Gulf Refining Co ofc S Dixie hghwy 9100
Gulf Refining Co filling sta Washington av 9117
Gutermuth J V Grant Fla .... Call L D

H

Harrell & Moseley Micco Fla .... Call L D
Hay I M Dr ofc Prospect av 120
  Res Magnolia pk 102-J
Henley King S r 2200 S Washington av 103-J
Henry Steam Laundry 520 Mclaren 7-J
Hicks Grace Mrs 239-W
Hicks I K Dr ofc Realty Arcade bl 56
Hicks I K Dr r 1609 New Haven av 239-J
Hockstra Chas r S Dixie hwy 64-J
HOLMES TREZEVANT
  Office 414½ New Haven av 179
Hopkins Sue Miss r 114 Lincoln av 176-M

Seen above are Melbourne telephone directory listings from 1931.

Houchins J W r N Dixie Highway........ 140-J
Huggins Harvey Malabar Fla..........Call L D
Hunter J P r 939 New Haven av...............243

I

Indialantic Beach Casino Indialantic Beach......9188
Indialantic Bridge Toll House 114
Indialantic Corp 155 New Haven av..........16
★INDIALANTIC HOTEL Indialantic Beach......160
Irwin Fred C r 205 Indian River av..........94-W

J

Johnson R S r 212 Lincoln av...............231

K

Kempfers Market 320 New Haven av.........43
Kempfers Market Hopkins Fla..............9115
Kennedy H C r Indian River av..............49-J
Kennedy H C Furniture Co S Dixie hwy....... 101
Kittredge G H r Indian River Bluff.........200-R
Knight Friley r 636 Lincoln av............215-W
Krider J A r Country Club Colony...........151-M

L

L & L FREIGHT LINES INC
....72
Lathrop E C r 616 Lincoln av...............241
Lathrope E C 17 Melbourne av...............59
Leslie & Hodges groc S Dixie hgwy...........87-W
Liggett's Drug Store 226 New Haven av........ 29
Lotz Geo W r 10 Roosevelt.................28-J

M

MacDowell L G r 3 Strawbridge av...........208-J
Maddox Cafe 128 Washington av.............9191
Martin John C r Riverview dr..............254-J
McMullen W G r New Haven av...............130-W
Melbourne Airport Kissimmee Highway....... 706
Melbourne Battery and Ignition Co 9141
Melbourne Beach Casino Melbourne Beach....Call L D
Melbourne Chamber of Commerce 120 Wash av..105
Melbourne City of
City Hall 237
Fire Department 15
Police Dept Chief's Res 406 Palmetto av..147
Welfare Board 146
Melbourne Electric Co 25 Melbourne av........ 12
Melbourne Filling Station Washington av......9195
Melbourne Hardware Co 304 New Haven av.......57
Melbourne High School 50
Melbourne Hospital Prospect av..............120
★MELBOURNE HOTEL THE 66
Melbourne Motors Inc Strawbridge av...........73
Melbourne State Bank 231 New Haven av....... 4
Melbourne Times 17 Waverly pl 150
Melbourne Wholesale Grocery Co........... 26
Melbourne & Tillman drainage dist 155 Nw Hvn av 46
Men's Shop The 42 Melbourne av...........86-J
Mentons Store Kissimmee Highway............ 703
Midway Camp S Dixie Highway 9183
Midway Chevrolet Co garage 133 Washington.... 110
Mid Way Market Mid Way Camps............87-J
Miegel Richard E r 205 Melbourne av........ 164
Minton O C r 38 Begenca.................230-W
Monogram Cafe 327 New Haven av..........9187

Moore Geo W r Second av...................202-W
Mullins J F Dr ofc dentist Flat Iron bl..........38

N

Nagel M I Mrs r 301 Bluff Walk............233-J
NuGrape Bottling Co Orange av..............187

P

Palm Service Station 500 Washington av......106-J
Patchen G W Dr ofc Flat Iron bl............. 6
Patchen G W Dr r 112 Columbus............214-W
Peel David atty ofc Flat Iron bl.............. 54
Peel David r 820 Strawbridge av............ 251
Peeler J A r Palmetto av 58-W
Pennington O E r 50 Waverly...............9086
Peyraud H S r 43 Helen 35
Pierce C W r 400 Indian River av............131
Police Dept Chief's Res 406 Palmetto av........147
Porcher J L r 540 New Haven av...........104-W
Post Office U S Govt 240
Postal Telegraph Co ofc 206 New Hvn av..Call Postal
Prairie J B r Riverfront.....................277

R

Rath William r Kissimmee Highway............704
RITE WAY CLEANING CO
Vernon pl 33
Rodes Jno B grocery 9 Melbourne av.......... 23
Rodes Jno B r 212-W
Rodes M B r 201 Orange av 219-J
Rollins Chas E Jr r Shannon av Indialantic Bch 165-W
ROTGERS DAIRY
Kissimmee Highway 702
Rowe R L r 10 Oak.....................156-J

S

Sanitary Sea Food Mkt 116 Washington av....47-J
Schell Lucille Miss r Flat Iron Hotel bl........34-J
Scott B F r Irwin......................142-W
SCOTT'S SERVICE STATION
South Dixie Highway 9197
Service Garage 201 New Haven av............ 31
Shull B E r 44 Front.....................42-J
Simmons G M r 637 Lincoln av...............127
Ofc 46
Sinclair Refining Co S Dixie Highway........183-J
Snarr E C r 97 Lincoln av..................175-J
SOUTHERN BELL TEL AND TEL CO INC
For reporting trouble with your
telephone call ....Repair Service
For subscribers not listed call......Information
Manager's Office 9000
Standard Oil Co Bulk Plant S Dixie Highway.... 81
Standard Oil Co New Haven av..............9116
Standard Oil Co Service Station No 117.......9186
Standard Oil Co Service Sta No 118
S Dixie hgwy 191-J
Starr M Miss r 318 Indian River av.........176-J
Stephens Hotel Strawbridge av..............9192
Stewart Arthur H r Indiatlantic Beach........226-W
Stewart Chas H r 123 Lincoln av.............246
Stewart Funeral Parlors 236 New Haven av.......1
Night and Sunday call 218-J
STEWART HARDWARE CO
236 New Haven av.................... 1
Stone J S r 136 Stone 248-J

These are additional listings in the Melbourne telephone directory from 1931.

MELBOURNE Str—Wil 7

ROTGERS SUPERIOR DAIRY PURE MILK AND CREAM

KISSIMMEE HIGHWAY **TELEPHONE 702**

Strange J W Dr r 708 Lincoln av 291
Sun Oil Co Washington av 60
Sweetland E G r 636 New Haven av 249-J

T

Texas Co The ofc Hopkins 207-W
Tubbs W G r 508 Melbourne av 220-J
Tucker P E r 9 Hickory av 170-M
Turck Thressa r Indialantic Beach 226-R

U

U S Post Office (See Post Office)

V

Valentine Chas r 38 Front 42-W
Van Croix Theatre Washington av 9196
Vaughn W G 204 Realty Arcade 185
Vinciguerra Louis r 49-W
VorKeller Albert r 117 South Front 238

W

Wade E H r 132-M
Wallace Elizabeth C r Orange Spot Pk 124-W
Warren J B r Country Club Colony 168-W
Warren N N Indian River Bluff 252-J
Welch W N r 649 New Haven av 130-J
Welfare Board Hallwood pl 146
Wells Wm T Mrs r Washington av 229
Western Union Telegraph Co
Ofc 317 New Haven av ...... Call Western Union
Will C A r 706 Palmetto av 128-J
Williams E B r 102 Palmetto av 176-W

FLORIDA POWER & LIGHT
ICE
DEPARTMENT
COMPANY

Buy Your ICE From The
Wagon or Truck With The
ORANGE OVAL EMBLEM
It is Pure, Clear, Solid Ice
FULL WEIGHT GUARANTEED
Dixie Highway and Seminole Ave.
(Melbourne)
TELEPHONE 2

By 1931, Melbourne had almost 200 telephones and Eau Gallie had 40. Telephone etiquette messages from Bell Telephone warned customers that calling the wrong number was like knocking on the wrong door. Customers were reminded to be polite and check numbers in the directory. It was hardly necessary, as Mrs. Coe, the operator, had all the numbers memorized anyway.

8 Bar—Wes EAU GALLIE

CASH STORE MEATS—GROCERIES & FEEDS **Tel. 1**

EAU GALLIE, FLA.

(By arrangement with the Western Union Telegraph Company any telephone subscriber of this exchange may have charges for messages received or sent by Western Union Telegraph Company charged to his telephone and collected with his telephone bill.)

Barbour P D r........10
Barr Tom Jr r S Dixie Highway........44
Brooks Department Store 408 Highland av........9105
Brooks S F r........34-J
Bryan J S r........64-J
Burton O L r Pine........37-J

C

Cox W R r Housten........66
Creel W J Dr r........29

E

East Coast Lumber & Supply Co ofc........15
Eau Gallie Alemite Sta S Dixie hgwy........9107
Eau Gallie City of........35
Fire Dept........35
Eau Gallie Pharmacy........9

F

Fire Department........35
Florida East Coast Ry Co
Ticket Ofc........3
Freight Ofc........83
P S White Waiting Room........9106
Florida Power & Light Co Highland av........61

G

Gleason Co The Gleason bl........8
Gleason George W r........32
Gleason W H H r........23

H

Hodgson A R r........31
Holzborne J........73

K

Karreck J E........1
Kempfers Market Dixie hgwy........9103
Knapp Katherine McLaren r Young........50

M

McCormick A........67-J
Merrow L A r S Dixie Highway........45
Mitchell H H r Hyde Park........48-J
Moore Lydia S r Hyde Park........48-J

O

★OLEANDERS HOTEL........100
Oleanders Service Station Dixie Highway........9104
Osteen Paul L r........36

P

Paddison Gertrude Mrs r........38

R

Railway Express Agcy Inc F E C Depot........20
Rast B F r Dixie Highway........60-J

S

Scheible C E r........41
Seawright J A r Oak........40-J
SOUTHERN BELL TEL & TEL CO INC
Manager's office........9000

T

Taylor C L r Ninth........4-J
Torrence J E r........65
Torrence Jessie L Mrs r Dixie Highway........42-J

W

Western Union Telegraph Co........68

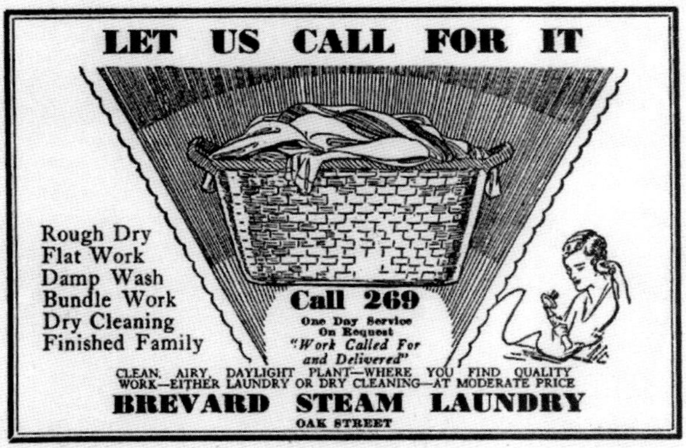

Seen above are Eau Gallie telephone directory listings from 1931.

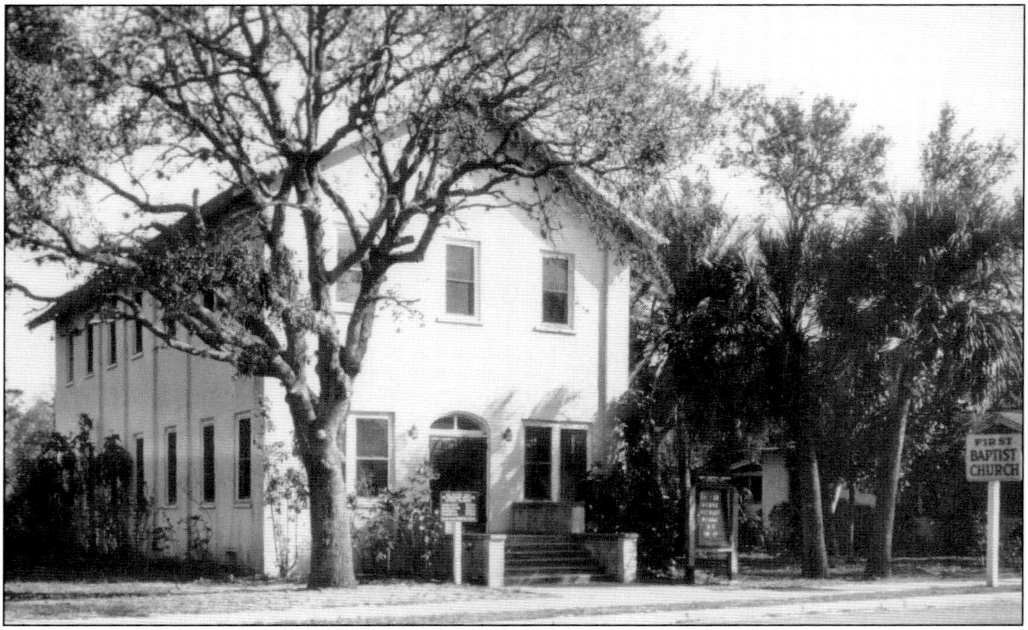

The First Baptist Church of Melbourne was organized in 1921 and the sanctuary on New Haven Avenue was completed in 1924. Rev. J.E. Pate was the pastor. The building still stands at the corner of New Haven and Livingston. In 1951, the congregation of the church built a new sanctuary next to this one. In 2000, the church sold the property and moved to a larger building on Dairy Road.

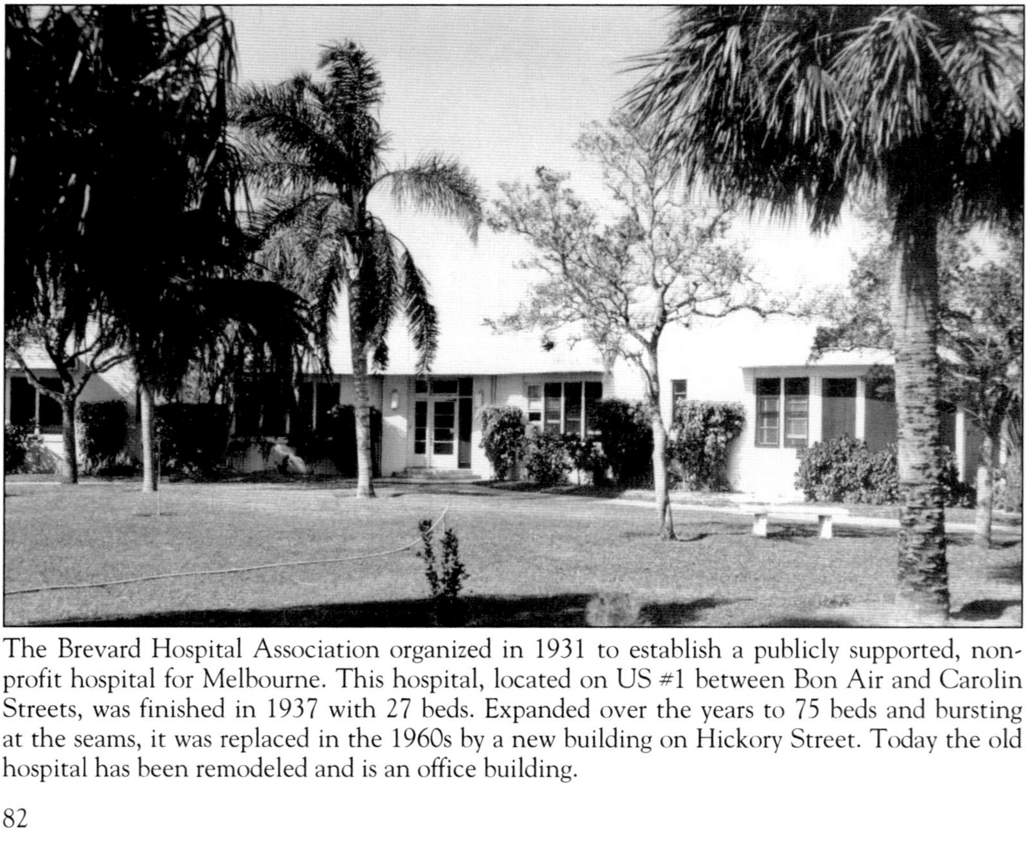

The Brevard Hospital Association organized in 1931 to establish a publicly supported, non-profit hospital for Melbourne. This hospital, located on US #1 between Bon Air and Carolin Streets, was finished in 1937 with 27 beds. Expanded over the years to 75 beds and bursting at the seams, it was replaced in the 1960s by a new building on Hickory Street. Today the old hospital has been remodeled and is an office building.

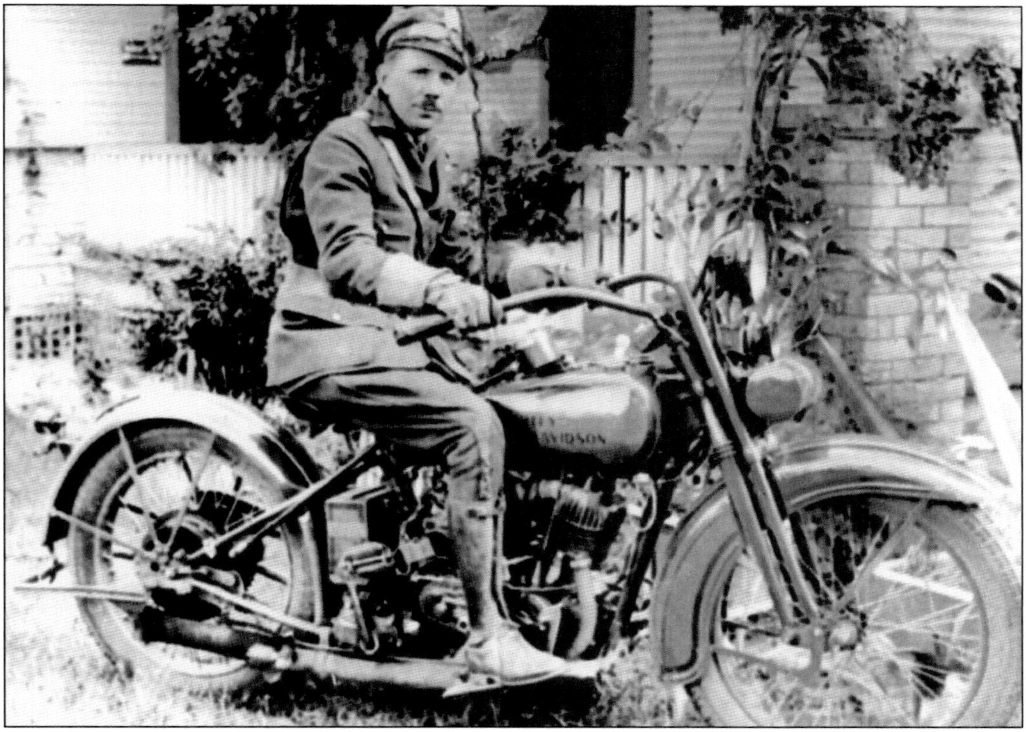

The photo above is of Melbourne's first motorcycle policeman, Frederick W. Jernigan. The early motorcycle policemen in Melbourne and Eau Gallie used their own vehicles and kept track of mileage. This photo of Jernigan was taken in 1924.

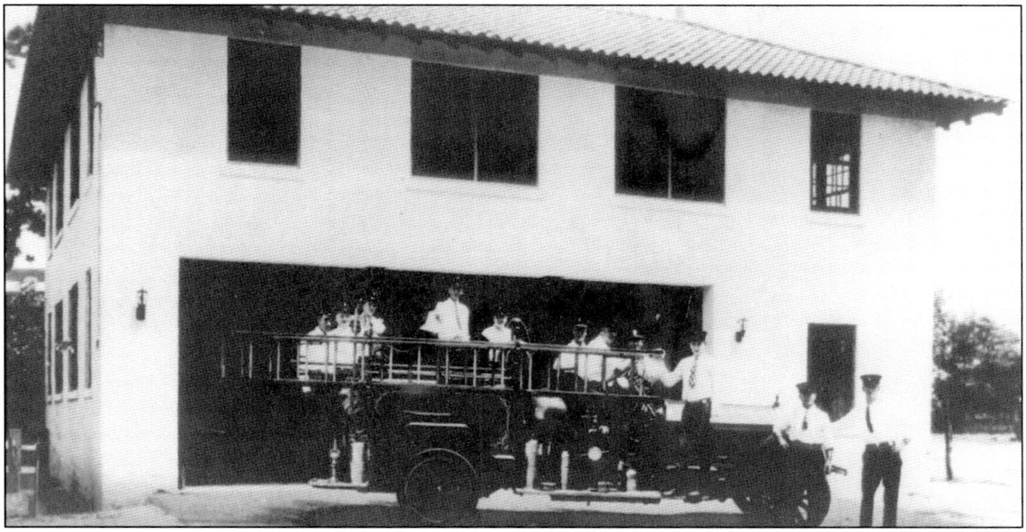

Melbourne's Volunteer Fire Department was organized in 1916. Frank Bennett became the fire chief in 1924. The department got its new engine in 1925 and this photo was taken in 1926 at Melbourne's new city hall on Strawbridge. Claude Beaujean was the chief at that time. The early fire engines could pump water from the creek to douse a fire, but one serious problem was the lack of fire alarms. After the Carleton burned the second time, Melbourne installed a siren to beckon volunteers in emergency. The historical records of Eau Gallie and Melbourne are strewn with destruction, as the wooden buildings and bridges caught fire frequently.

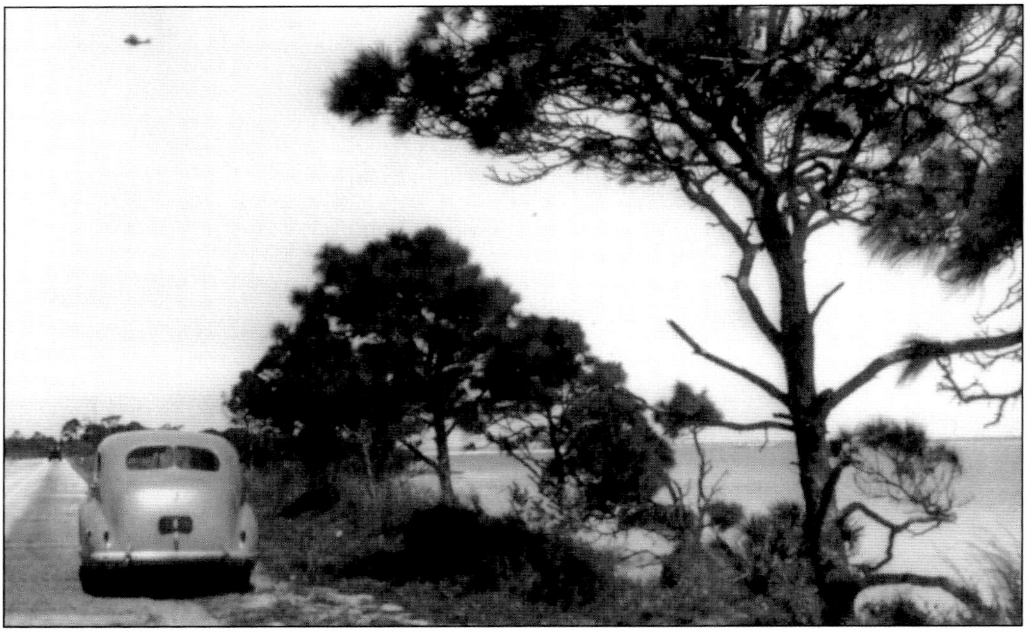

By the late 1930s, when this photo was taken, the automobiles and highways had come a long way in a single generation. Compare the Dixie Highway photo at the beginning of the chapter with this one. Through Melbourne and Eau Gallie, US #1 was paved, had a centerline, guardrails, and a cleared shoulder solid enough to use for parking. Note the airplane heading for the Melbourne-Eau Gallie airport.

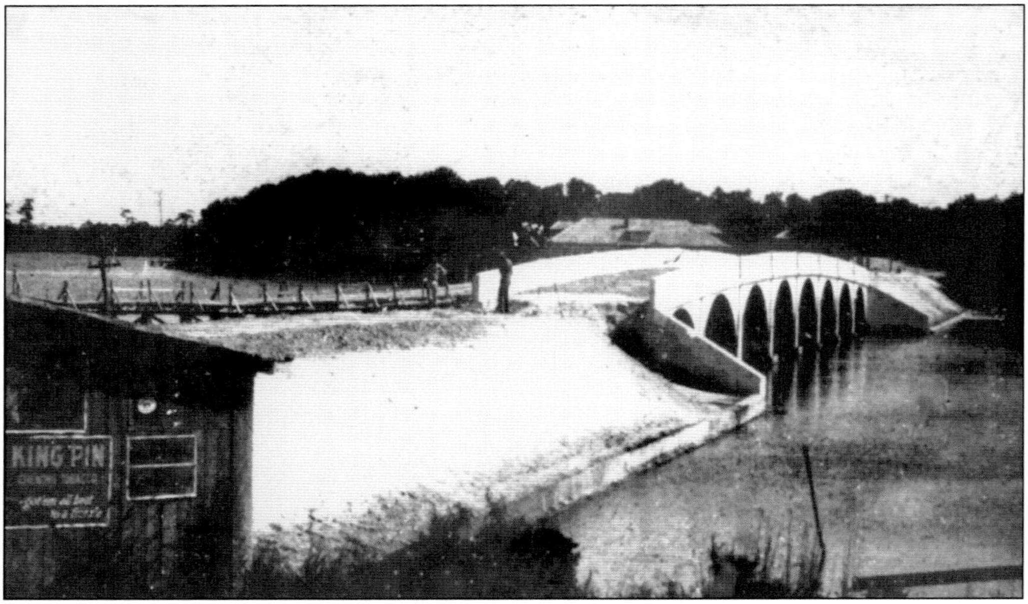

This new concrete bridge that carried US #1 over the Eau Gallie River is another sign of modernity. It is the "Humpback" Bridge under construction in the mid-1930s. Its predecessor, at left, was a wooden bridge constructed in 1924. It burned only 10 years after it was built. At one time, church congregations and private businessmen raised money to connect the community by building bridges. By the 1920s, the government provided its citizens with modern—and fireproof—access to the rest of the state.

Four

THE WAR YEARS

Eau Gallie and Melbourne were pulled out of the Great Depression the same way the rest of the country was—through federal spending. The New Deal provided "commodities" to the needy. Works Progress projects put the unemployed to work and built local infrastructures. However, the real national recovery came with the war.

In South Brevard County, the two greatest economic catalysts were the Naval Air Stations—one in Melbourne and one on the barrier island north of Eau Gallie. After the war, the Banana River Naval Air Station became Patrick Air Force Base. Patrick and Cape Canaveral were to be the home of the United States Space Program by the late 1950s. The Melbourne Naval Air Station's property and buildings became assets in that city's economic transformation as well.

World War II changed much in American history, as our country became a global power and a leader in technological revolution. Melbourne and Eau Gallie began to feel the effects of that change even before the war was over. The pioneer isolation was long past. The dependence on tourism and transportation systems was already assured. With the war, the fortunes and character of Eau Gallie and Melbourne became inextricably tied to the national economy, identity, and purpose.

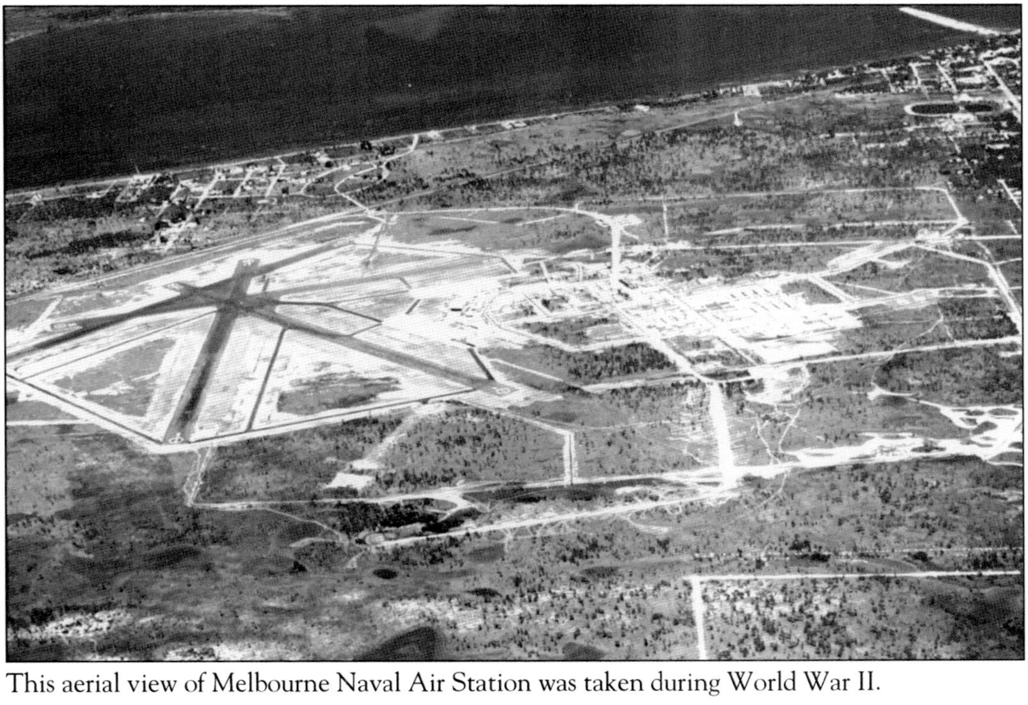

This aerial view of Melbourne Naval Air Station was taken during World War II.

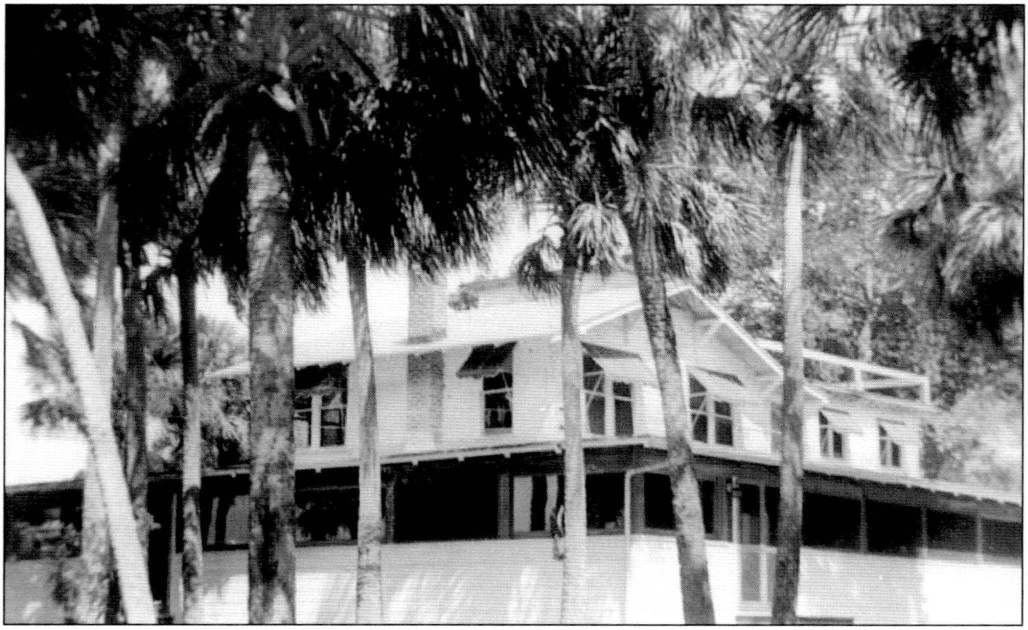

After the United States entered the war, the Banana River Naval Air Station became a seaplane base, and the Melbourne-Eau Gallie Airport became a fighter pilot training base, with auxiliary fields at Malabar and Valkaria. There were more than a thousand men stationed at the Melbourne Naval Air Station, most of them young pilot trainees. The building shown above is the Castaways Club, a favorite recreation spot for locals and military men that continued to be popular after the war. It is located on Castaway Point in Palm Bay.

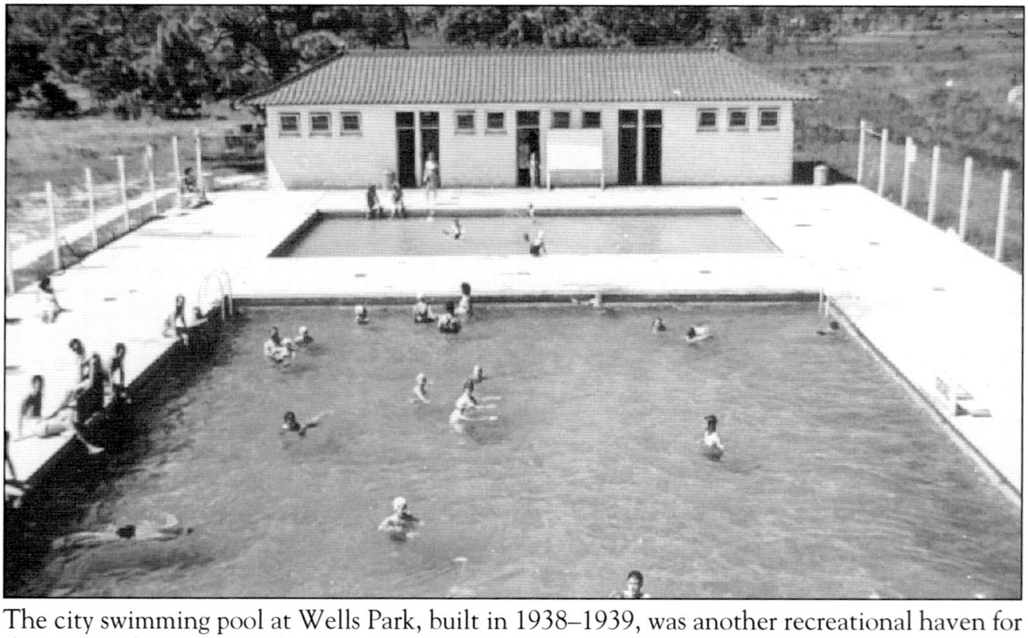

The city swimming pool at Wells Park, built in 1938–1939, was another recreational haven for the Navy pilots. The pool was open part-time for the general public and part-time for military personnel. Located between Hickory and Oak Streets south of Hibiscus, the pool continued to be a joy in the lives of Melbourne children for several years. Currently, the site is being prepared as a park to honor the 65 men who lost their lives at the training station during the war.

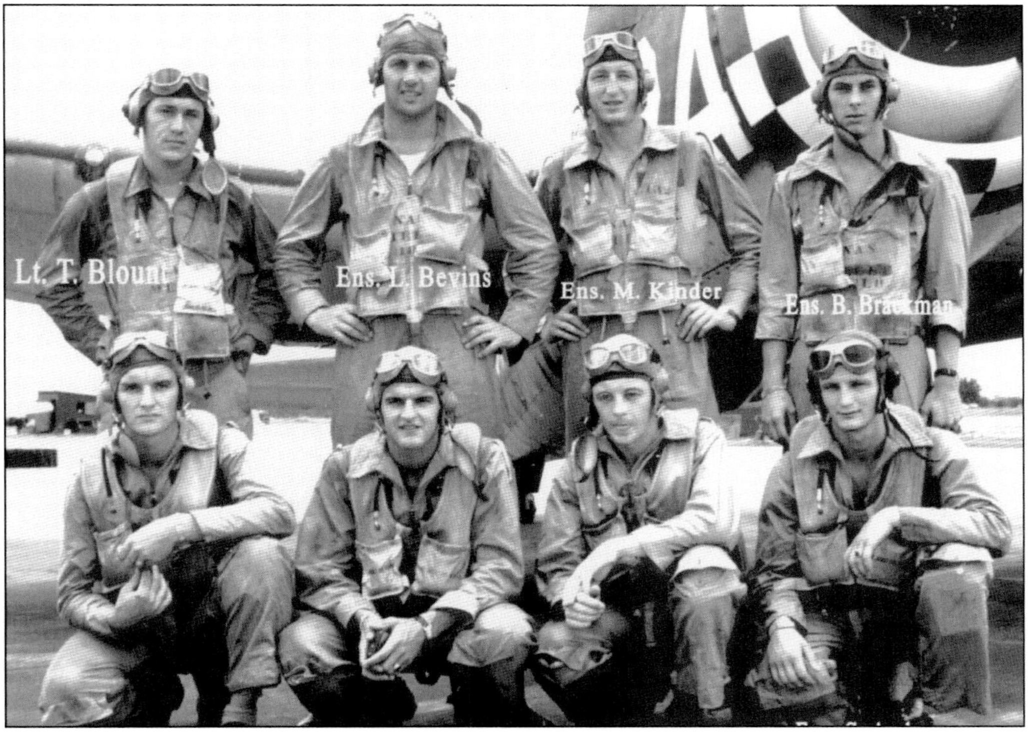

This group of flyers is Operational Training Class #198. In the front row are Ens. C.M. Craig, Ens, P.D. Grossnickle, Ens. William R. Barnett, and Ens. C. Anderson. In the back row are Lt. T.E. Blount, Ens. L.L. Bevins, Ens. M.E. Kinder, and Ens. B.R. Brackman.

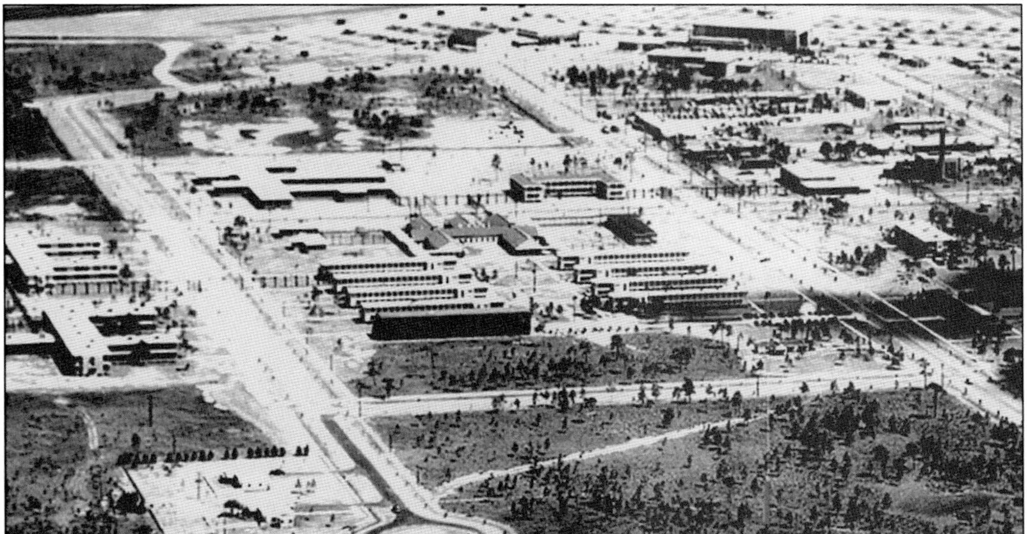

This view of the Melbourne base shows officers' quarters on the left, enlisted men's barracks in the front center, and the base hospital behind these on the left. At the center of the photo are the barracks for the WAVES. The large three-story structure behind them is the training building, and there are more training buildings, a fire station, and garage at the right rear. To the left and not visible in this view is the POW compound which held 250 men. The airfield is visible in the first photo of this chapter.

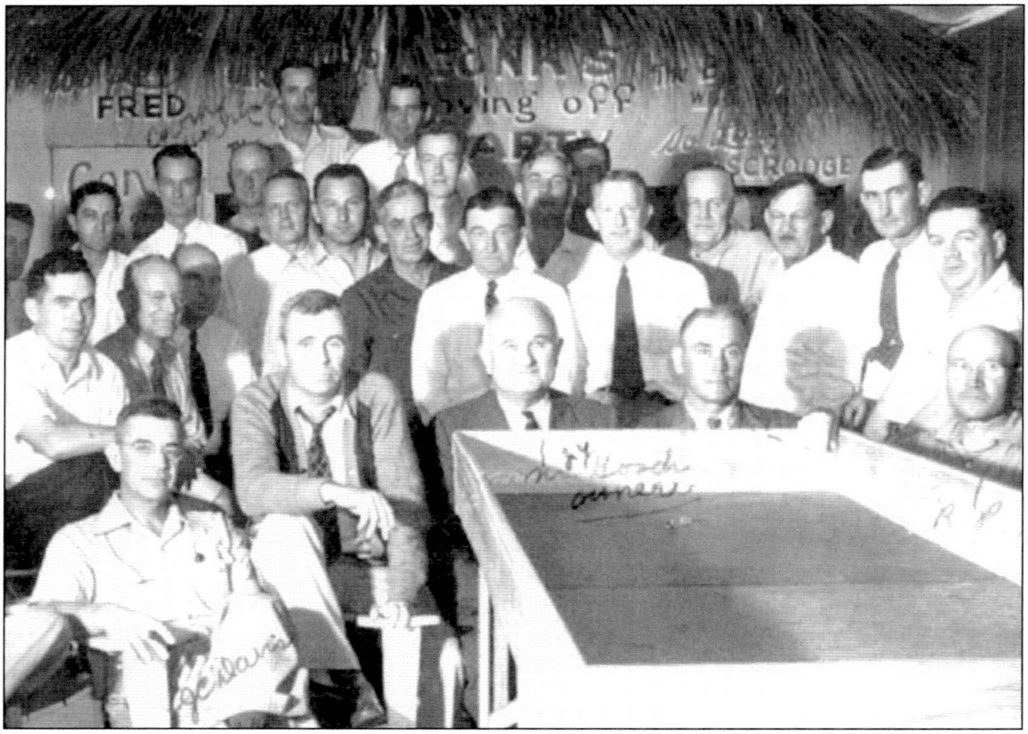

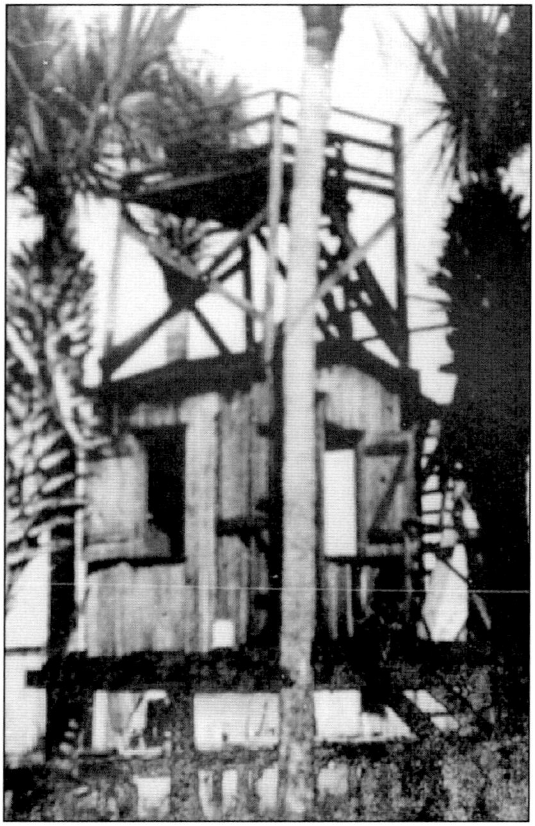

Here a group of construction engineers and supervisors pose for their picture at a planning meeting for the Melbourne Naval Air Station in 1942. Included are J.C. Davis, J.Y. Gooch, and R.P. Silva. Non-military construction in Eau Gallie and Melbourne was at a near standstill during the war, and the base had the priority on building supplies. No wonder there was such a housing shortage!

Submarines prowled off the coast, occasionally torpedoing ships. Local residents were trained as aircraft and submarine spotters. They volunteered to take four-hour watches in the observation towers, which were connected by radio to the Coast Guard in Fort Pierce. The Melbourne Beach tower, shown here, was eventually torn down.

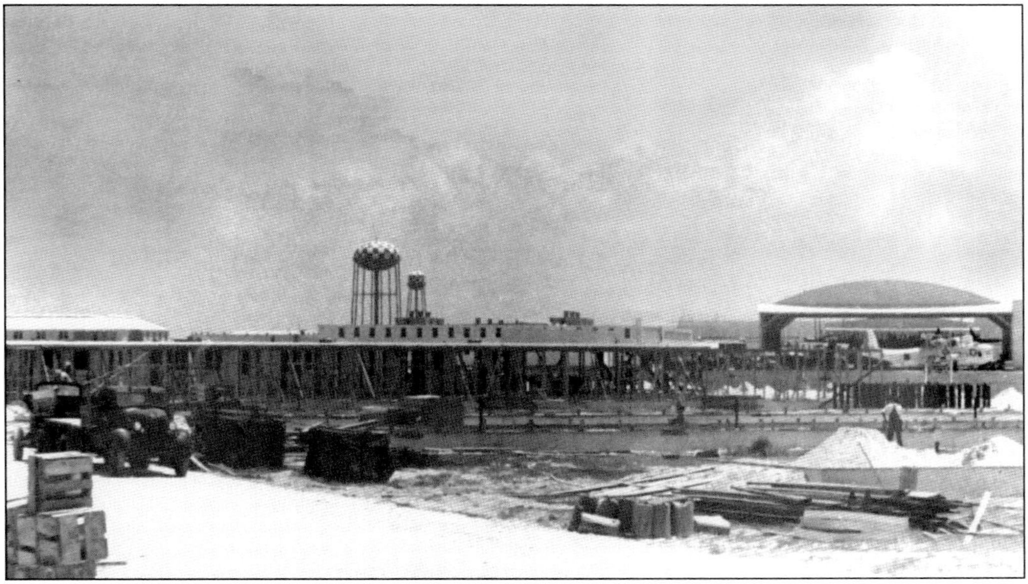

This photo shows the Banana River Naval Air Station under construction in 1940. It was the first Naval Air Station built on the Florida east coast and was intended as a permanent seaplane base. The fighter planes used at the Melbourne and other Florida training fields were repaired and maintained here. The Station was designated as the Joint Long Range Proving Ground in 1949, and then became Patrick Air Force Base in 1950. The base covers almost 2,000 acres from the Banana River to the Atlantic Ocean.

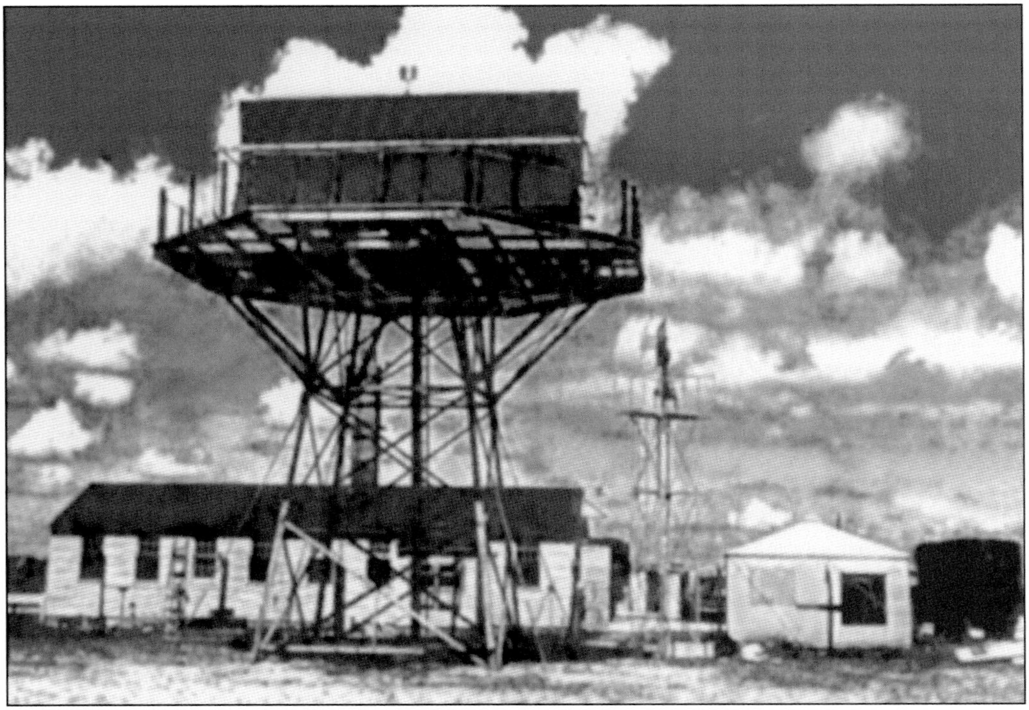

The photo above is the radar station at Canova Beach. The station maintained radio and radar contact with pilots in the training program.

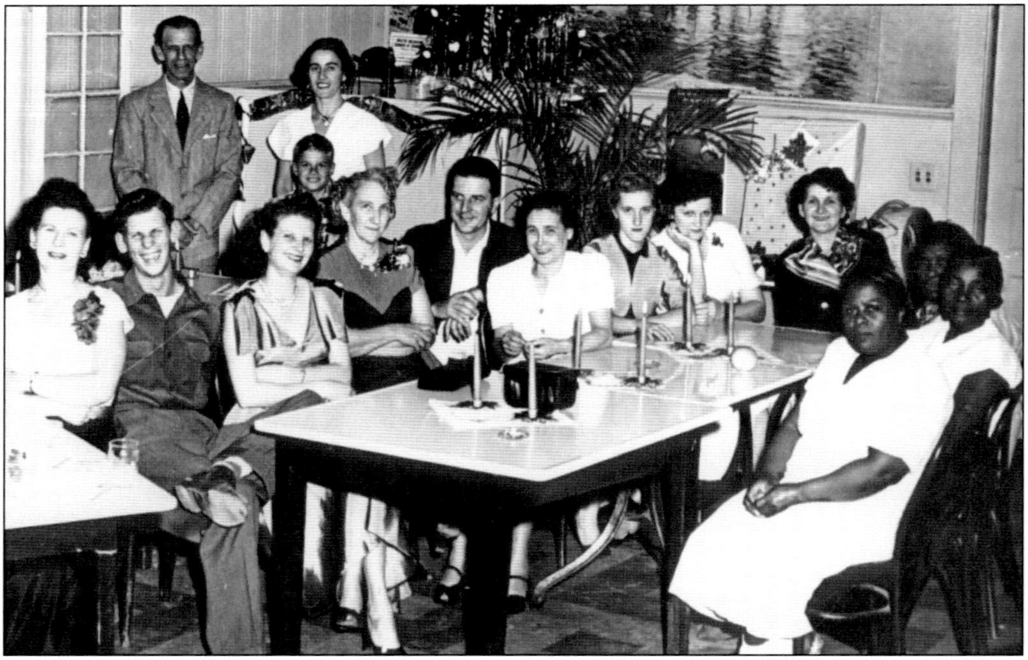

In the scene above, customers and staff pose at the Ever Ready Café. The diner, which opened in 1930, was in an adjoining dining car. It stood at the corner of US #1 and Strawbridge and was torn down when the highway was widened. Owners Charlie and Lottie Smith ran the popular restaurant and specialized in the deviled crabs they caught in the Indian River.

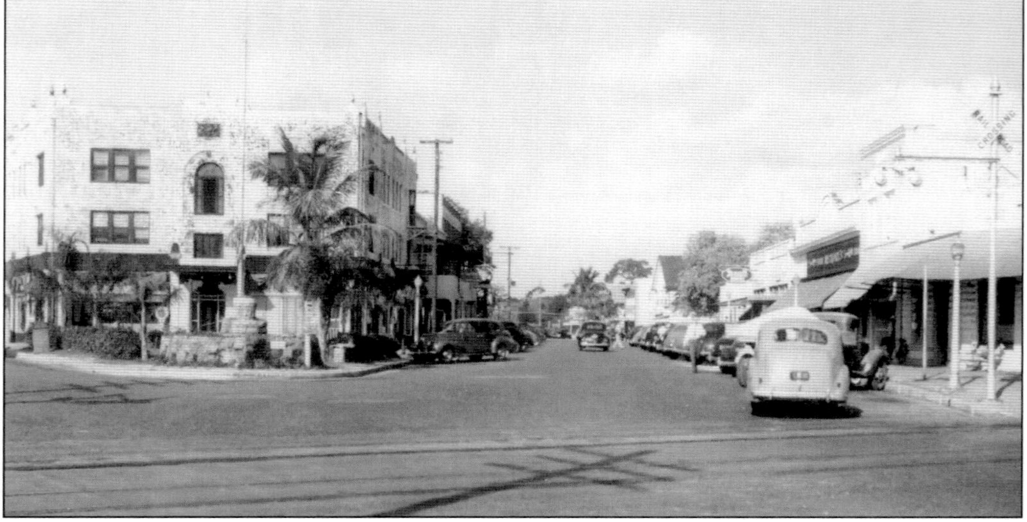

The war brought new experiences to the local population—blackouts, rationing, bond drives, aircraft and submarine spottings, and the frequent crashes of pilots in training. During this time, the influx of personnel and the construction of the Naval Air Stations brought economic recovery to Eau Gallie and Melbourne. Their civilian populations grew rapidly, improving business for the locals. Above is a wartime view of New Haven Avenue from the FEC tracks west. The Flat Iron Building, erected in 1925, stands behind Campbell Park. The bandstand has been removed with street widening, and downtown Melbourne has taken on the appearance that it maintains to this day.

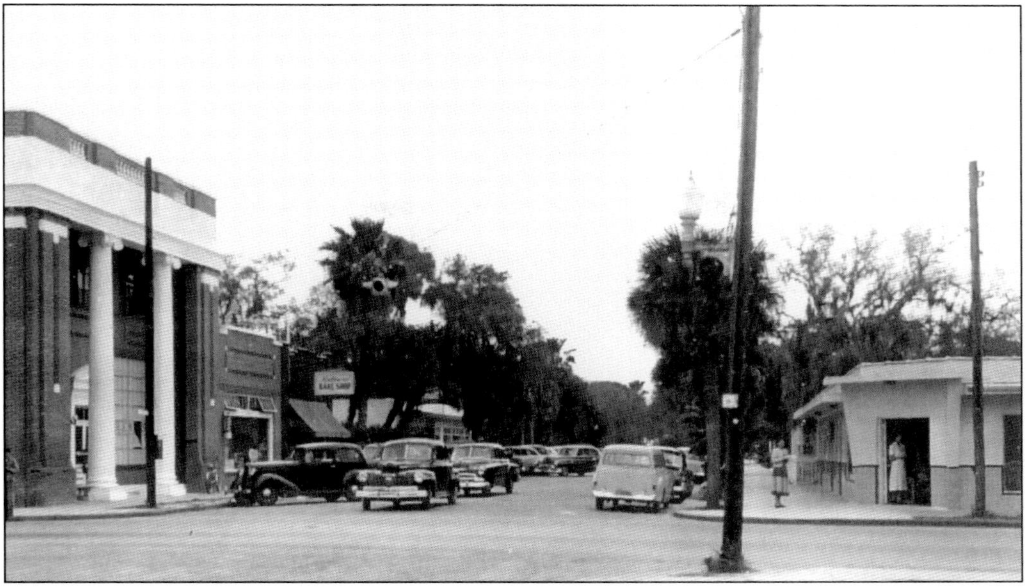

These two 1940s views are of downtown Eau Gallie. The top photo shows Highland Avenue, looking south from Eau Gallie Boulevard. The date is approximately 1948, and like Melbourne's downtown, the buildings seen here are relatively unchanged today. Mathers Bake Shop, on the left, is still in business at the same location. The lower picture, taken in 1941, shows the State Bank of Eau Gallie, constructed in 1924, at the corner of Highland and Eau Gallie Boulevard. The Oleanders Hotel is visible at the left. The Eau Gallie Pharmacy preceded the more modern structure seen at the right in the upper view.

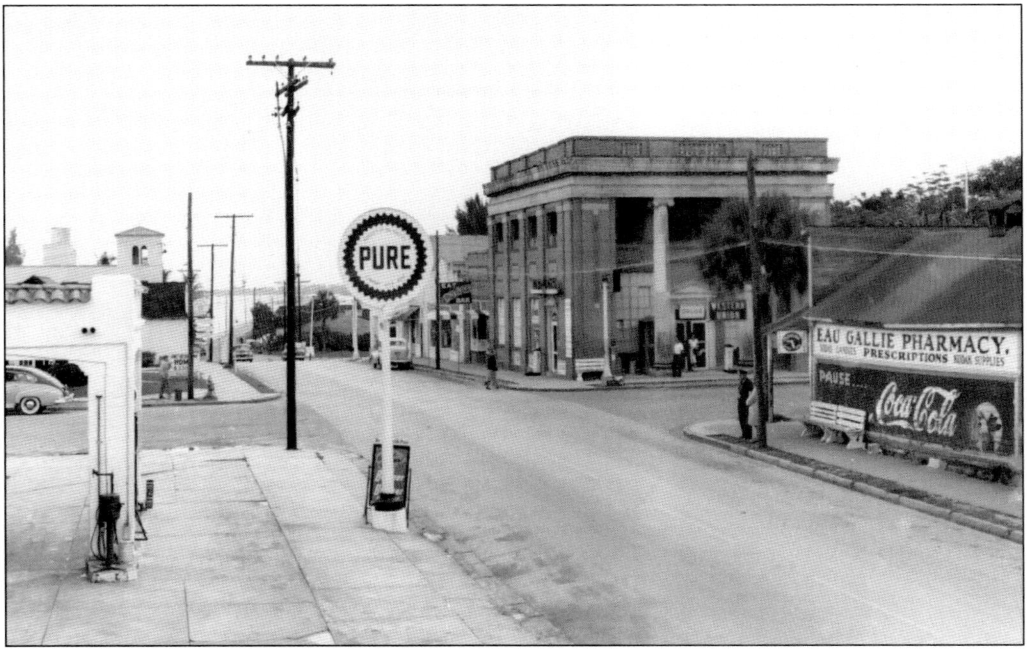

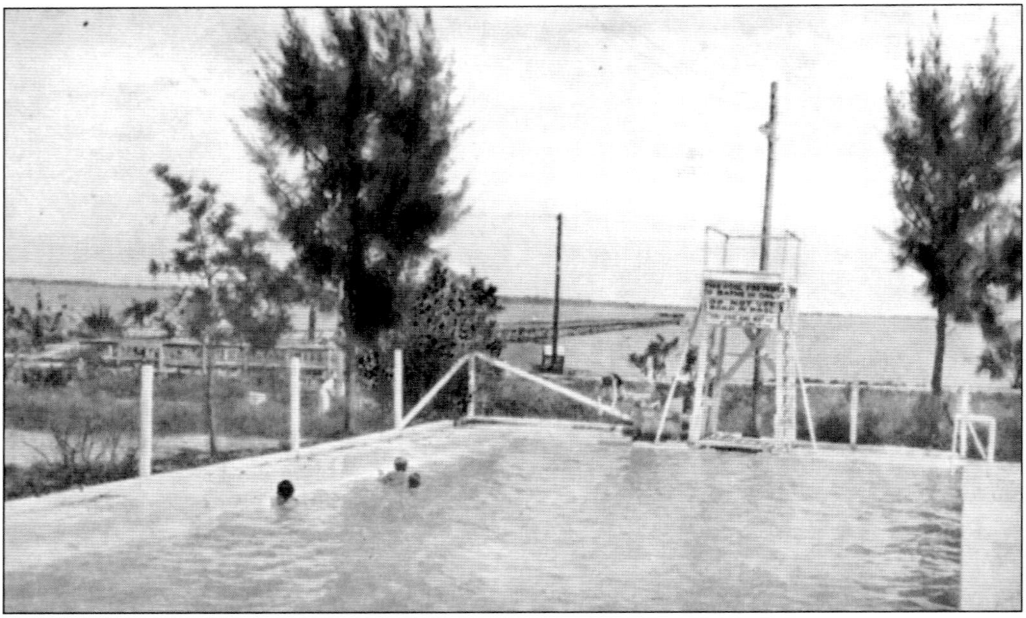

The four pictures on these pages are of Midway Colony, named for Melbourne's role as "The Midway City." Founded in 1922 by Art and Dolly Ratleff, the Midway Tourist Camp was a year-round residence for carnival people and new Florida arrivals. Later, it catered to Tin Can Tourists and winter visitors. The swimming pool, fed by an artesian well, overlooked the Indian River and the camp's 400-foot fishing pier.

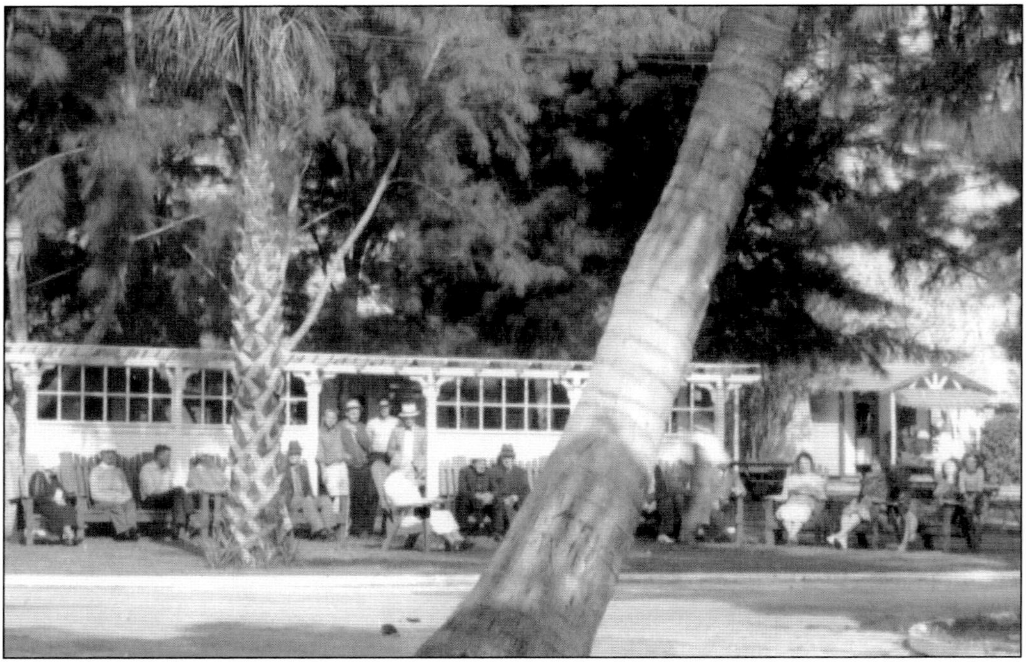

The community was closed during the summer, but residents returned year after year, creating a close-knit community. Activities, which were for members of the colony only, included dances, plays, sporting events, a colony newsletter, and social gatherings. The residents had a community building, and a store, as well as recreational opportunities.

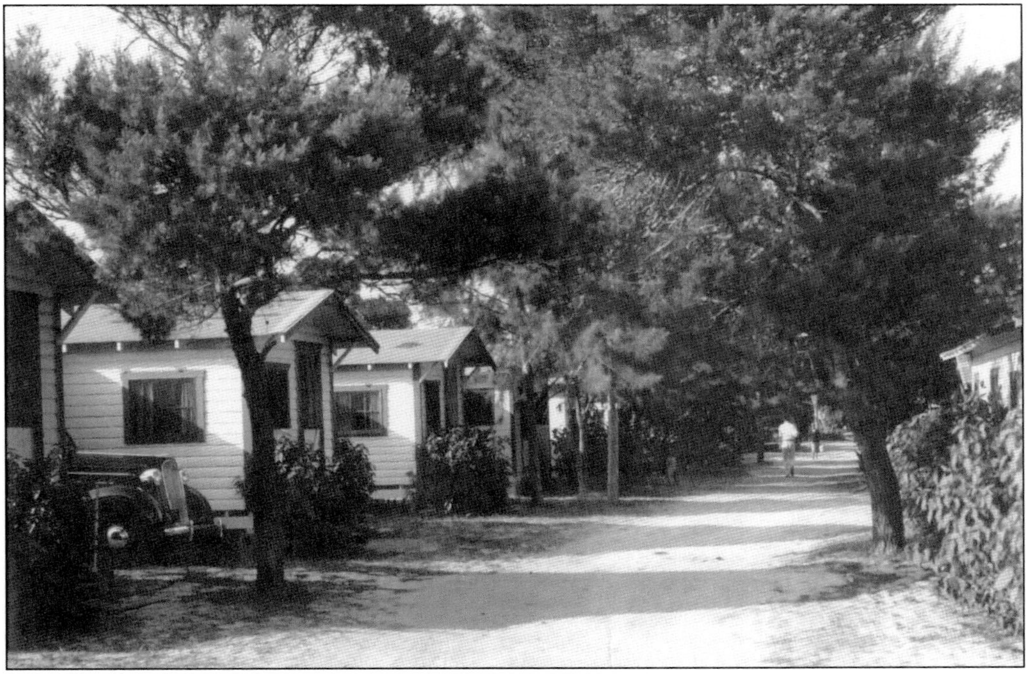

The Fenner family owned Midway Colony during its heyday from the 1940s through the 1960s. During the war, their 150 cottages were full, many occupied by military couples. The Colony also boasted a trailer camp area, as shown in the photo below, which was taken in the late 1930s. There is little left of the cozy enclave today, and most of its former grounds are in parkland. A few of the original cottages do remain and can be seen west of Riverview Drive.

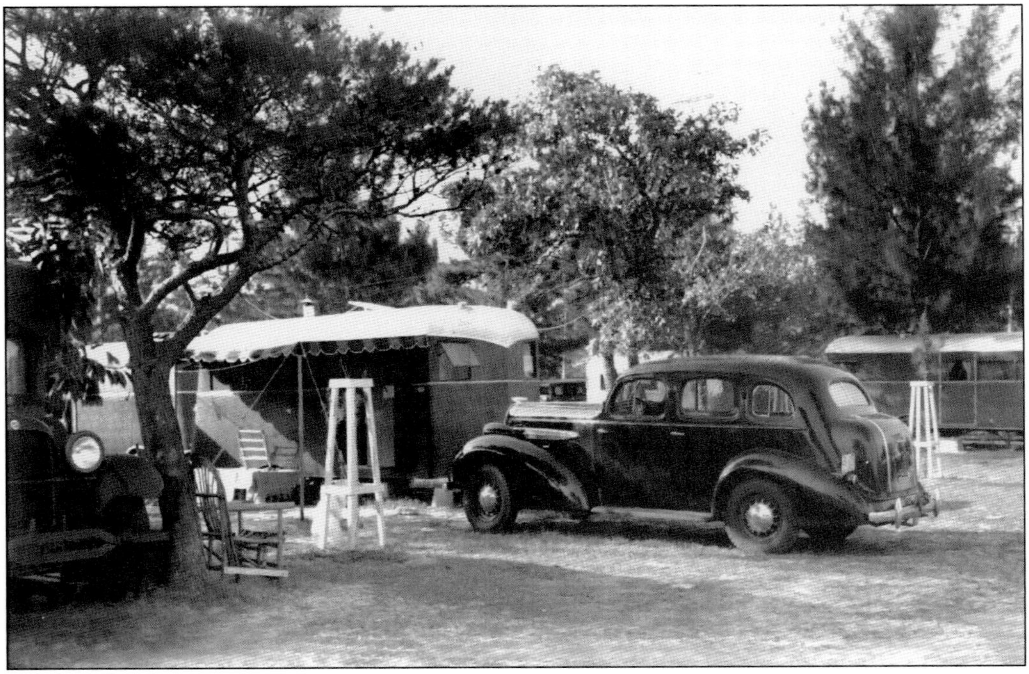

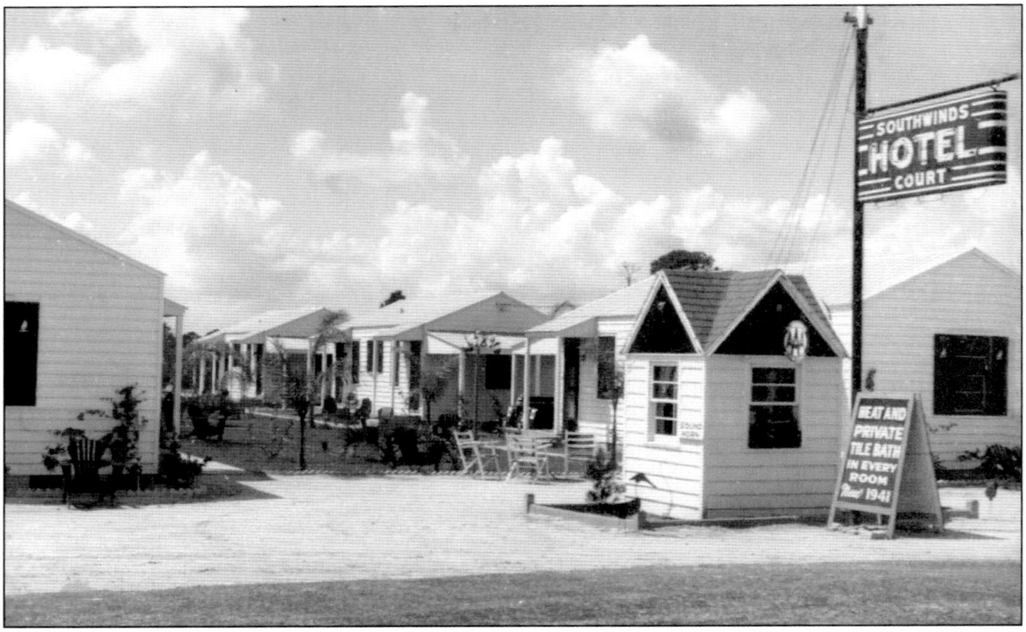

During the war, when housing was in such short supply, every available apartment or cottage was rented. The landlords of the area saw a reversal of the doldrums of the Depression when tourism virtually died. During the war, occupancy was up but tourism was limited. After the war's end, there was a sharp rise in tourism just as there had been after World War I. Automobiles poured south and a new emphasis was placed on vacation activities and special destinations.

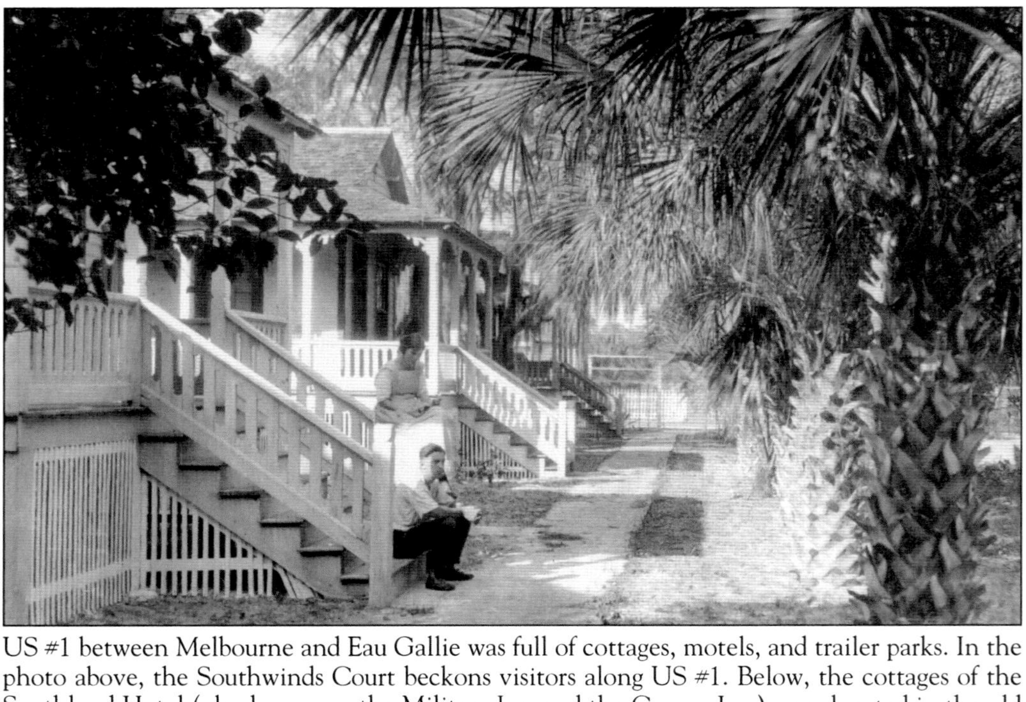

US #1 between Melbourne and Eau Gallie was full of cottages, motels, and trailer parks. In the photo above, the Southwinds Court beckons visitors along US #1. Below, the cottages of the Southland Hotel (also known as the Military Inn and the Canary Inn) were located in the old Eau Gallie section south of Young Street.

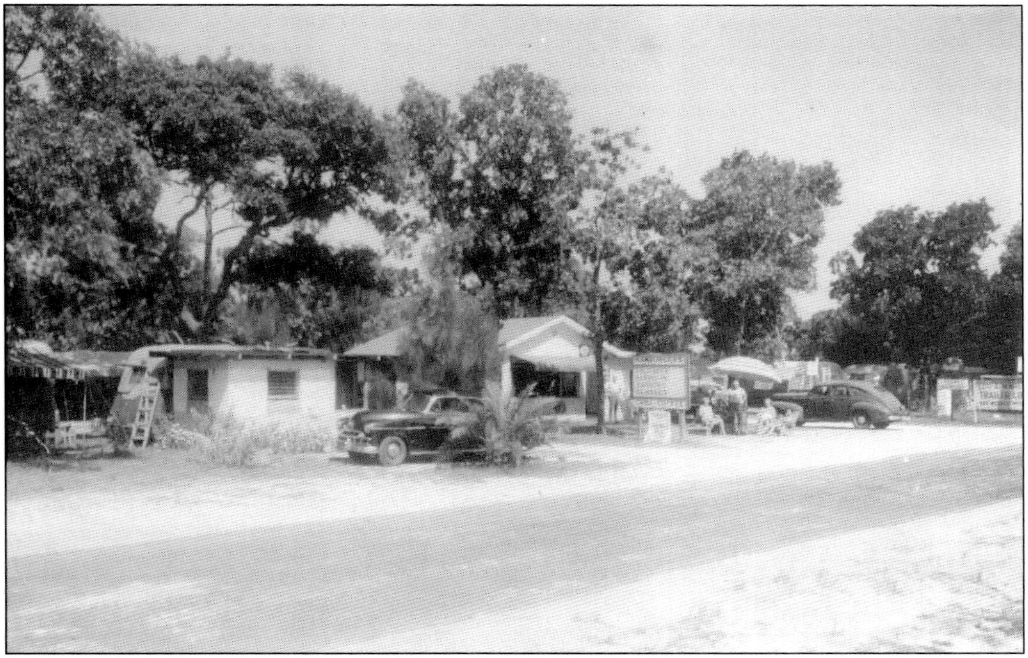

These traveler havens were located in north Eau Gallie on US #1. The top photo is of Lou and Marlin's Trailer Park, and the lower view is of the Rocky Water Camp and Amusement Park. Similar to the Midway Colony, Rocky Water Camp provided a community environment for visitors. These small villages provided a store where residents could buy groceries, gasoline, and bait. There were also campsites, a swimming pool, shuffleboard and horseshoe courts, and a small café. Rocky Water Park has hosted generations of visitors and year-round residents. Owned by the Stouts, Rocky Water was full during the war and the immediate post-war period. The camp is still in operation today.

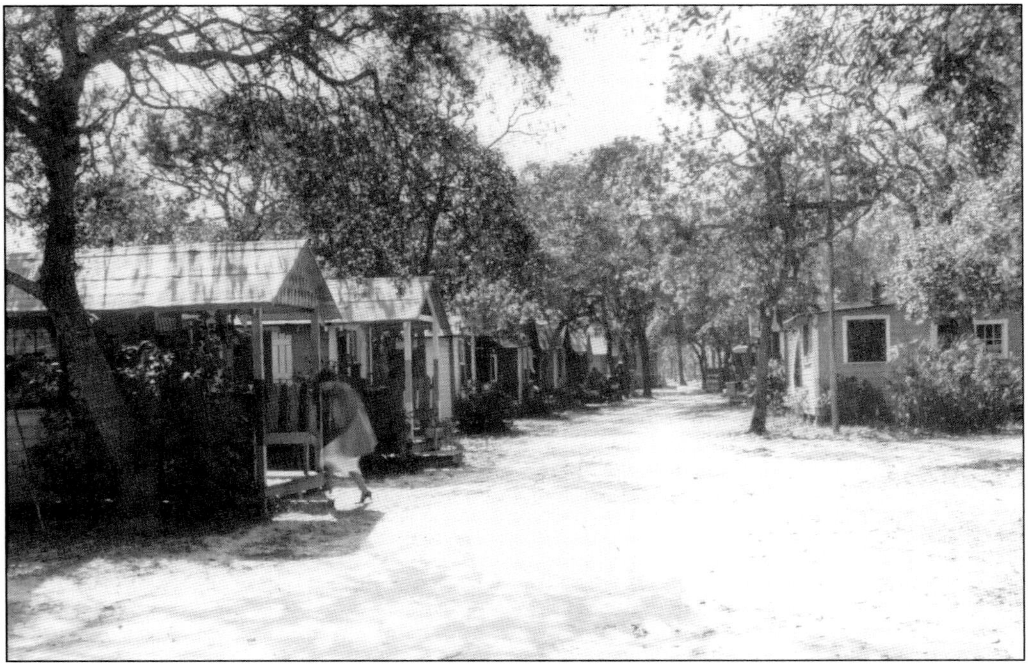

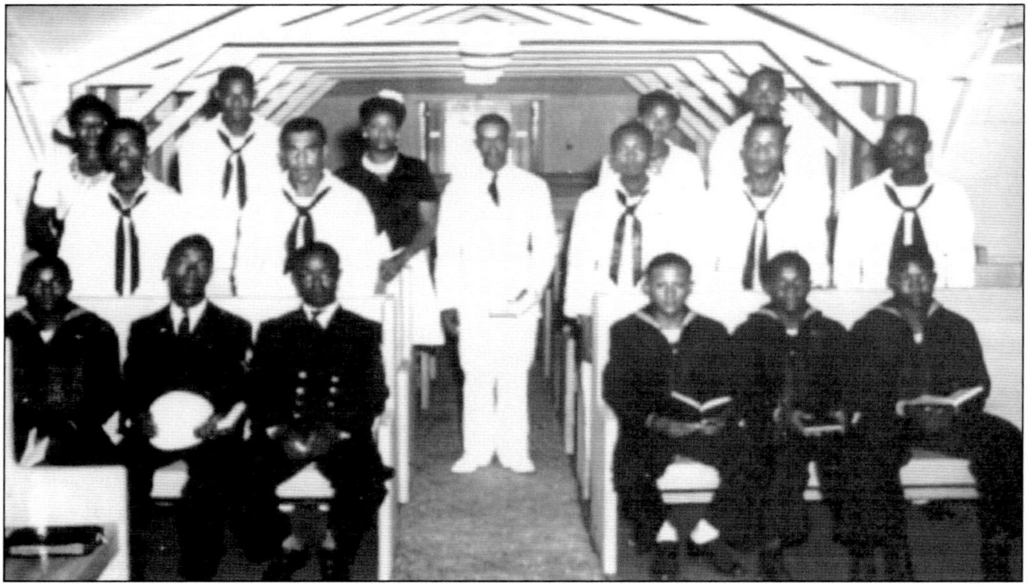

The United States Armed Forces were still segregated during World War II. In this photograph, taken at the Melbourne Naval Air Station, black sailors at the base assemble in the chapel that was built for their religious services. It was not until 1947 that Truman desegregated the military and it took a few more years for the ruling to take significant effect.

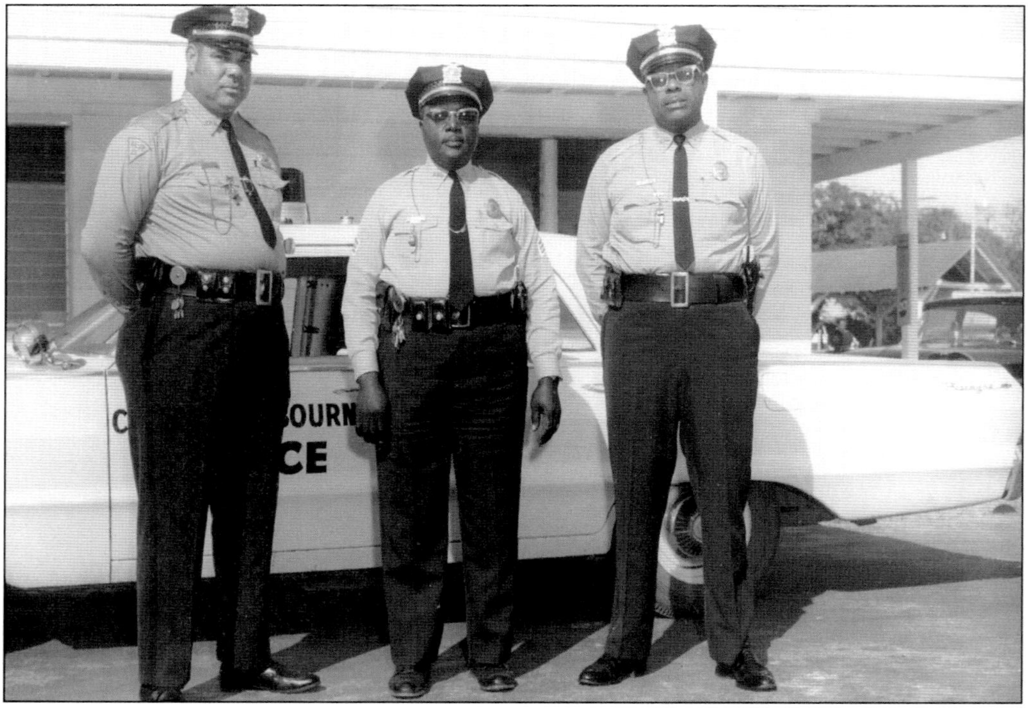

After years of pressure from Harry Lawrence and other leaders in South Melbourne, the City hired James R. Ryoland in 1947 as Melbourne's first black officer. He served for two years with no uniform, provided his own gun and car, and became a solitary police force for South Melbourne until the 1960s. Ryoland was eventually joined by other black members of the force. Here, Sergeant Ryoland stands with Foster Thayer on the left and James Thayer on the right.

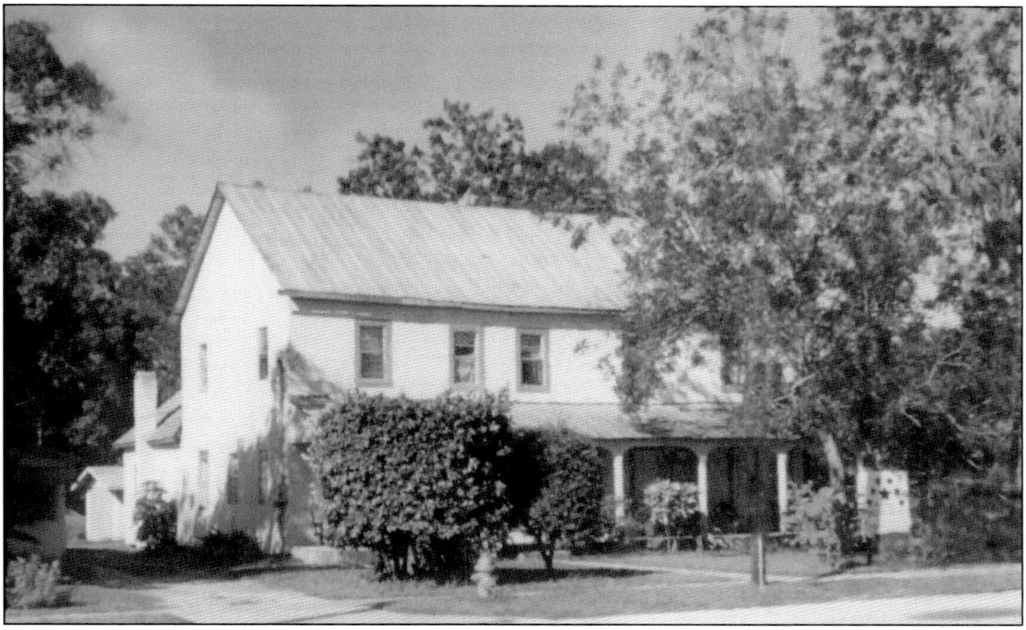

South Melbourne's history is filled with stories of courage and persistence. Martha Hankins's life is surely one of the most inspiring. Born in 1892, Hankins came to South Melbourne in 1937 and purchased the former Hopkins Hotel. She and her daughters worked near Okeechobee in the mucklands, picking vegetables in order to pay for the house.

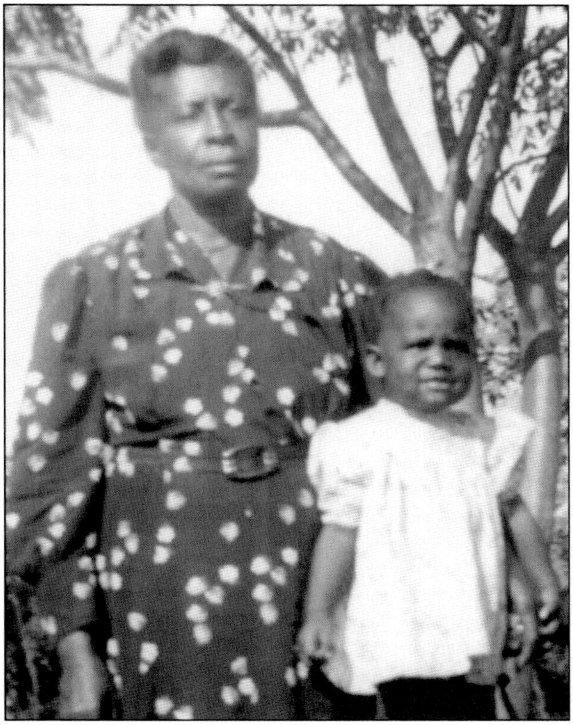

Hankins organized the local Triumph, the Church and Kingdom of God in Christ, and supervised the construction of two churches. She operated her house as a Rescue Mission for those in need and made seven trips to Monrovia, Liberia, founding and maintaining a mission there. The Rescue Mission, pictured above, is still owned and operated by the family. At right, Rev. Carol Williams Glanton, at the age of two, stands with her grandmother, Martha Ann Hankins.

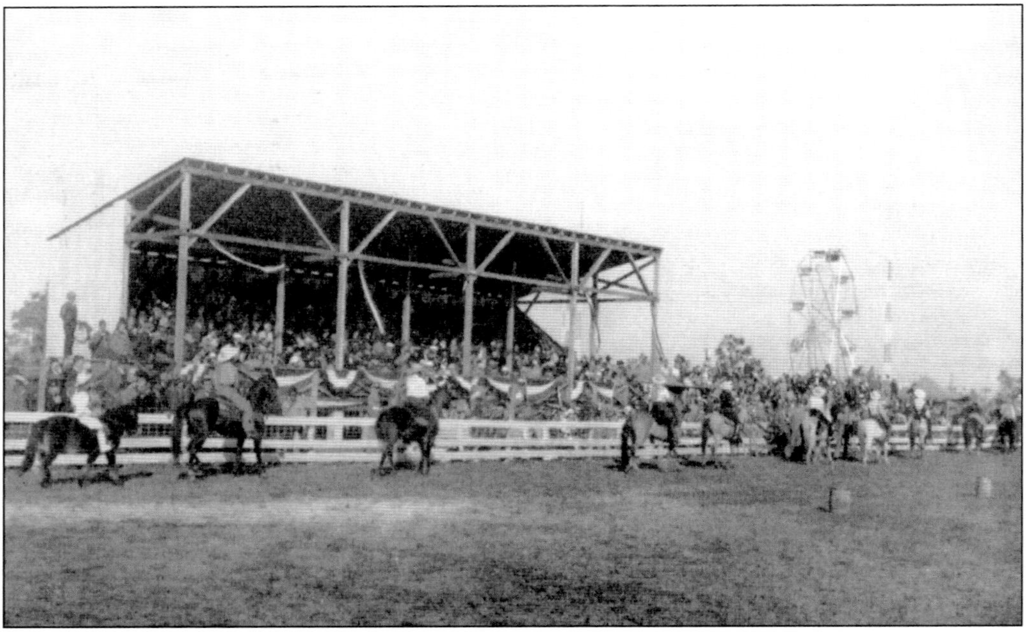

West of Eau Gallie and Melbourne was cattle country and home to the area's largest land-owning families. Here is a scene from the Eau Gallie Annual Rodeo and Fair during the World War II era.

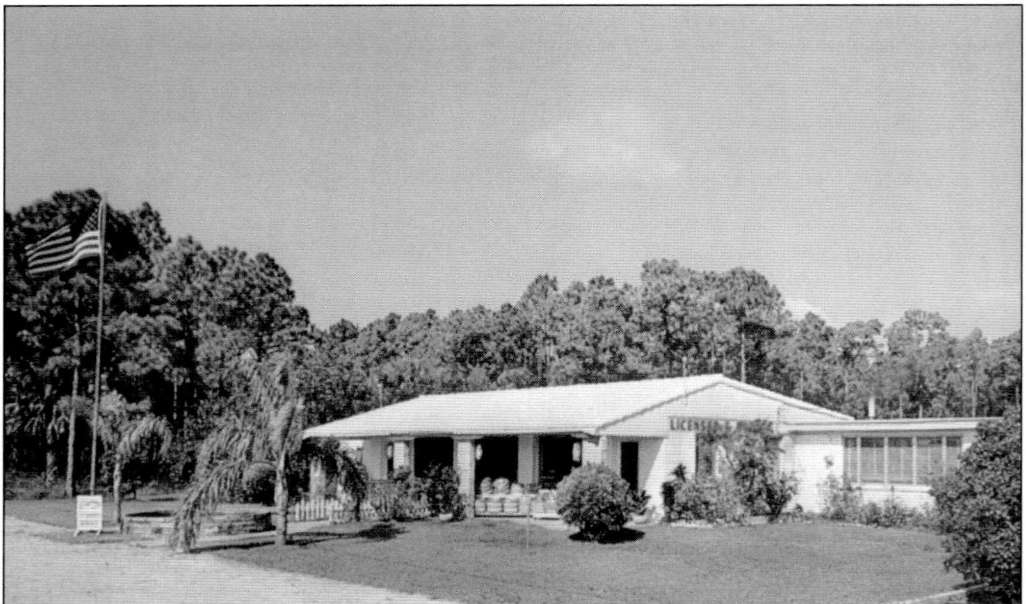

Indian River citrus fruit was grown and sold along US #1 and in areas west of Melbourne and Eau Gallie. Here is a view of Houser's groves, whose sales office was on West New Haven Avenue. Houser's enhanced its appeal when it added a petting zoo in the 1960s.

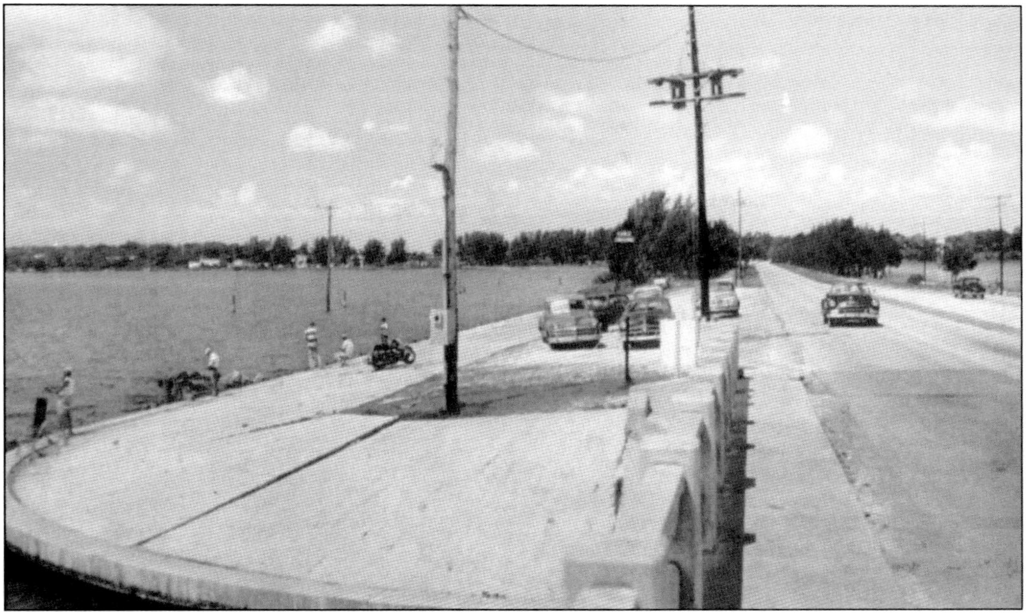

Melbourne replaced the wooden bridge across the Indian River with a new causeway and steel drawbridge in 1947. This view is of the concrete apron on the eastern end of the drawbridge. The photographer is facing east. The causeway had broad shoulders and Australian pines planted in semi-circles around picnic tables. The bridge was usually lined with people fishing.

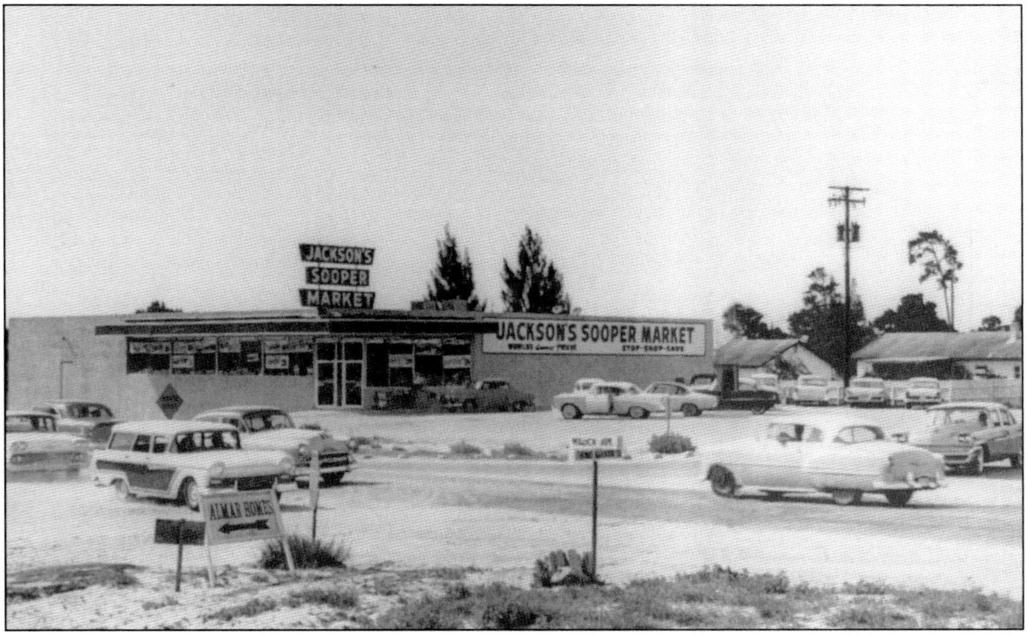

As soon as the war was over, housing starts shot up. This photo shows the intersection of US #1 and Thomas Barbour Drive in the 1950s. The sign in the left foreground points to the just-opened Almar Homes subdivision. Behind the new grocery store is another housing development—Loveridge Heights. This will be Eau Gallie and Melbourne's new look for the next decade, as palmetto and pine make way for concrete block and asphalt. Jackson's, later the Big Apple, is a marina today.

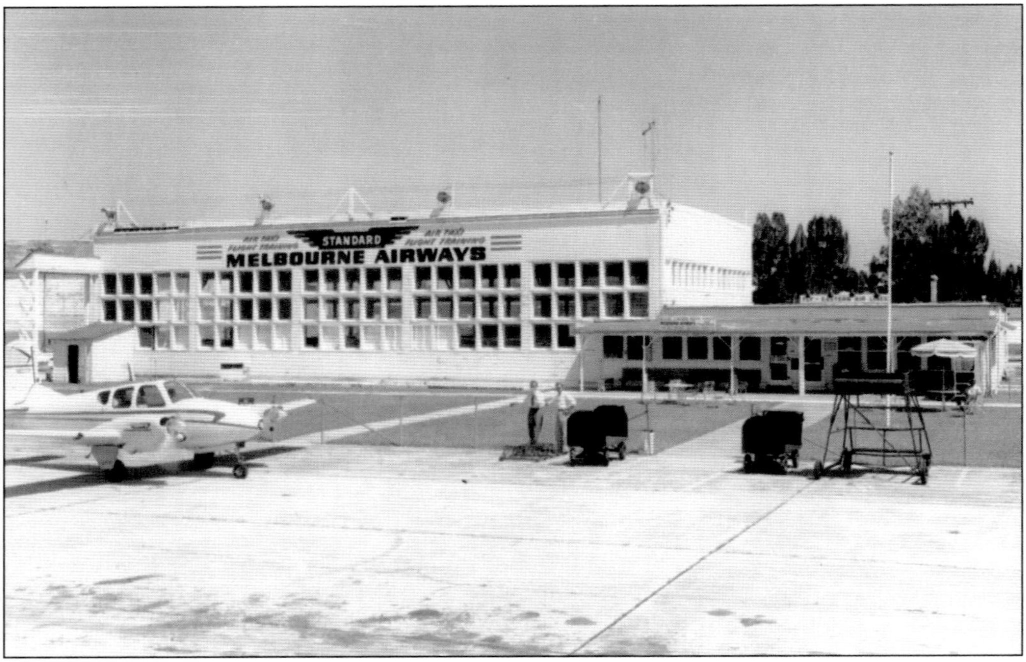

City fathers considered Melbourne's original airport site west of town to be too far from town. They welcomed instead, a new location between Melbourne and Eau Gallie, slightly west of the Dixie Highway. In 1934, the first flight arrived, and the first carrier, Eastern, began service in 1953. National Airlines added Melbourne to its schedule in 1963. The photo above shows the hangar at the airport in 1956.

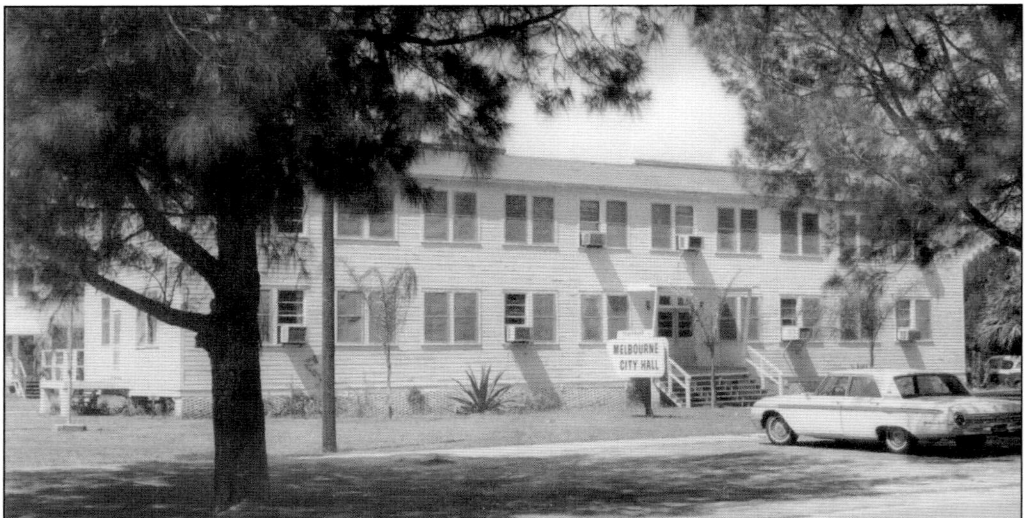

In 1947, the United States government ceded more than 2,300 acres to the City of Melbourne when it decommissioned the naval base at the airport. Above is one of the base's wooden buildings that the City inherited. Several base buildings subsequently housed a number of new companies and organizations, the best known of which was Radiation (later Harris). Others included DBA Systems, HETRA Communications, Collins Aviation, FIT Aviation, Instrument Corporation of Florida, Sebastian Radio, Custom Craft, the Minnesota Twins, and the Indian River Players.

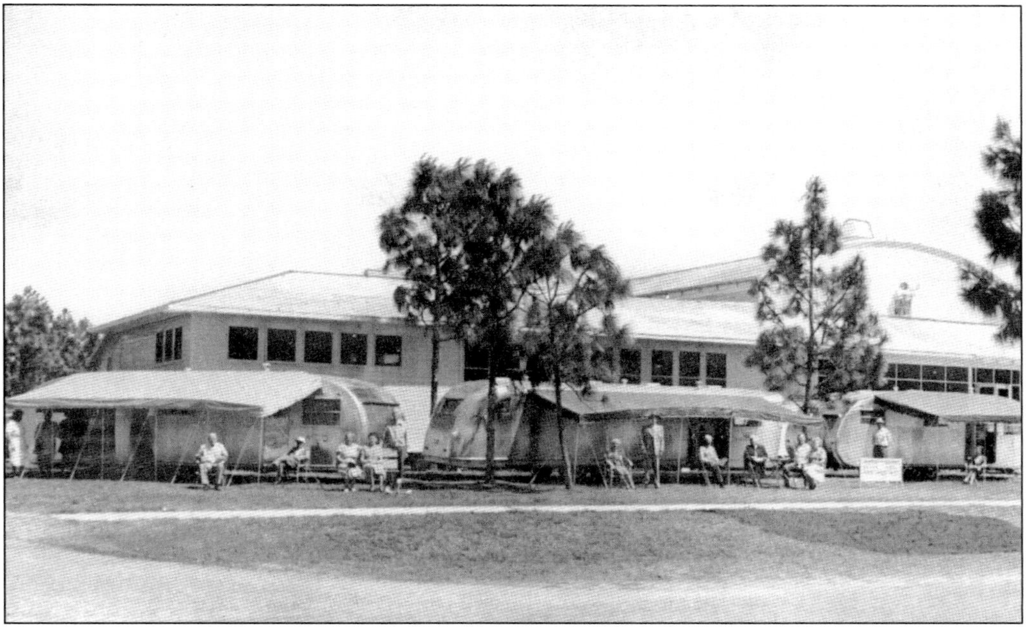

In 1950, the Tin Can Tourists helped set up Trailer Haven on the grounds of the former base. The Community Center building above is the last of the wooden structures at the airport. The trailers on the front lawn are sales models. Trailer Haven advertised 30 by 40 foot lots with city water and sewer. In 1969, the Airstream Park and Land Yacht Port o' Call opened on property leased from the airport.

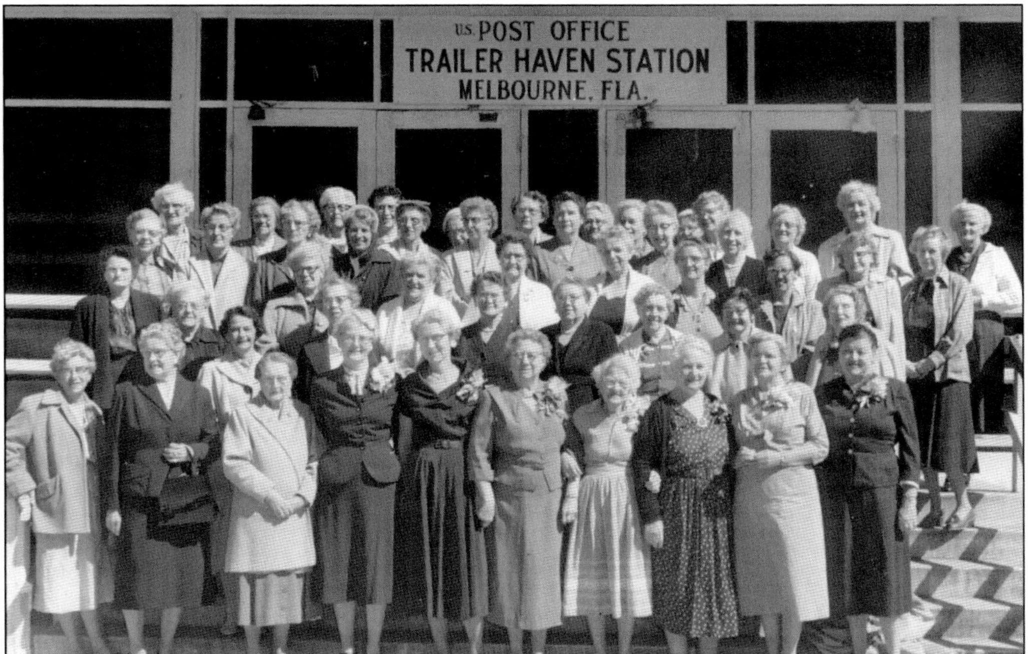

From the beginning, Trailer Haven has elected officers and published a newsletter. Here the Trailer Haven Women's Club gathers on the steps of the community center at Christmastime, 1950.

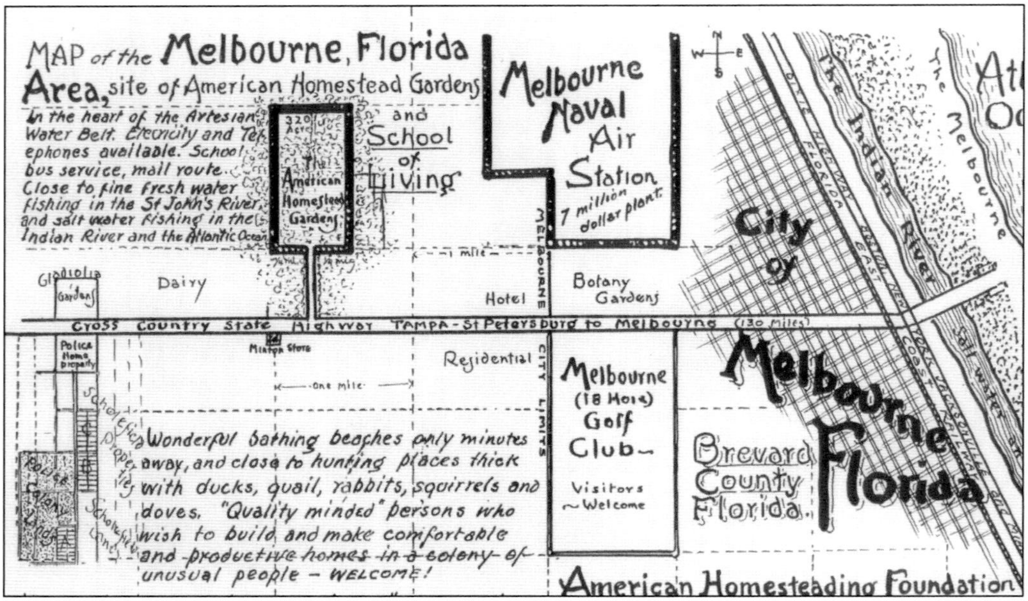

In 1946, the American Homesteading Foundation (AHF), organized in Dayton, Ohio, came south and set up a planned community of self-sufficient colonists. Their idea was that gardening, cooperative living, creative work, and home-based manufacturers would supplement or even totally supply income for residents. The group purchased land in and near a picturesque oak hammock west of Melbourne.

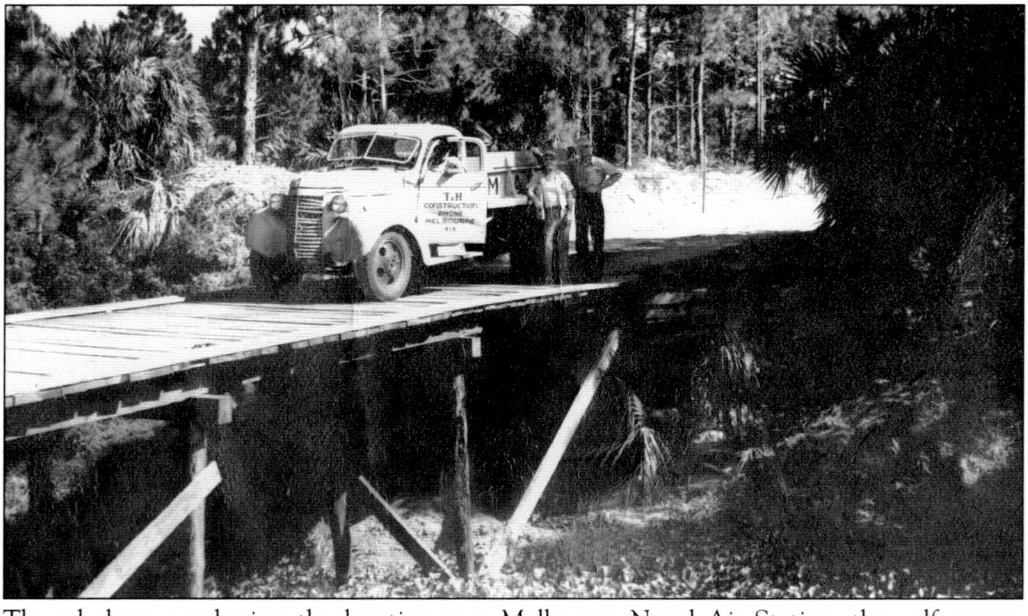

The ad above emphasizes the location near Melbourne Naval Air Station, the golf course, Botany Gardens (formerly Magnolia Park), the City of Melbourne, the Indian River (an "arm of the ocean"), and the Melbourne Beach. The goals of the group were also educational, and residents of the American Homesteading gardens would be supplied with a "School of Living," a fine library, and eventually, a graduate university. The scene below shows Melbourne Village Manager, Norman Lund, with villagers and contractors, Tynan and Halverson, on the AHF's first bridge into the village in 1950.

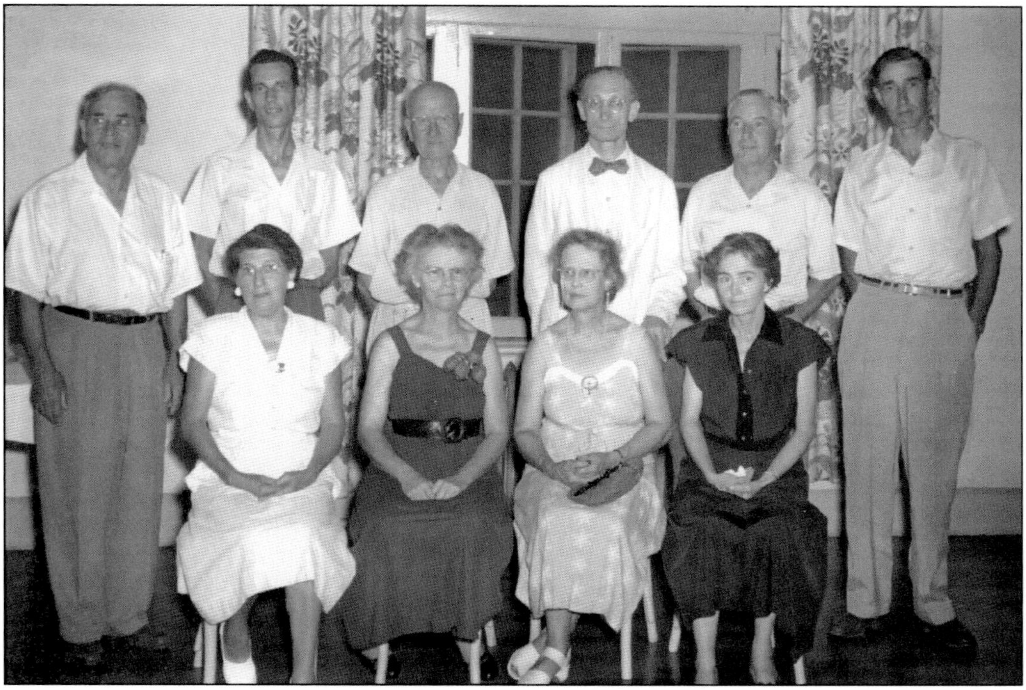

Founders and organizers gather for the fourth annual meeting in 1950. In the front row are, from left to right, Gertrude Martin, Elizabeth Nutting, Virginia Wood, and Margaret Hutchinson. The latter three are the founding mothers of Melbourne Village. In the back row, from left to right, are Arthur Tippie (manager of the cooperative store), Wayne Taylor, J. Horton, Ralph Borsodi (a centrist proponent whose ideas the founders followed), George Tynan, and Frank Rothery Sr.

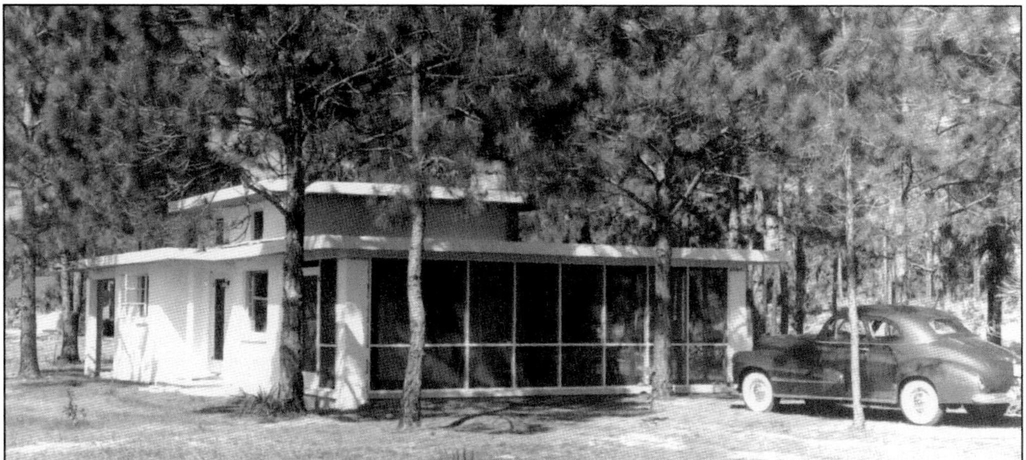

True to the self-sufficiency ethic, villagers economized and improvised while building their houses. Some residents lived in temporary cabins or travel trailers at first. Others used the smaller wooden buildings from the Melbourne Naval Air Station as components for their homes. The old community center, now planned for renovation, was brought down the river on a barge from the Banana River NAS, now Patrick AFB. The village style emphasized native Florida settings and natural ventilation. This photo shows Virginia Wood's airy house, the first built in the Melbourne Village.

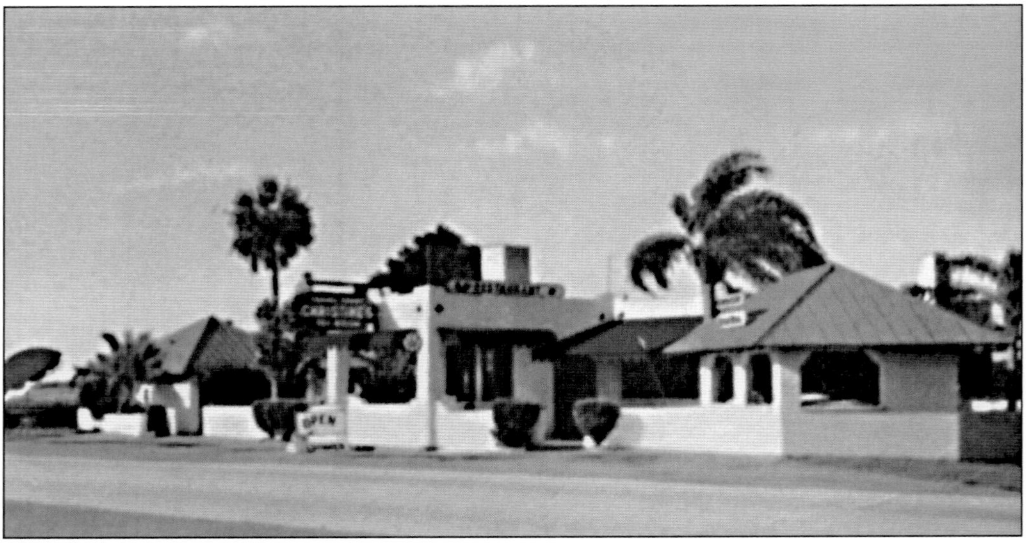

These photos show the expansion of Eau Gallie and Melbourne along US #1 during the 1940s and 1950s. Above is Christine's, a family restaurant owned and operated by Judith and Jorge Lopez. Christine's was seven miles north of Eau Gallie Boulevard, a long way from the center of town. Lopez' career served as an example of the size, mobility, and cohesiveness of the expanding Eau Gallie-Melbourne community. Beginning in 1959, he commuted 15 miles south to the newly constructed Southwest Junior High School at the southern edge of Melbourne. There, he taught Spanish to the Baby Boom children of families brought to the area by the Space Program. By the mid-1950s, Melbourne and Eau Gallie had become one community unified by a federal highway and a common economy.

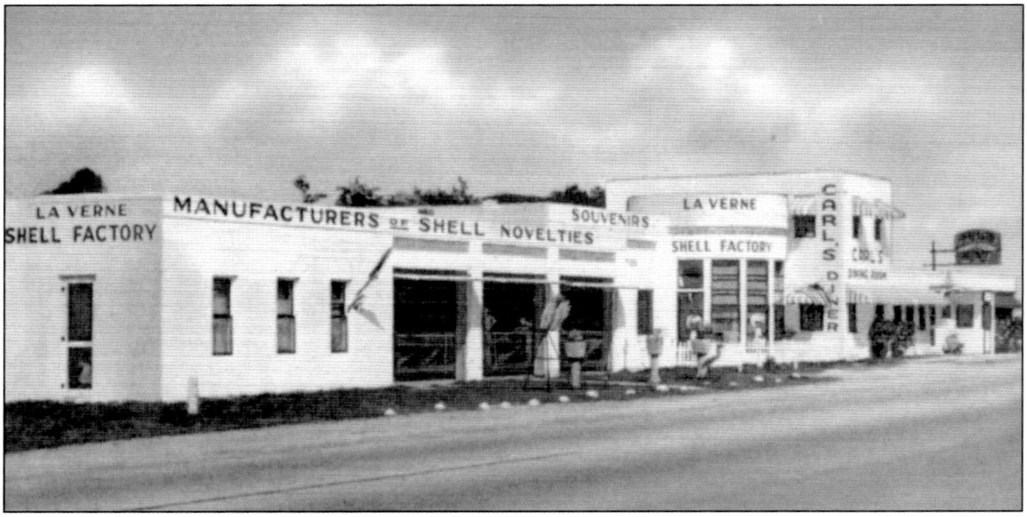

The view above shows Carl's Diner and La Verne's Shell Factory, located south of Melbourne on US #1. The community bandshell on Front Street, begun in 1948, is dedicated to Gamer. His restaurant was popular with locals and with the many travelers who stopped at La Verne's for a souvenir on their trip south.

Five

The Space Program

In 1950, the World War II–era Banana River Naval Air Station became Patrick Air Force Base and the Long Range Proving Ground. After the launch of Sputnik in 1957, the U.S. tried to outpace the Soviets in guided missile development and space exploration. NASA was formed in 1958, and Patrick AFB and the missile facilities at Cape Canaveral became the center of a national scientific endeavor. The Space Race became the driving economic and ideological force behind Eau Gallie and Melbourne's development. This photo of the Technical Laboratory at Patrick shows the base's location, between the ocean and the Banana River. The missiles in front of the Tech Lab are proudly displayed as testimony to national and local achievement.

From 1940 to 1960, the population of Melbourne and Eau Gallie increased from 5,330 to 24,203. After 1955, Federal "impact funds" flowed into the county to help local providers deal with the strain of ballooning public service needs. In the next 15 years, the cities would be transformed into a united community with a well-connected infrastructure. In this final chapter, the unified Melbourne and Eau Gallie have become a new city with modern systems of transportation, communication, education, health care, retail, technology, finance, and public service.

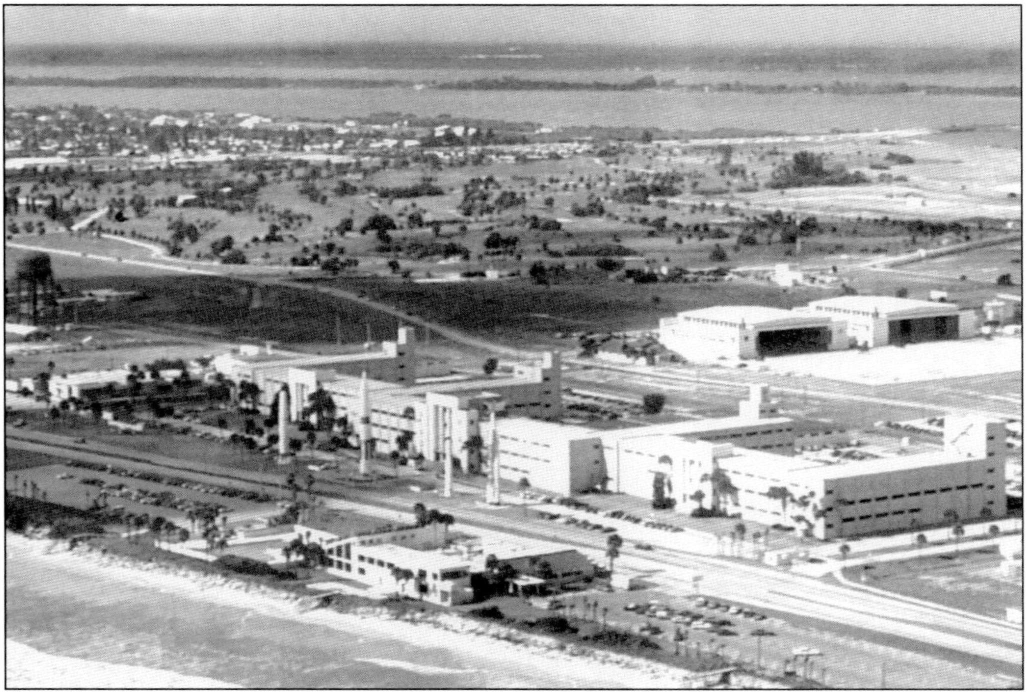

Above is Patrick Air Force Base, between the Atlantic Ocean and the Banana River, c. 1965.

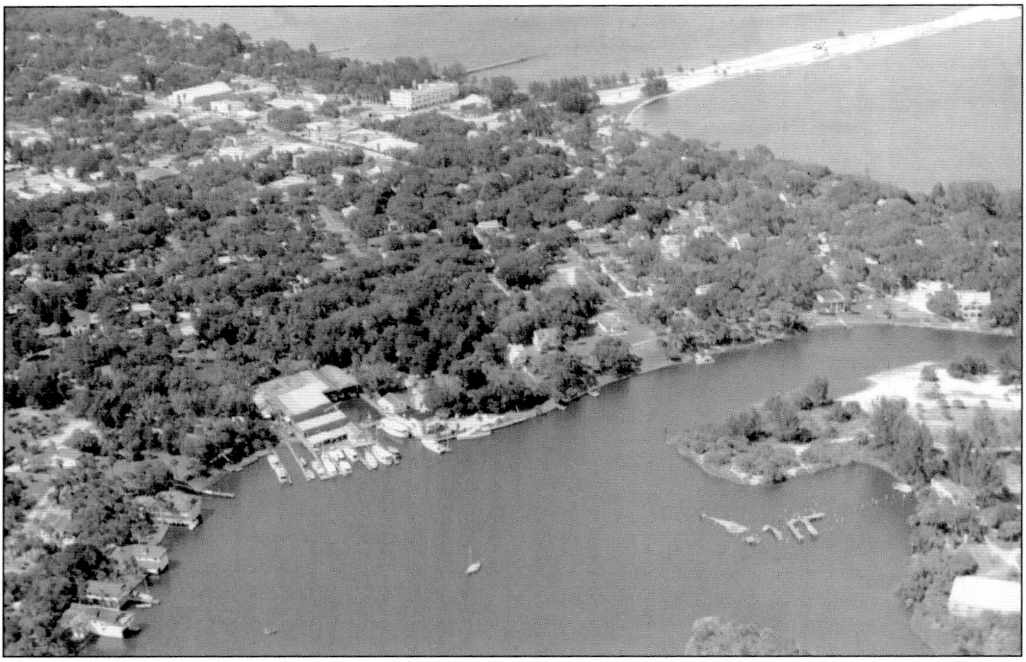

This aerial view of Eau Gallie shows the downtown area, the old riverfront district, and the new causeway across the Indian River. The causeway and W.J. Creel Bridge were completed in 1955. The aerial below is of Melbourne in 1959. The new US #1 Bridge across Crane Creek is complete, and development has clearly spread from the downtown area.

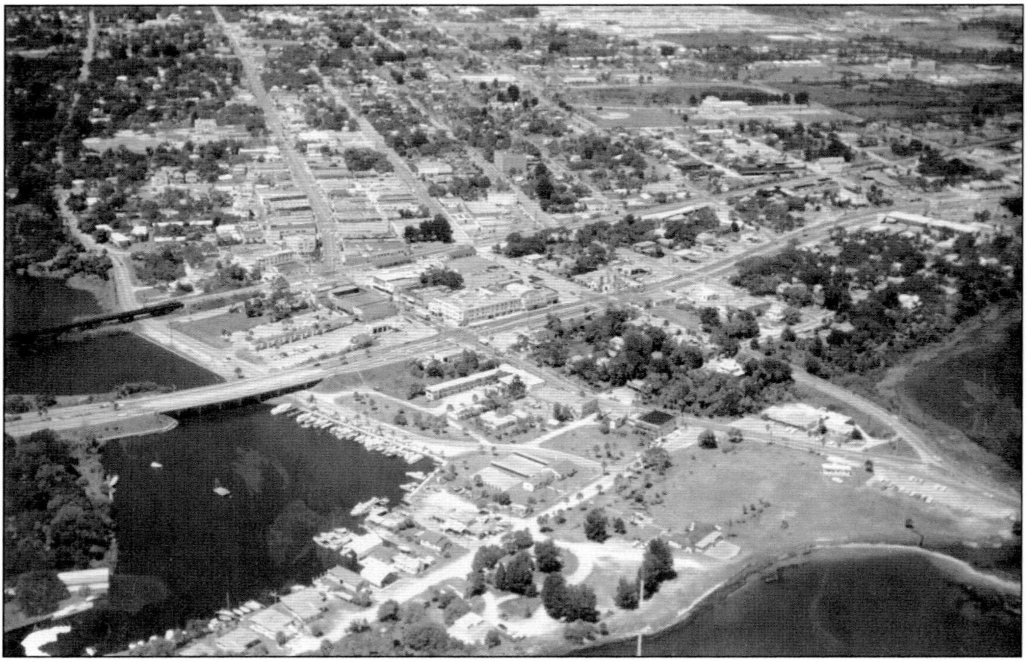

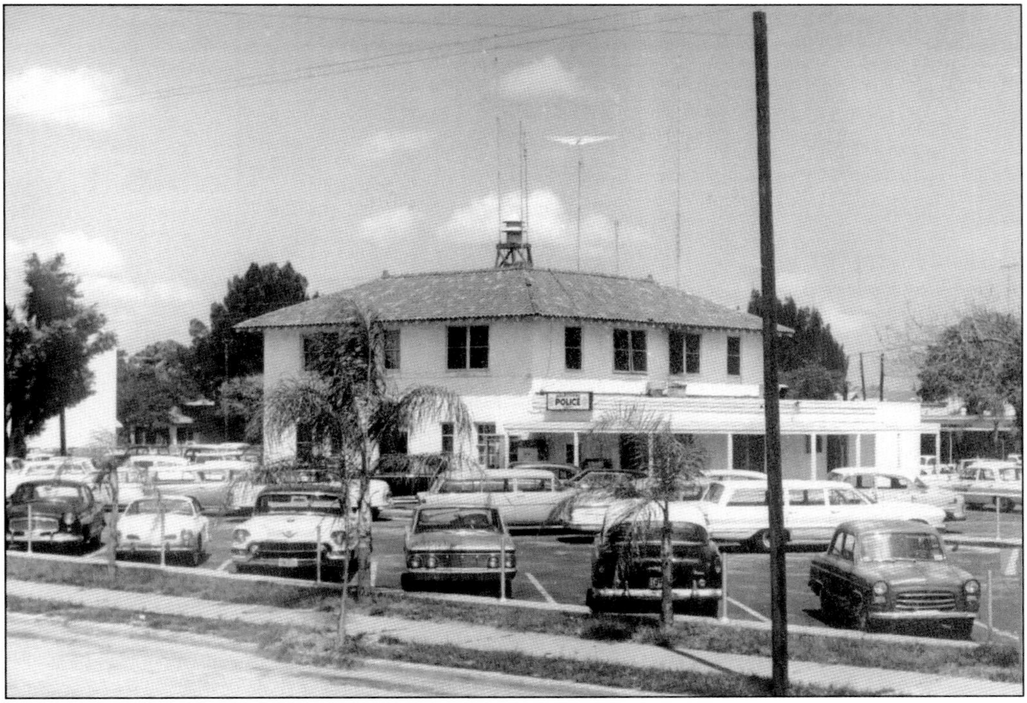

By 1960, when this photo of the old Melbourne City Hall was taken, technology and an increasing population had already begun to create changes. Below, police dispatchers Thera Adams, Thelma Newell, and Anita Gourlay communicate with patrol cars by radio.

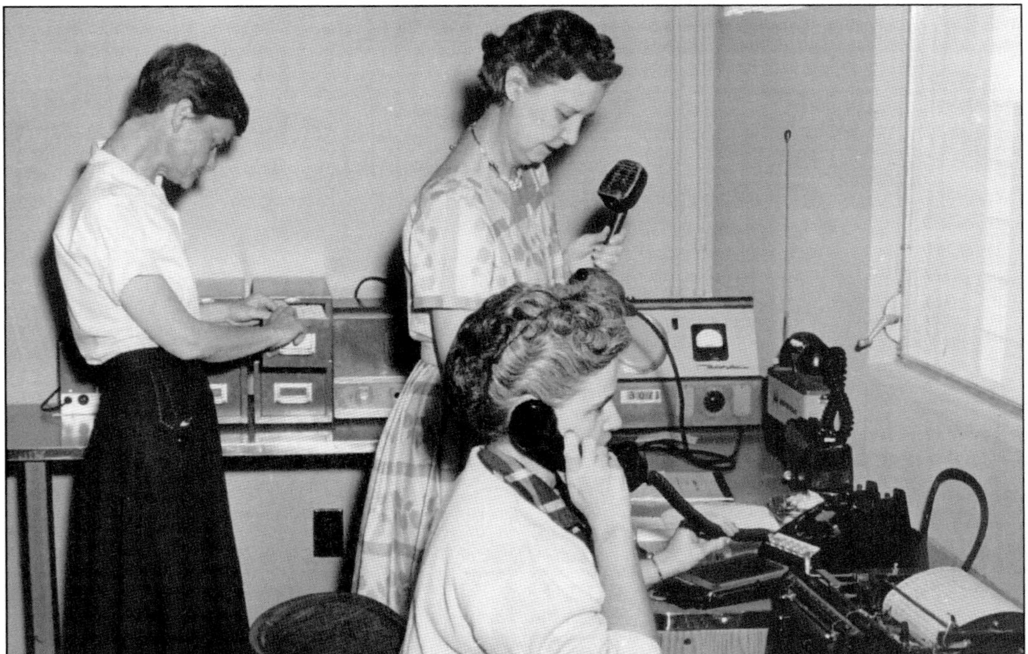

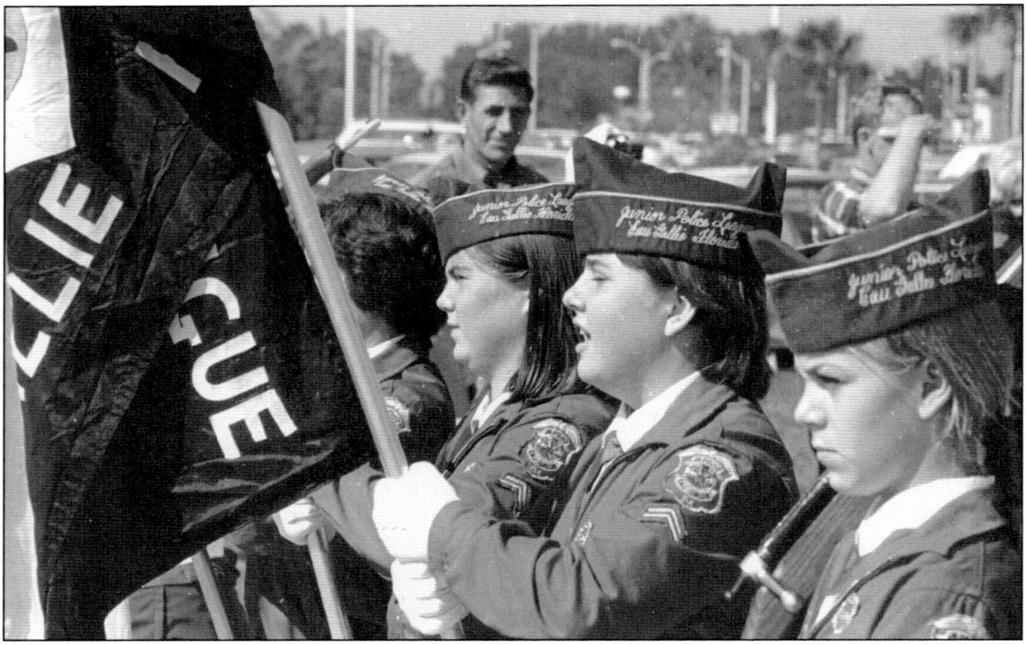

Eau Gallie's civic pride and community spirit continued to bring the city together in celebrations as it had in the past. Here, the girls of the Eau Gallie Junior Police League march in a parade in the early 1960s. Below, children gather for the city's Fourth of July bike race.

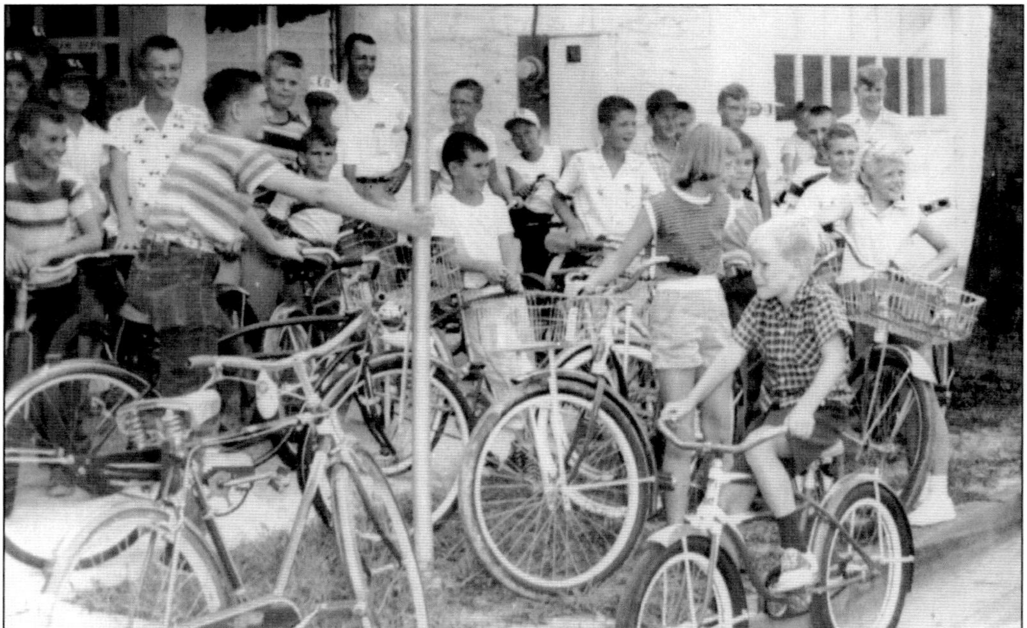

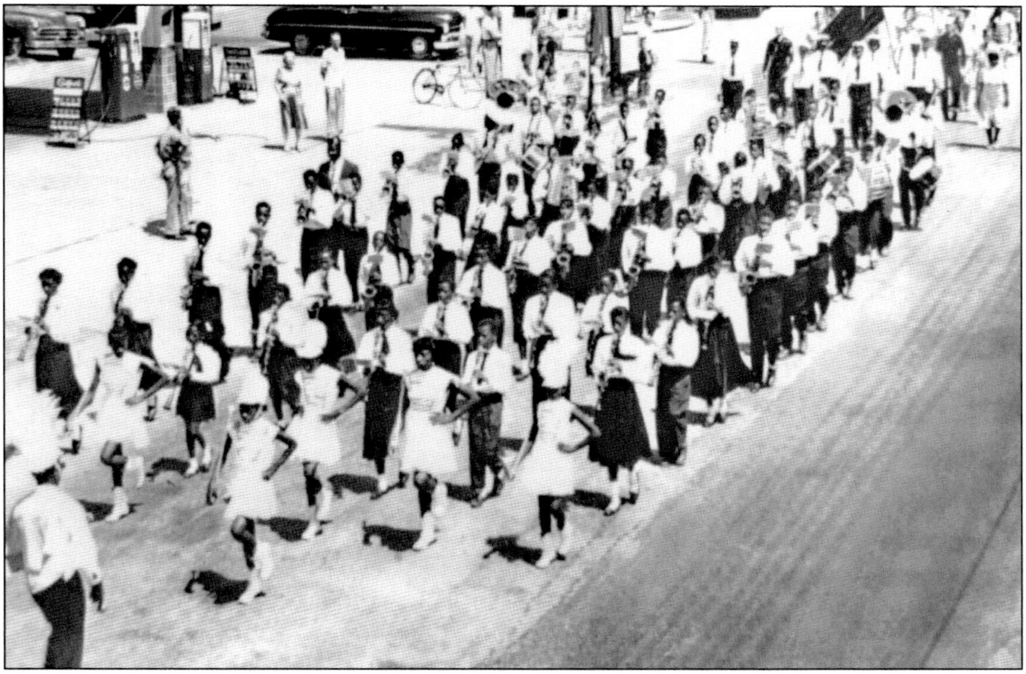

Above, the Stone High School Band marches in an Independence Day parade on US #1 north of New Haven Avenue in Melbourne. One of the greatest pleasures of the Melbourne parades was watching and hearing the unequalled flair and musicianship of the Stone High Marching Band under the direction of Philip Cooper. Melbourne had a segregated school system until 1965. African-American students attended the Melbourne Vocational (High) School from 1930–1953. They were bused to northern Brevard until Stone High was opened in 1957. After 1966, Stone became an integrated middle school and all 10th–12th grade students attended Melbourne High. The photo below shows another mid-1950s parade on US #1 preparing to cross the Crane Creek bridge. One of the charming facets of Melbourne life today is that old-fashioned community parades still take place.

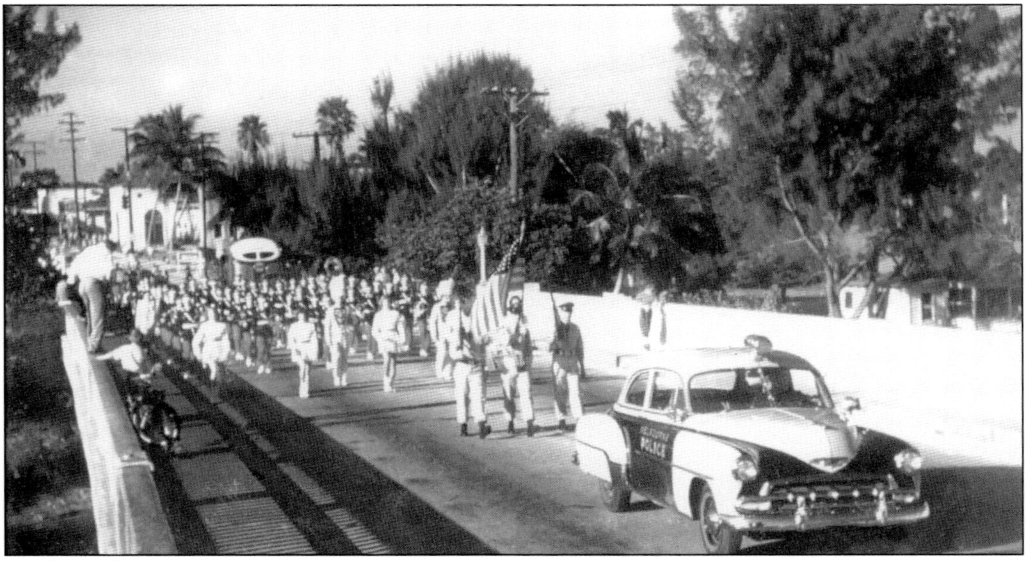

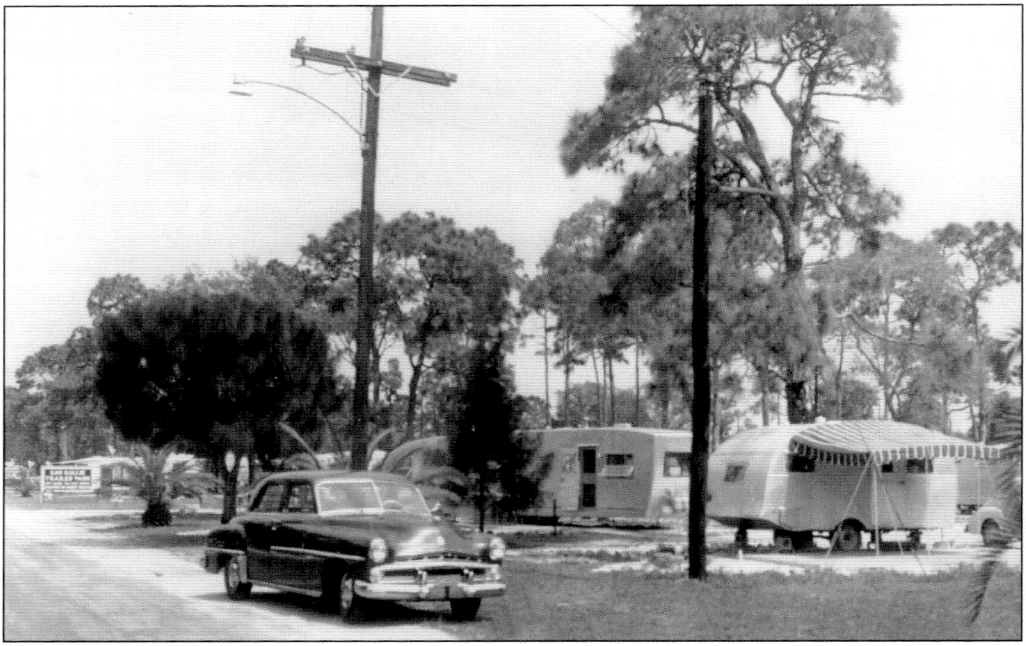

The Eau Gallie Trailer park, operated by James and Elizabeth Rickert, was located on Magnolia Avenue between Eighth and Ninth Streets. The view here is looking south. The same corner ten years later is in the photo below, which was taken looking north. The Shell station and Royal Castle have now replaced the trailer park.

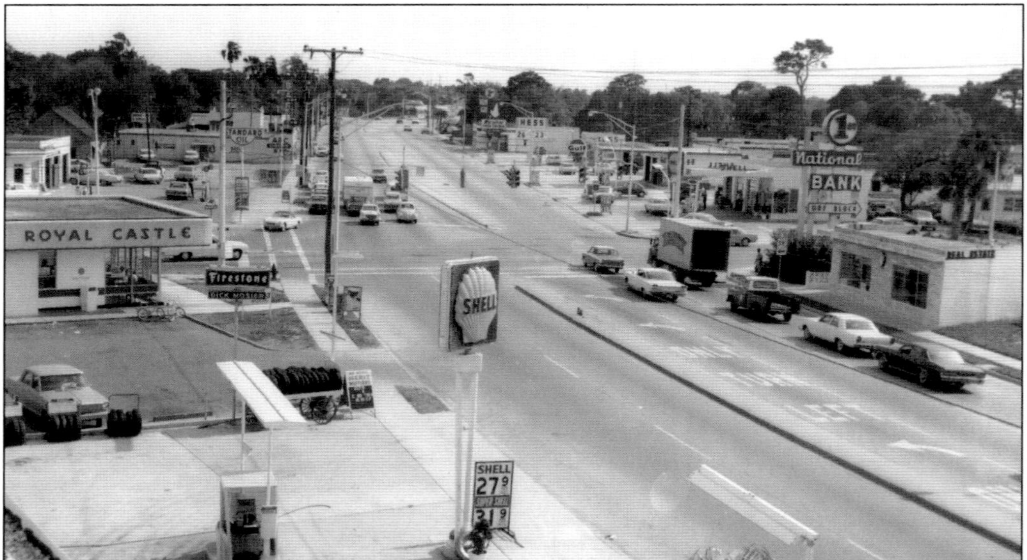

The life of Melbourne and Eau Gallie may not have depended on gasoline sales to the extent it had in the 1920s, but gas stations were still dominant along US #1, New Haven and Eau Gallie Boulevard. On the east are Dick Mosier's Firestone Tire Sales and Shell Station, the Royal Castle Drive-In, and Joe McClendon's Standard Oil. On the west are Tom Doran and Arthur Nicolai's Shell Station, Cecil Hart's Gulf Station, the new Hess Station, and Maryland Fried Chicken, another fast food drive-in restaurant. This view shows how much the local economy depended on the automobile.

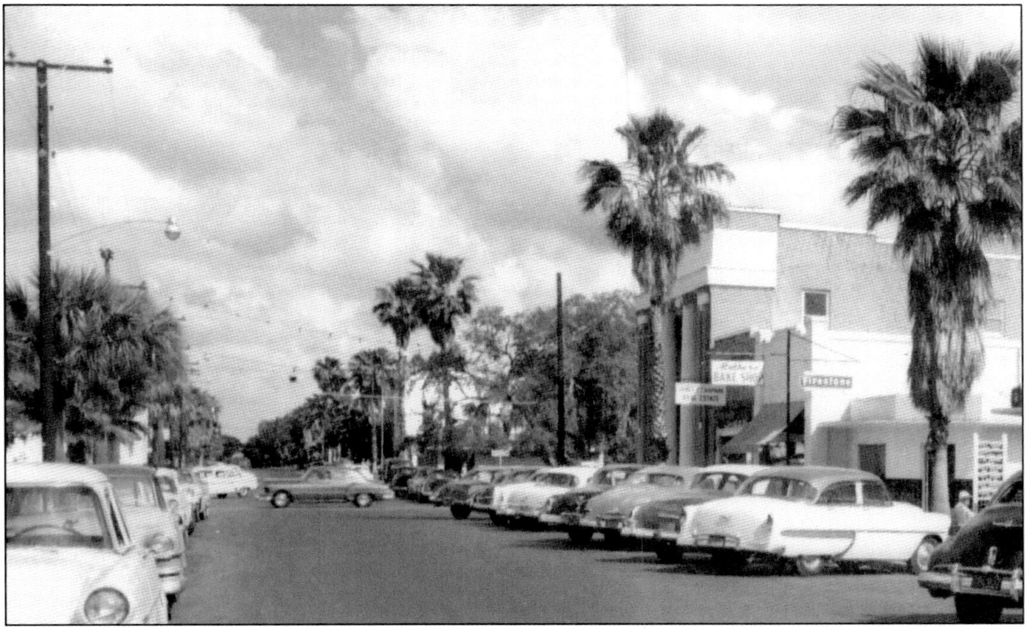

These two pictures show the Highland Avenue business district in Eau Gallie during the 1950s. They evoke the atmosphere of mid-century small-town life that was being replaced by commercial areas with highway accessibility and large parking lots. New subdivisions and shopping centers pulled essential businesses away from the old districts during the 1960s. The buildings seen here—the Coleman (below), the Eau Gallie Bank (above, right), and others—remain to this day. The Mathers' family bakery is also still in the same location. Older shopping areas like this are preserved architecturally because major access roads are routed around them rather than through them. They may look much the same, but the type of commerce in the older downtown business areas has changed.

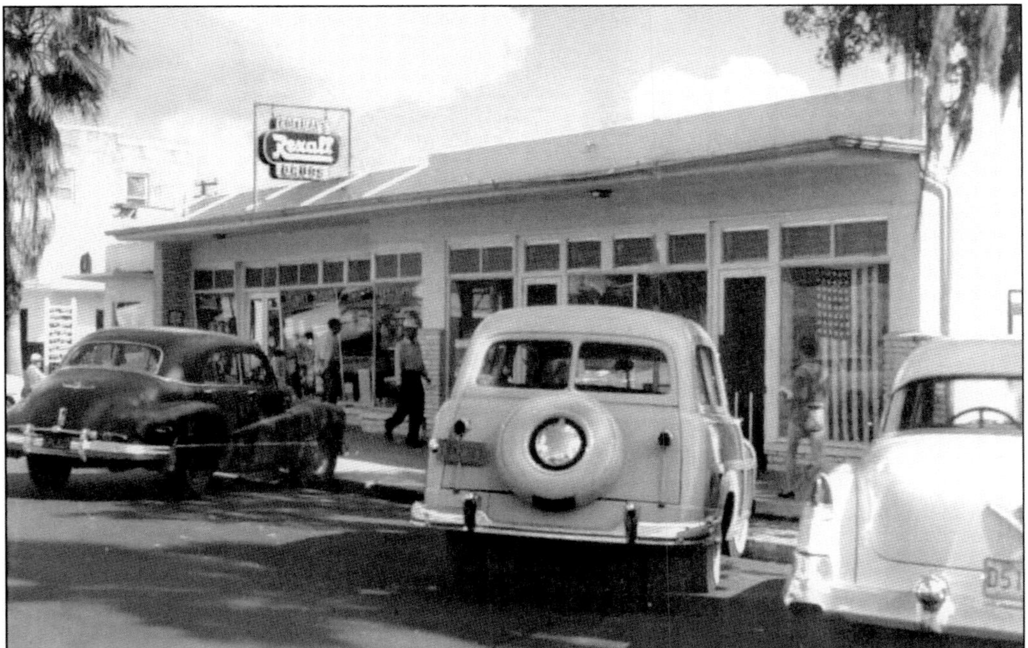

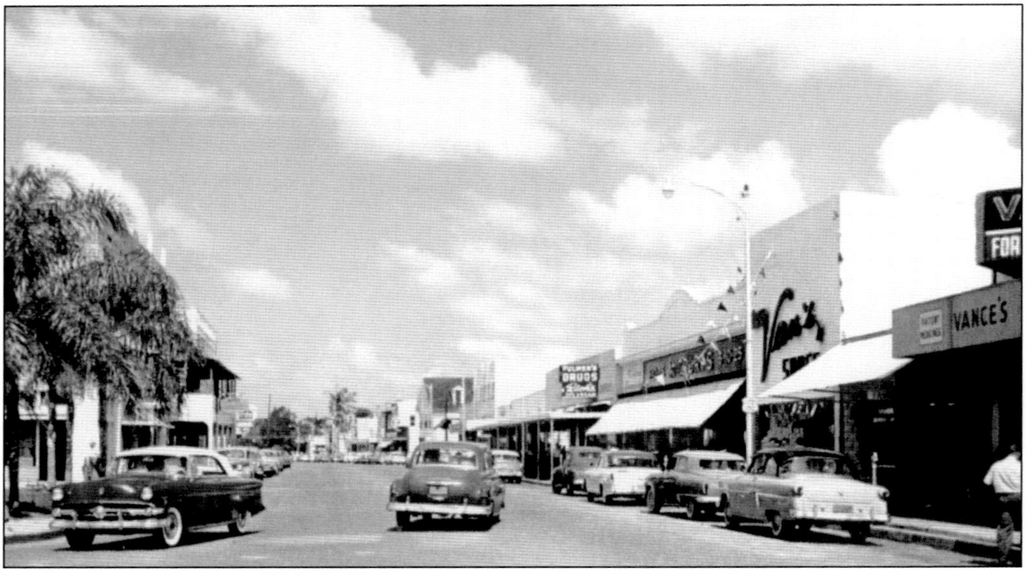

These views of downtown Melbourne in the 1950s are similar to those of Eau Gallie. They were both distinct central business districts defined by major crossroads. The Melbourne Hotel, managed by Sidney Platt, dominated the US #1-New Haven intersection, where a neon sign hung high and pointed the way to the beaches. Fulmer's Drug Store, owned and operated by Milton and Eloise Fulmer, was a local chain with several stores in Brevard County. In the scenes above and below, older buildings have been modernized and retrofitted to keep up with the needs of a mid-century commercial center. The Melbourne downtown area declined with the innovation of shopping centers. It later revived in a new form after a widened US #192 was re-directed to the street one block north of New Haven. Like many other downtown districts today, the area is filled with antique and specialty shops and is pedestrian-friendly.

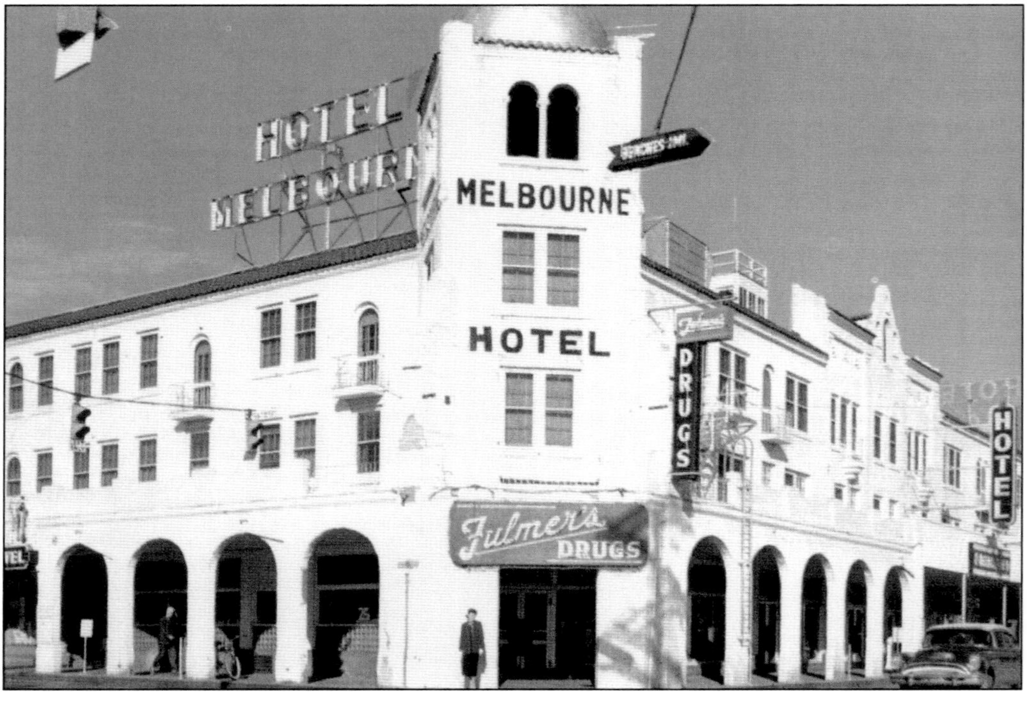

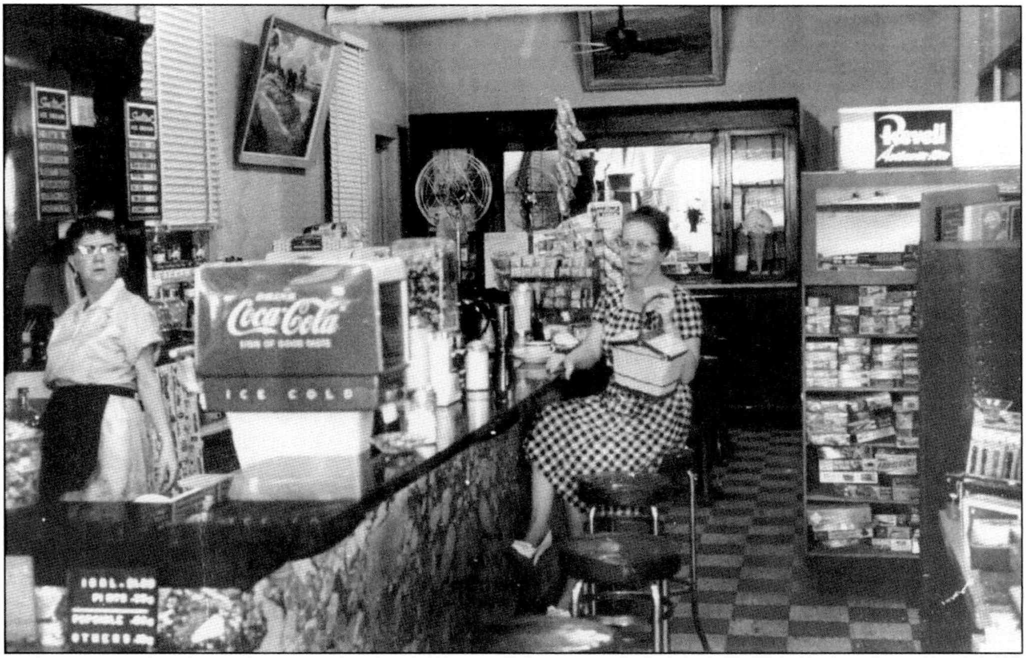

These photos afford a glimpse into the early 1960s. Above, Mary Louise Stevenson sits at Henderich's soda fountain. Stevenson taught piano a few doors away and was organist extraordinaire at the First Methodist Church. Henderich's, on New Haven Avenue, was one of Melbourne's favorite gathering places, as was Shorty's Bar next door. Employees Dennis and Ronnie Meehan purchased Henderich's, moved the business across the street, and expanded it. Meehan's Office Products is currently at 900 East New Haven.

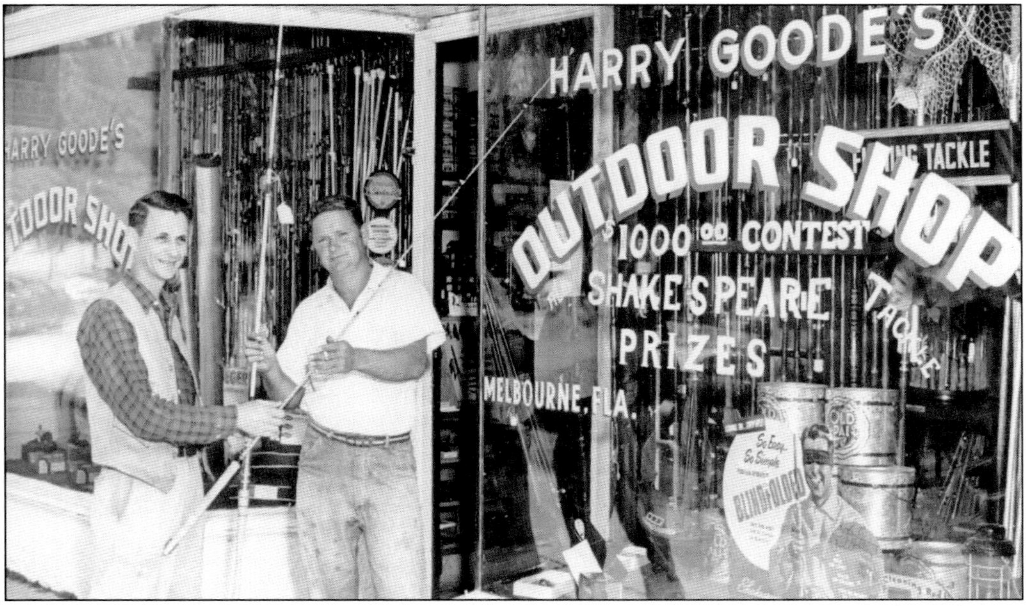

Harry Goode Sr. (left) stands on the sidewalk with a customer in front of his Outdoor Shop, a Melbourne institution and treasured emblem of its connection to the river and to the past. The store is in the Edge Building, built in 1920, right after the big fire. Located at the corner of New Haven and Front Street, it is still there today.

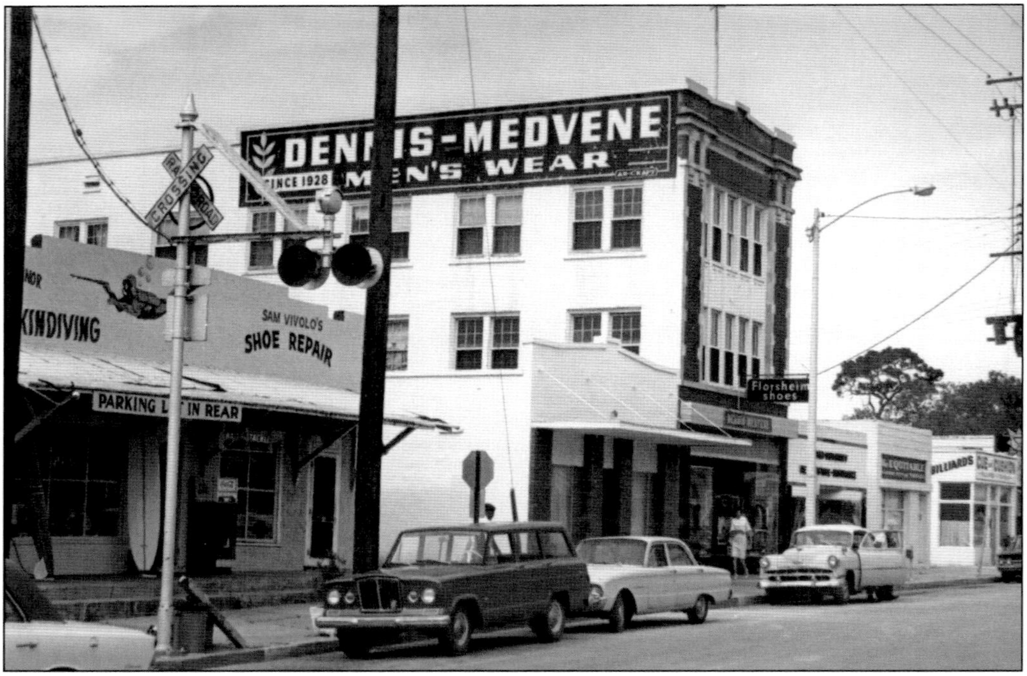

These pages continue the trip down memory lane with more early 1960s scenes of downtown Melbourne. This peek down Melbourne Court begins with Melbourne's old Post Office and Land Office building on the left. The businesses shown here, from left to right, are Jerry and Russell Hatt's Bait and Tackle Shop and Diving, Sam Vivolo's Shoe Repair, Dennis-Medvene Men's Wear, Rodes-Oudshoff Associates, Attorneys Jackson Vaughn and Tom Waddell, Cue and Cushion Billiards, and the Melbourne Bar.

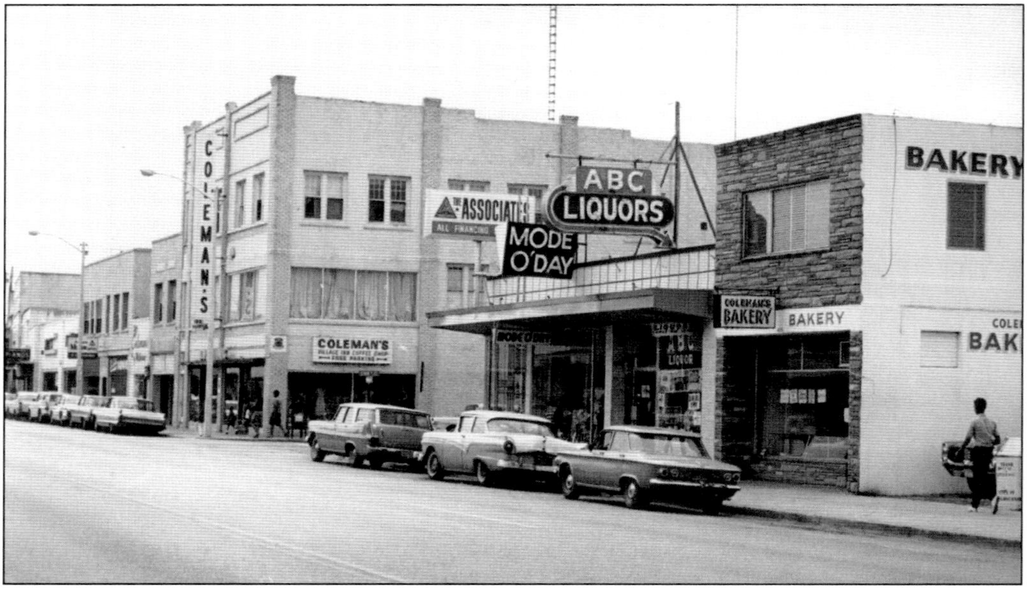

Looking east on New Haven, starting from the foreground at right, are Coleman's Bakery, ABC Liquors, the Mode O'Day Frock Shop, Coleman's Department Store, and Village Inn Coffee Shop. In the background are TV Emporium, New Haven News Center, DeLisle Hardware, Stott's Furniture, and Rinaldo's Music Store (located in the Melbourne Arcade).

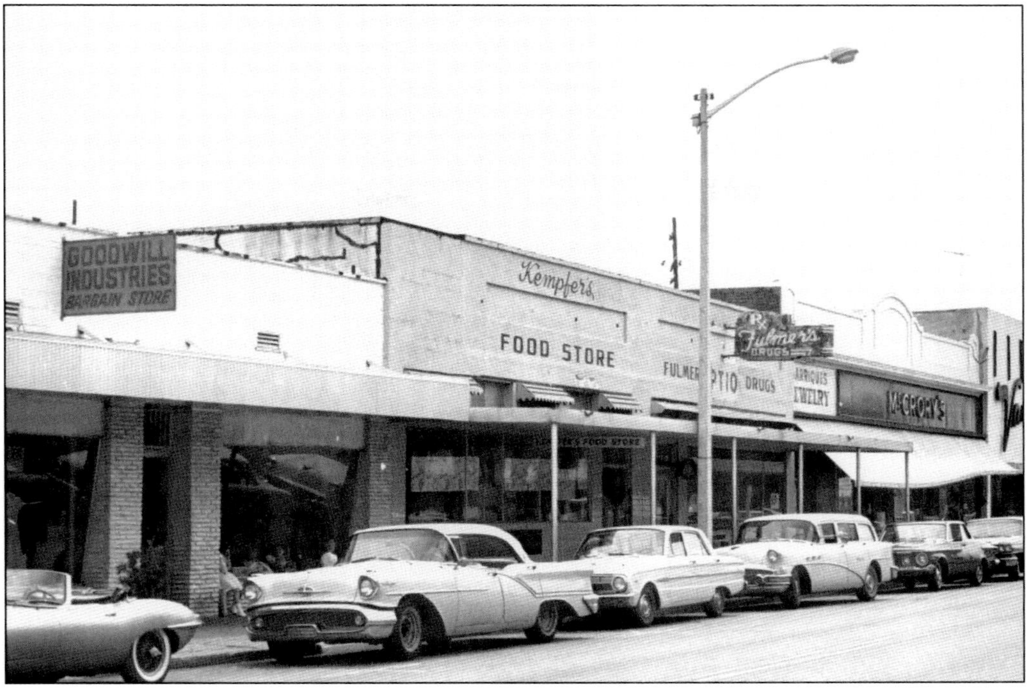

The Kempfers started their business in 1913 at Deer Park, the location of their farm. They opened Kempfer's Food Store on New Haven in 1923. The store, owned by Bob Kempfer, was known for its fresh vegetables and meats. The business is still in operation under the same name. From left to right, the stores in this photo are Goodwill Industries, Kempfer's, Fulmer's Drugs, Garriques Jewelry, McCrory's, and Van's Shoes.

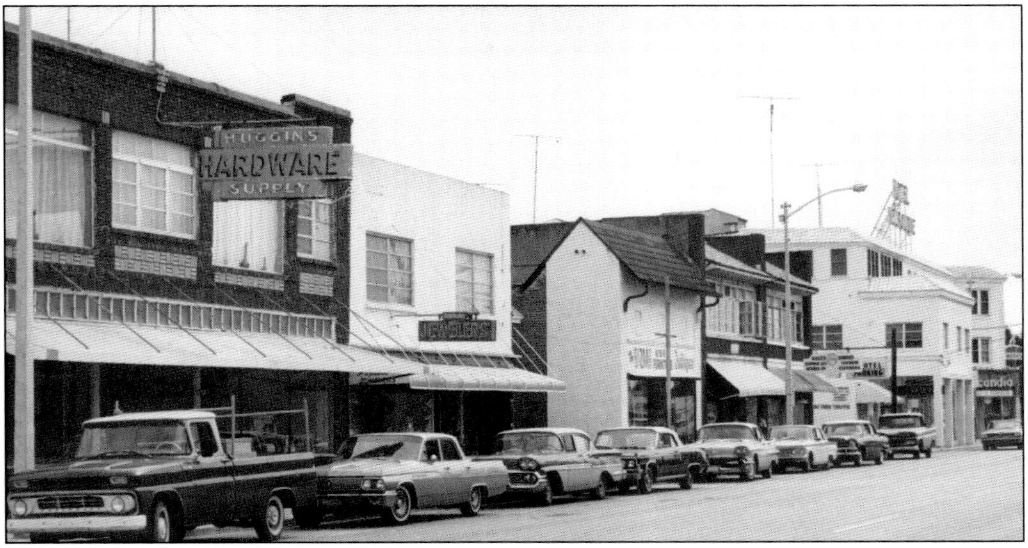

On the left in this picture is Huggins Supply Hardware, located in the old Stewart Hardware building, which was erected in 1898. For decades, there was a hardware store here, owned successively by C.H. Stewart, A.A. Stewart, Harvey Huggins, and the Struble and Meyer families. The building still exists as Christmas Cottage. To its right are Hopkins Jewelers, the Bazaar Antiques, John McLaughlin Real Estate, Kirby Vacuum Sales and Service, Hotel Melbourne offices, Scandia Furniture, and the Amoco Station.

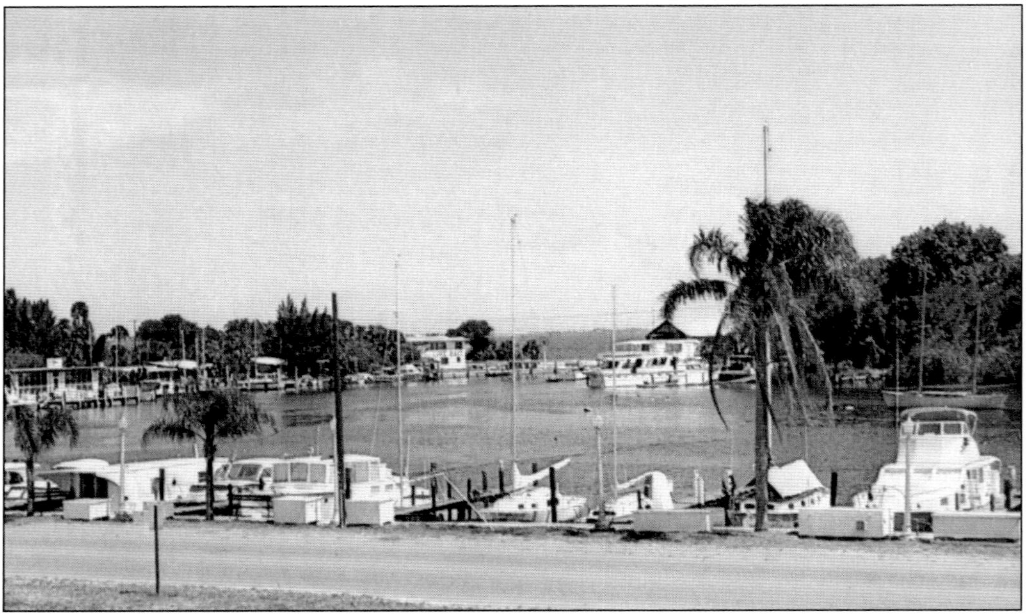

Melbourne Harbor in the 1960s was a modest presence in the town. Home to the Melbourne Yacht Club, established in 1886, and dredged in 1907 and 1931, the harbor was uncluttered and peaceful. Businesses in the harbor included the Melbourne Marina, the Indian River Marine Basin docks, and Hatt's Bait and Tackle.

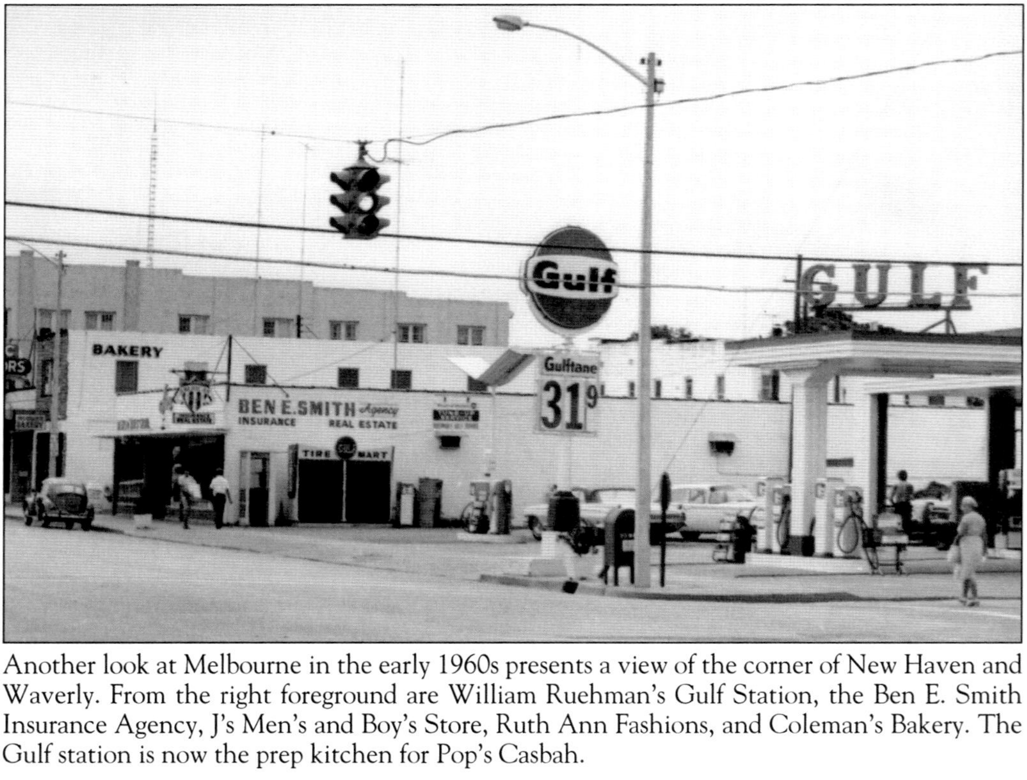

Another look at Melbourne in the early 1960s presents a view of the corner of New Haven and Waverly. From the right foreground are William Ruehman's Gulf Station, the Ben E. Smith Insurance Agency, J's Men's and Boy's Store, Ruth Ann Fashions, and Coleman's Bakery. The Gulf station is now the prep kitchen for Pop's Casbah.

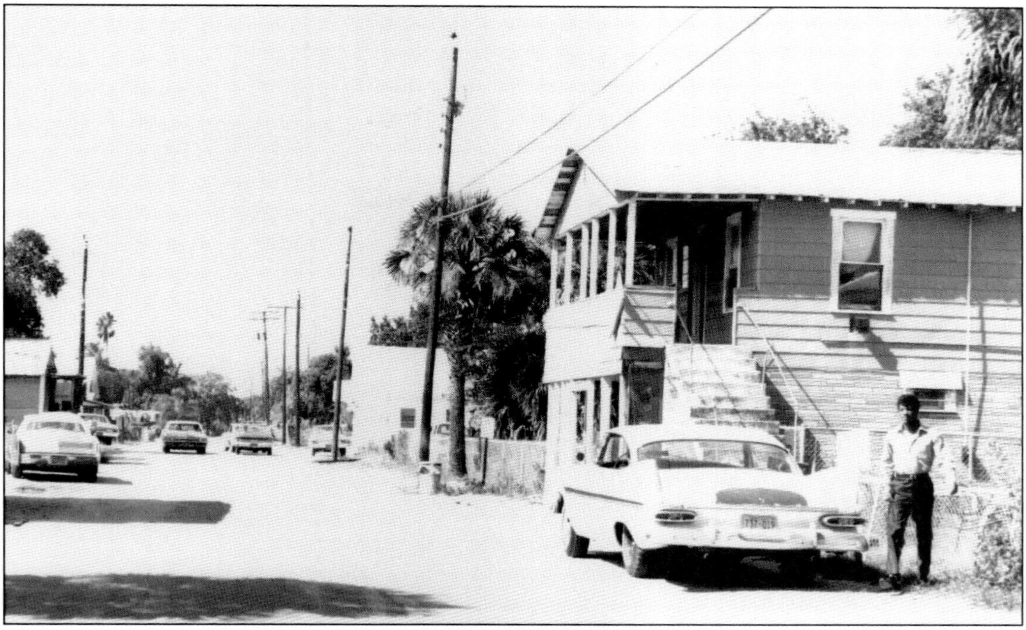

These views show popular businesses on Lipscomb Street in South Melbourne. Above is Mary Price's Grocery Store and Furnished Rooms. Beyond that is Line Street and the Church of God in Christ.

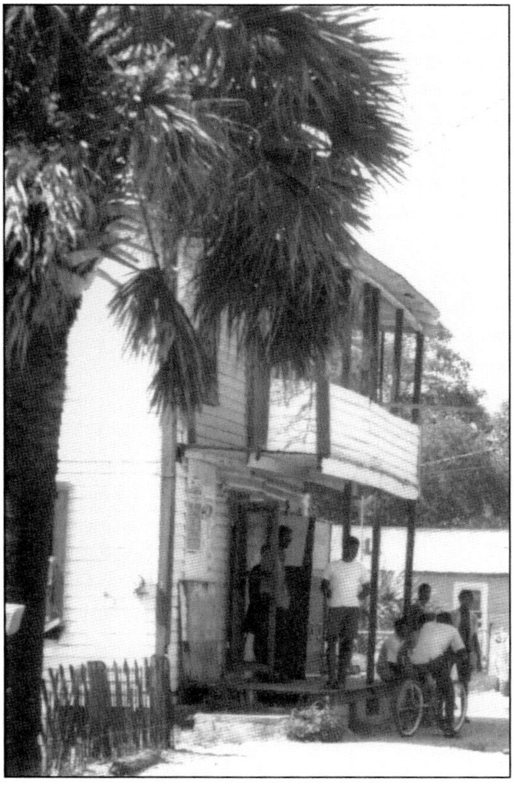

In the photo on the right is Charles "Sun" Bowman's Sunset Beer Garden Tavern and Rooming House. The South Melbourne Civic League worked with the City to beautify South Melbourne, improve drainage, and pave streets.

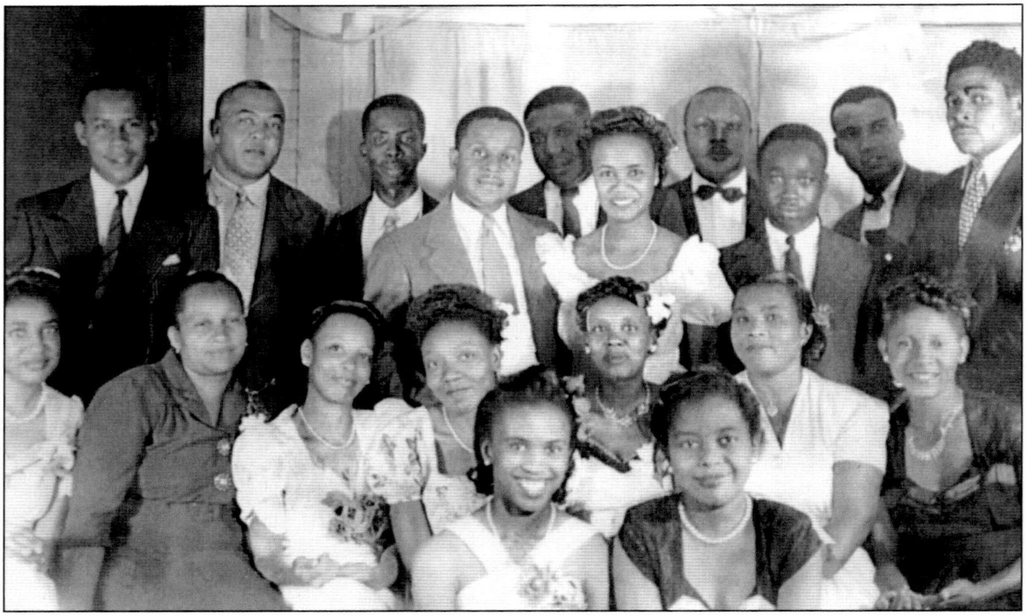

In the late 1950s, this group of South Melbourne citizens posed for this portrait at a banquet. From left to right, are (first row) Naomi Haines, and Essie Burgess; (second row) Phyllis Scott, Minnie Sealey, Eloise Taylor, Reba Rooks, Laura Williams, Angie Ryoland, and Hattie Mae Carr; (third row) Norman Coates, Naomi Coates, Kaiser Williams, and ? Stokes; (fourth row) Andrew Scott, John Sealey, J.W. Taylor, Louis Stokes Jr., J.R. Ryoland, and an unidentified person.

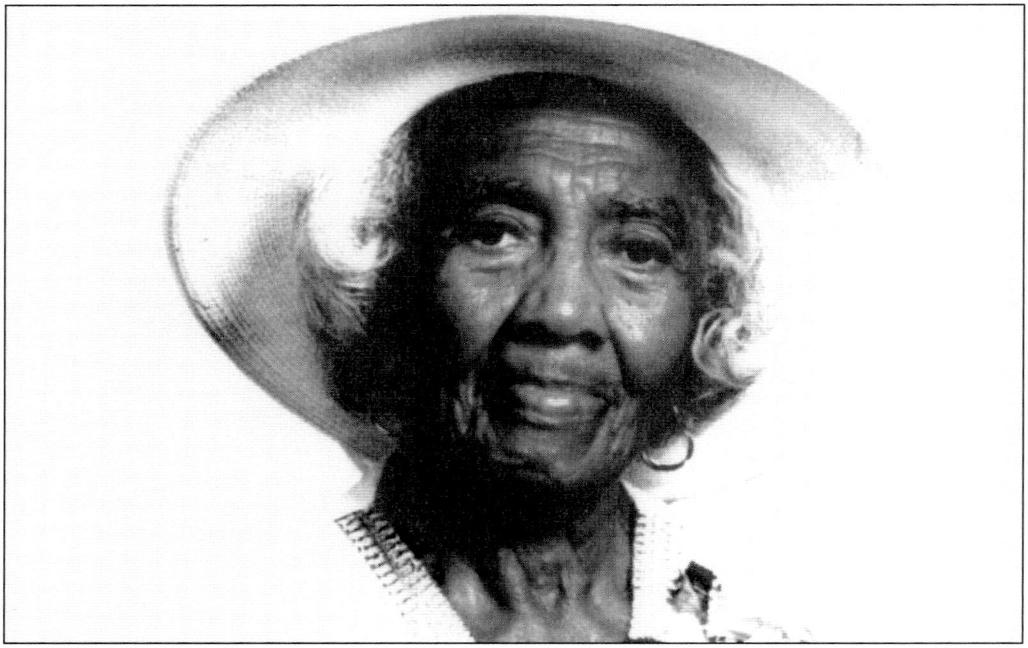

Cora Sims was the widow of Reverend Sims, who pastored at the Bethlehem Baptist Church in Titusville. "Mother" Sims worked at Patrick Air Force Base and attended the St. James Missionary Baptist Church in Eau Gallie. She was greatly respected for the benevolent work she did in her community for many years.

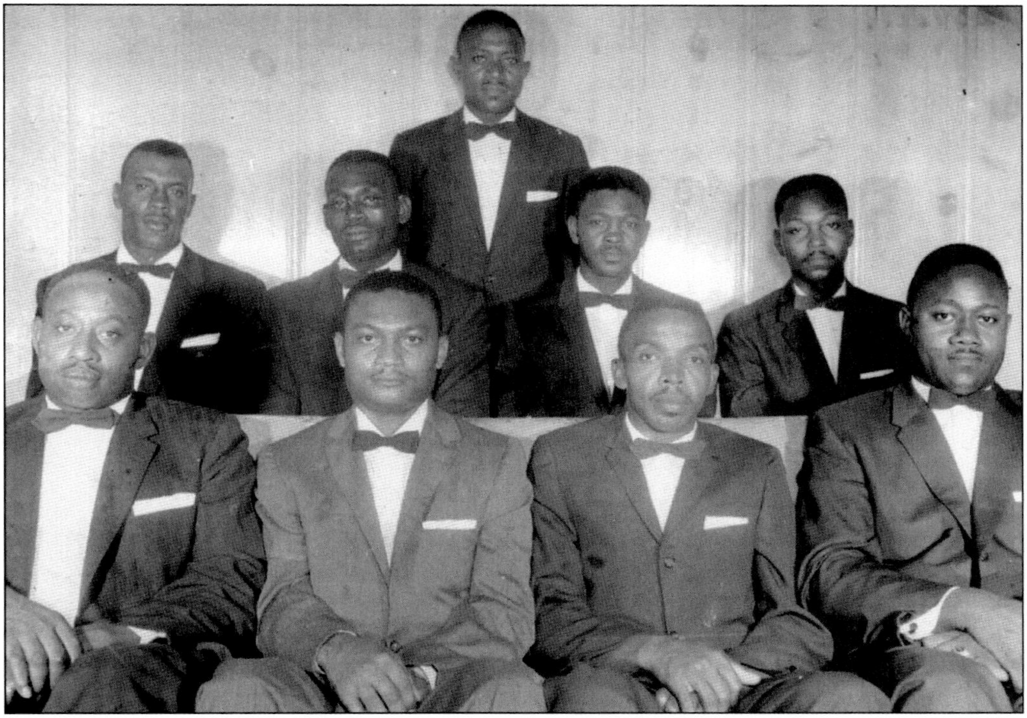

This photo is a portrait of the members of the Cavalier Men's Club in 1955. The group raised funds and gave local assistance to the NAACP during the struggle for Civil Rights in Melbourne in the 1950s and 1960s. From left to right are (front row) C.J. Robinson, Earl Burney, Moses Kitchen, and Jesse Buggs; (middle row) Rufus Caison, Robert Broomfield, Clarence Williams, and Lewis William. In the back row is Charlie Brightman. Broomfield, Buggs, Henry Jackson (not shown), and others led desegregation activities in Melbourne in the 1960s.

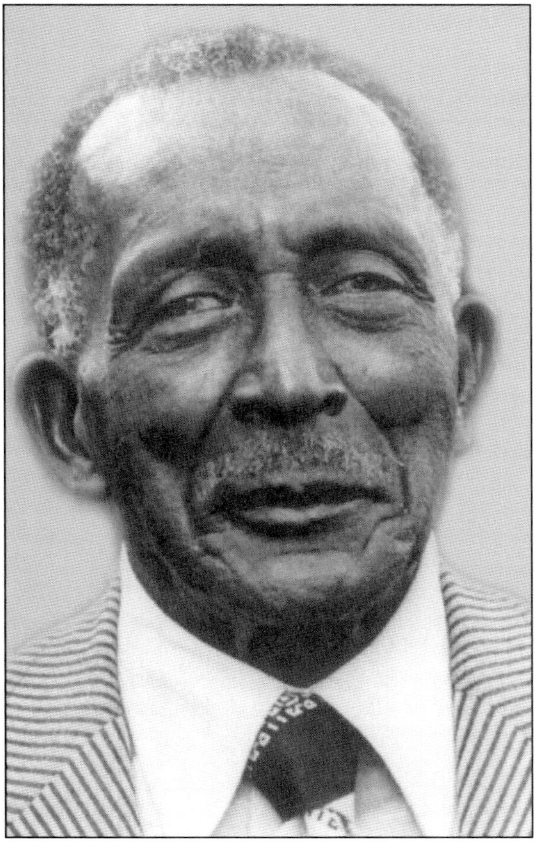

Harry Lawrence was a president of the South Melbourne Civic League. He initiated the movement to create Brothers Park on the site of the former Vocational School. As president of the Lipscomb Park Association, he worked with Councilman Ted Nichols (the first African-American City Council Member in Melbourne) to beautify South Melbourne and establish Lipscomb Park. Lawrence also served on the South Brevard Chamber of Commerce.

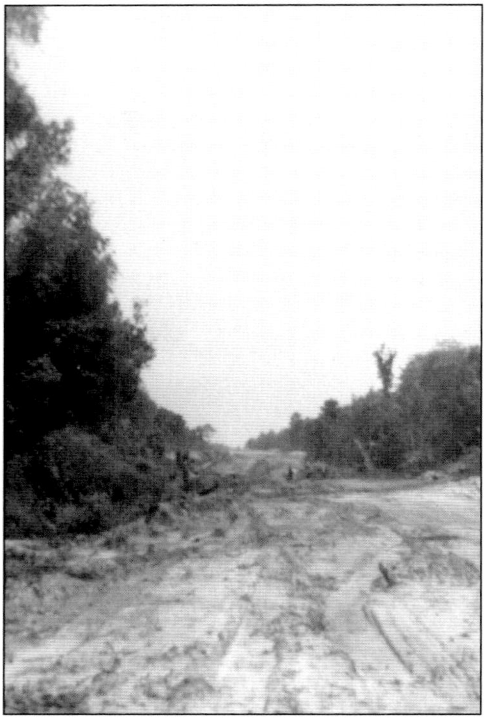

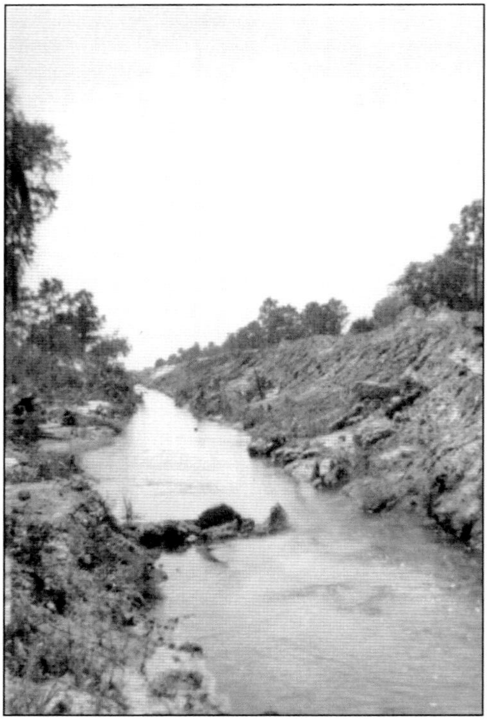

These three pictures document a typical Melbourne-Eau Gallie activity—road building. Shown here is the extension of Babcock Street over Crane Creek in 1958. Babcock ended only a half-mile south of New Haven at the time. When the creek was bridged, drainage ditches cut, and the road paved, Babcock became the major north-south artery west of US #1. Its construction created access to the development of South Melbourne, Florida Institute of Technology, numerous housing projects, and the greatest part of the City of Palm Bay. By the time Eau Gallie and Melbourne unified in 1969, Palm Bay was geographically larger than Melbourne. Babcock Street became a state highway extending beyond Brevard County, and Palm Bay's population grew to exceed that of Melbourne.

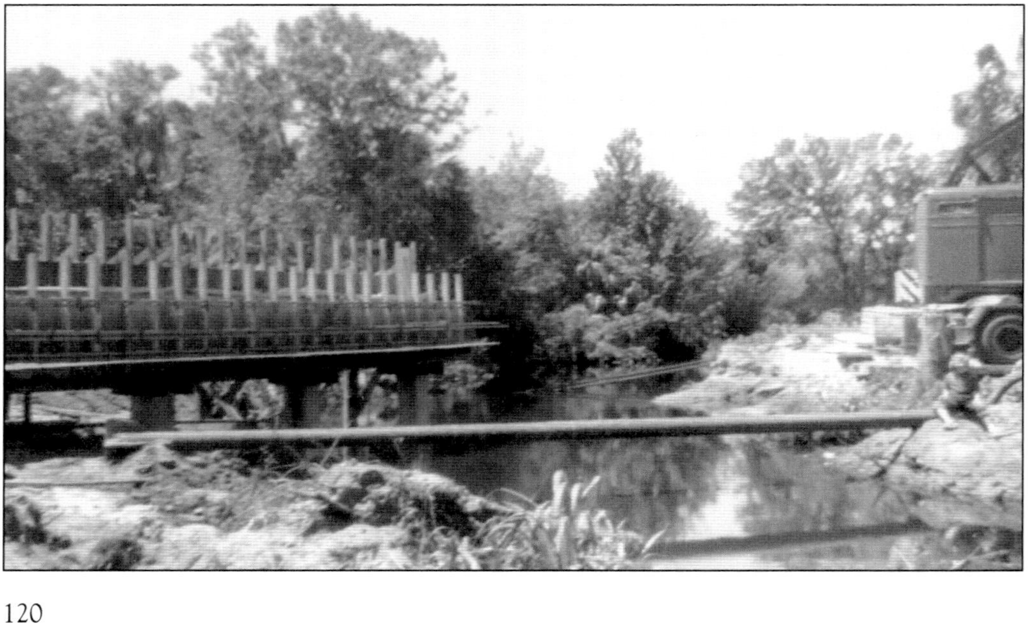

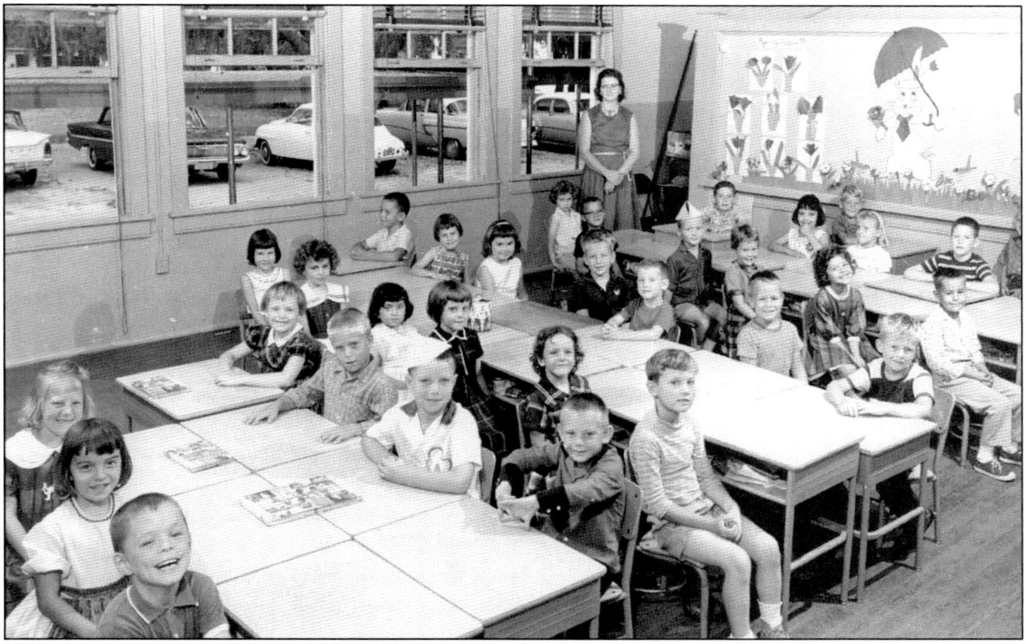

During the high-growth decade following the opening of the Space Program, Melbourne and Eau Gallie were swamped with the numbers of school children. By 1963, the newly built facilities included Melbourne, Satellite, and Eau Gallie High Schools; Stone High and Elementary; Eau Gallie and Southwest Junior High Schools; and University Park, Harbor City, Meadowlane, Indialantic, Sea Park, and Sherwood Elementary Schools. Older facilities still in use were Melbourne and Creel Elementaries. Even the Naval Air Station hospital was pressed into service as the Airport School, while the first portable classrooms cropped up at Melbourne High. Above, at Melbourne Elementary, is Mrs. Marjorie DeAngel's first grade in 1962. Below is Melbourne High School in 1963.

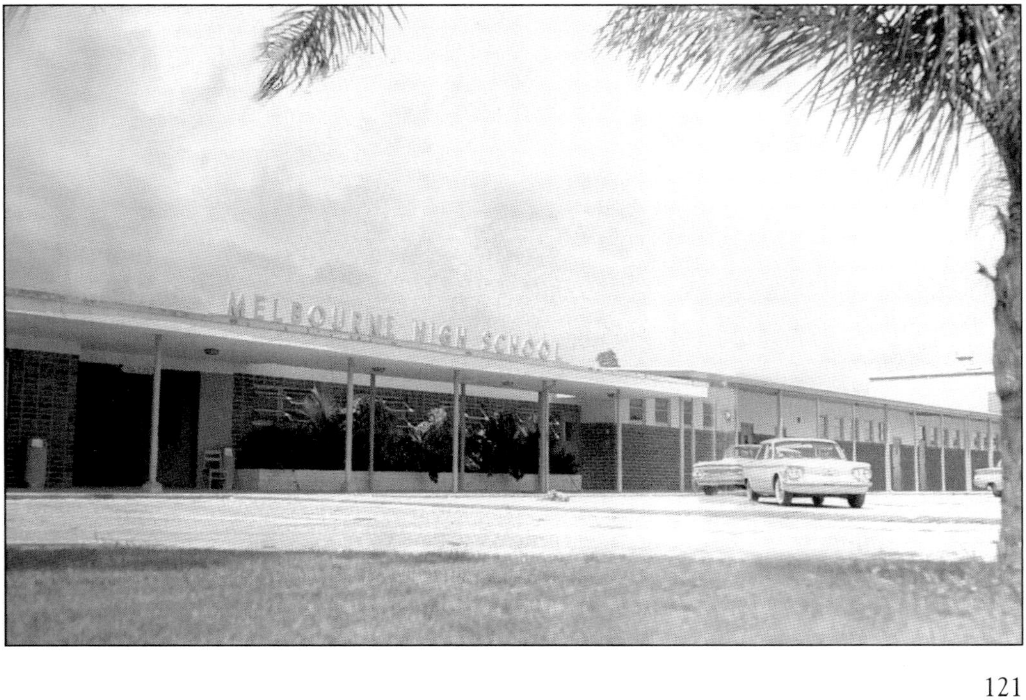

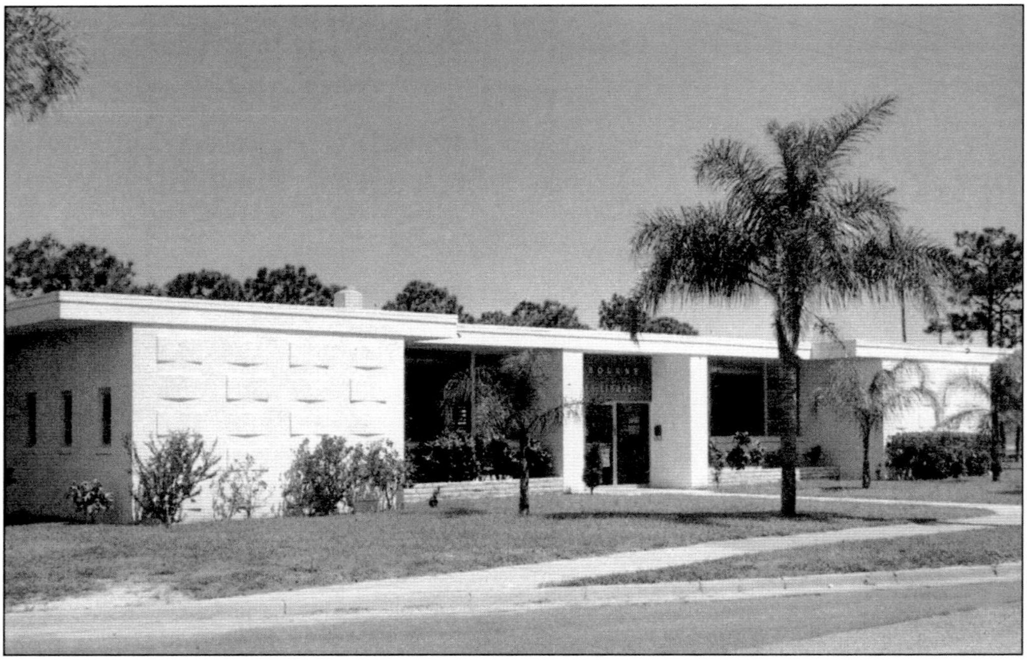

In the mid-1950s, Melbourne built a new library on Fee Avenue. By 1960, it had 10,000 volumes, and Eau Gallie's new library on Pineapple had nearly 12,000. In 1957, the first shopping center on Babcock Street opened for business. Its appearance was followed five years later by the construction of the Brevard Mall across the street. Other new area shopping centers and plazas included Sarno, Eau Gallie, Minton's Corner, West Gate, Fulmer's, Sears, South Patrick Shores, Atlantic, Indialantic, Indian Harbour, Port Malabar, and Palm Bay. Retail businesses grew as rapidly as the population.

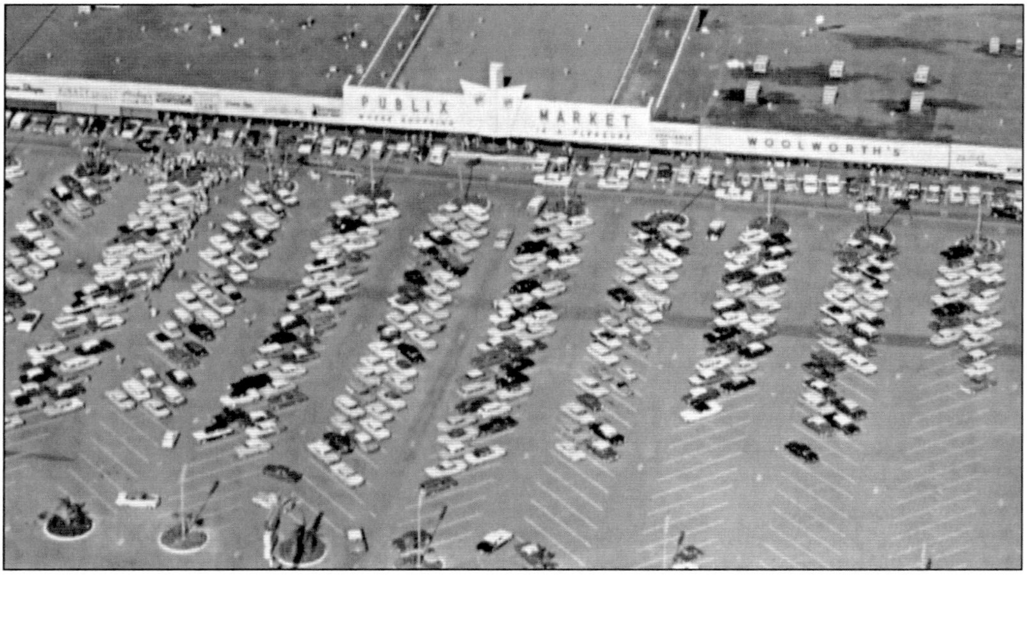

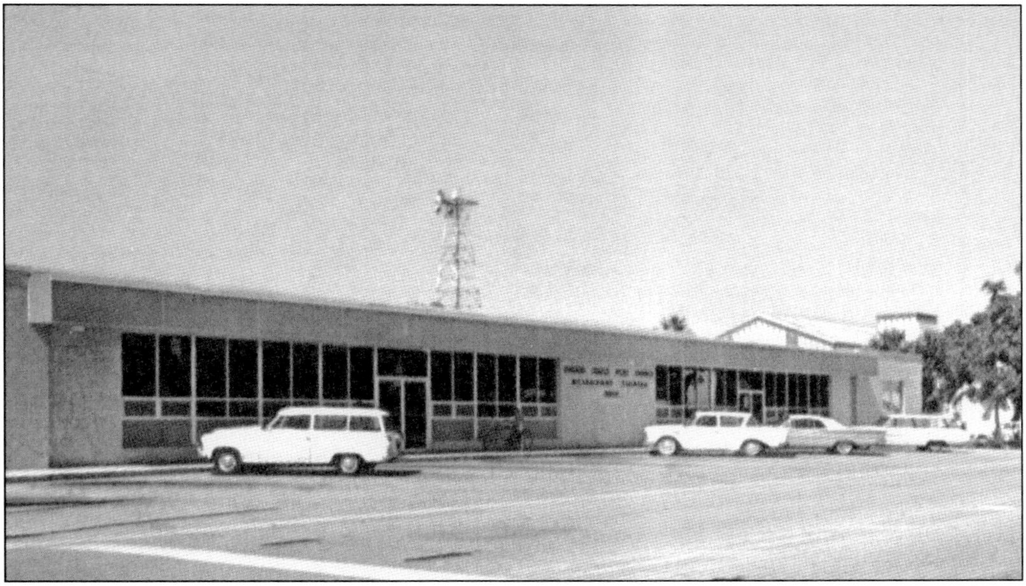

Shown above is the Melbourne Post Office on New Haven Avenue. Both Melbourne and Eau Gallie had new post offices in the early 1960s. In addition, a new branch of the Eau Gallie Post Office was opened in the Atlantic Plaza, and a Melbourne Branch was opened in the Melbourne Shopping Center.

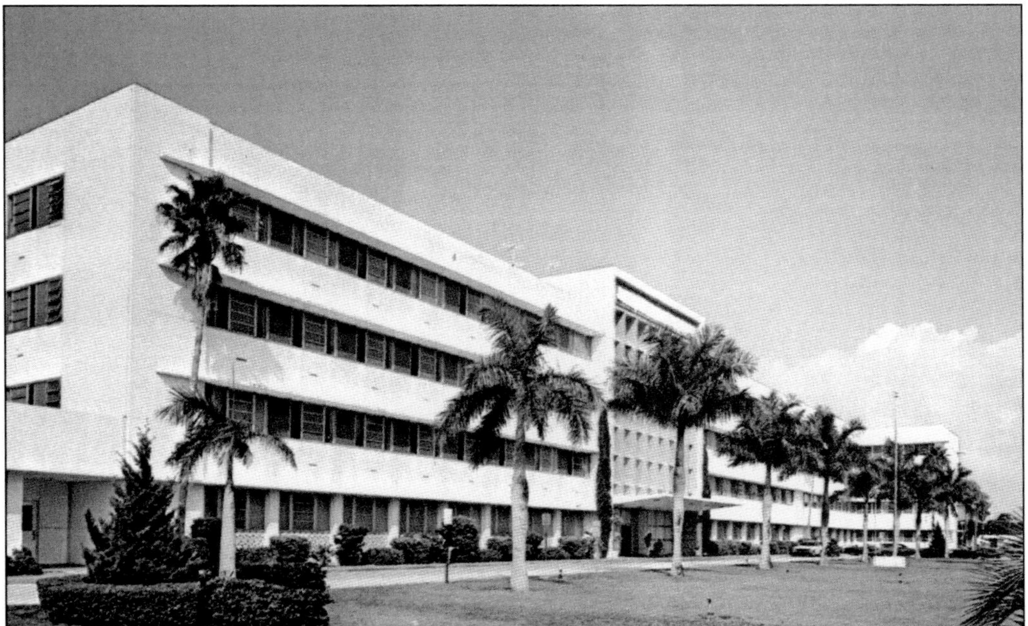

In the 1950s, the Brevard Hospital on US #1 was terribly overcrowded. Built in 1937, it had tripled the number of its beds to 75 by the time the City of Melbourne furnished the Hospital Association with 10 acres for a new building. The community raised funds enthusiastically, and the new hospital on Hickory Street opened in 1962 with 181 beds. Work began almost immediately on another wing. Before the decade was over, the hospital had nearly doubled in capacity.

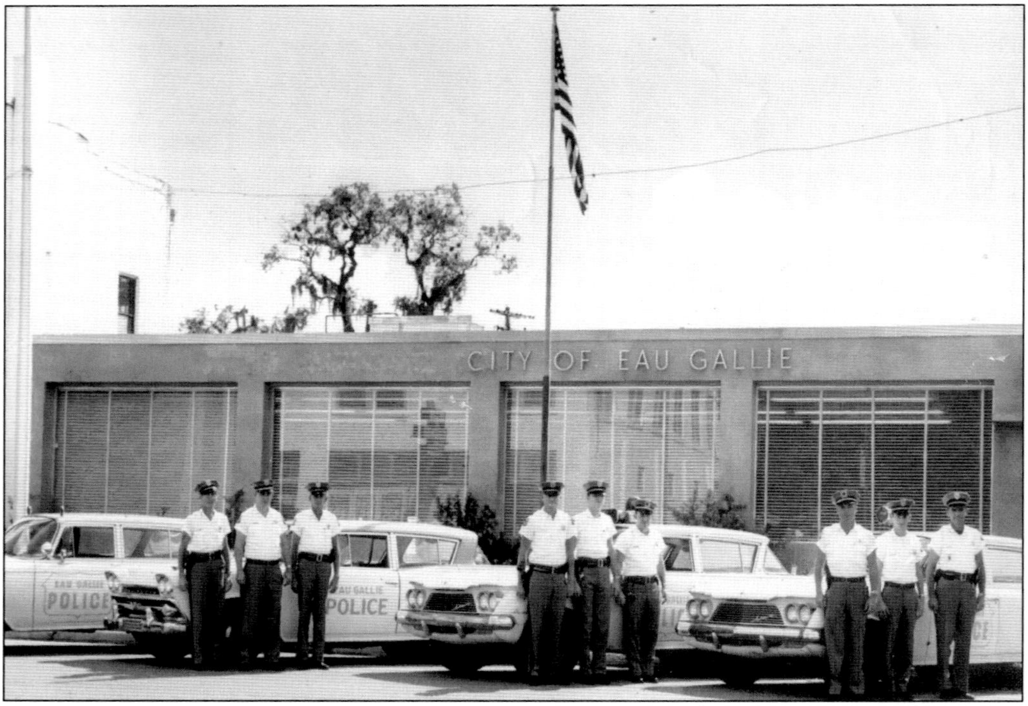

Eau Gallie and Melbourne had outgrown their municipal buildings by the 1960s. In this picture, taken in July of 1961, members of the Eau Gallie Police Force pose with their cruisers in front of the new Eau Gallie City Hall. When Eau Gallie and Melbourne merged eight years later, the new unified Melbourne Police Force occupied the building.

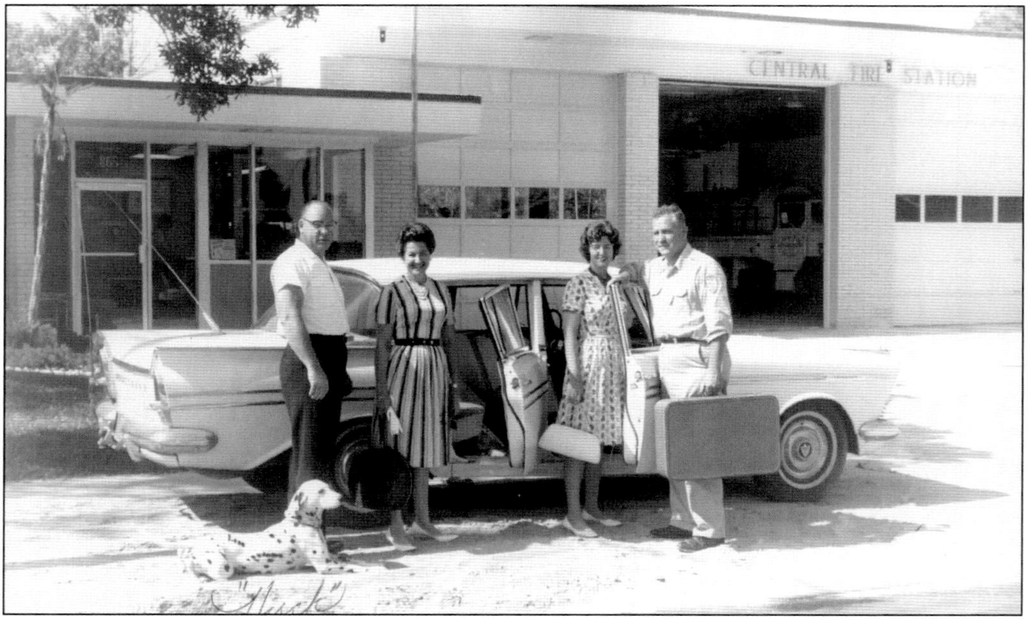

From left to right are Eau Gallie Fire Chief Dick Seitner and his wife, Violet, along with Jackie and Calvin Cook (volunteer firemen), as they prepare to leave for the State Firemen's Association Convention in 1963. The firehouse dog, Huck, poses with them in front of the new Central Fire Station on Eau Gallie Boulevard.

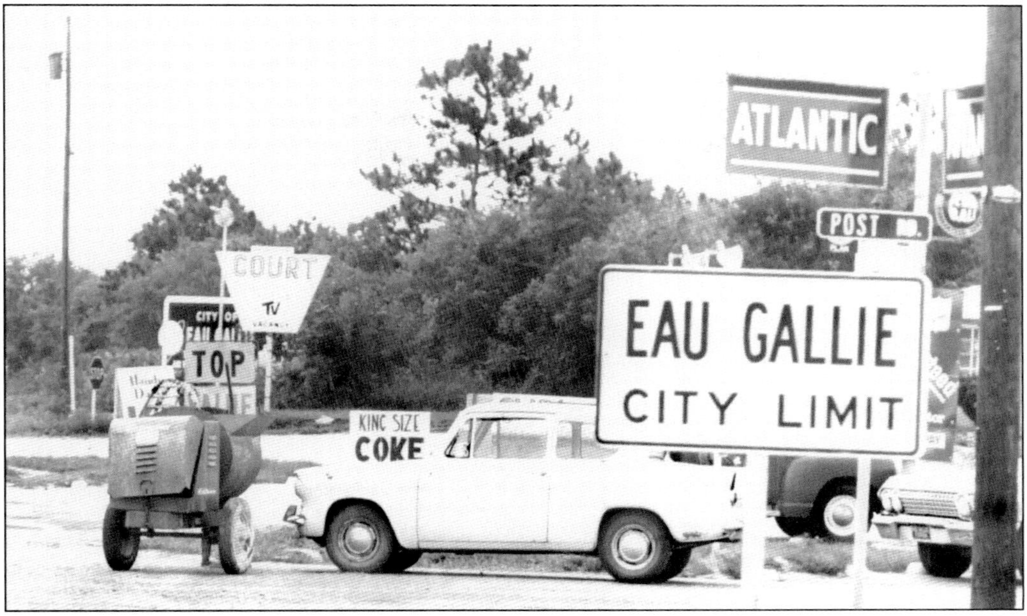

Eau Gallie city limits extended north to Post Road. Here, next to the Broadview Court and a newly built Atlantic filling station, residents of the Sherwood Forest subdivision turn west to go home. Under Eau Gallie and Melbourne's persistently blue skies and fluffy white clouds, Florida's muggy heat gave way to air conditioning while sandy scrub yielded to St. Augustine grass and sprinkling systems. Other new housing subdivisions in the cities were Ixora Park, Loveridge Heights, Almay Homes, Bowe Gardens, June Park, Magnolia Manor, Golf Club Estates, Hickory Hills, University Park, and Newtown. In Palm Bay, the massive Mackle Brothers' Port Malabar subdivision began the radical changes that would determine the future of the area immediately south of Melbourne.

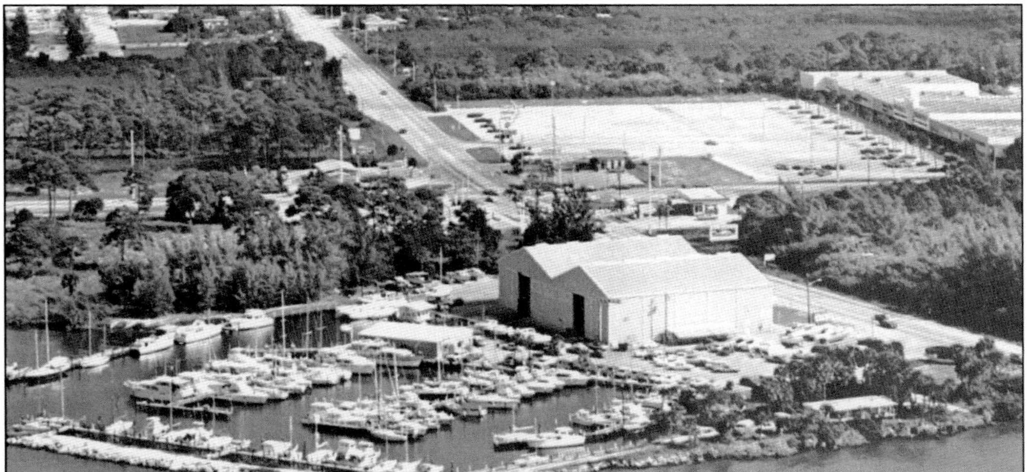

A small marina and trailer park named Anchor Cove developed into the Anchorage Yacht Basin in the late 1960s. The new facilities, located at the eastern end of Eau Gallie Causeway, include dry dock storage, repairs, sales, and slips up to 65 feet. The Eau Gallie Yacht Club moved to a nearby six-acre tract in 1961. Its new facilities had docking for 20 boats, a swimming pool, and an 8,000 square foot clubhouse with a restaurant and ballroom. In 1974, tennis courts were added. The club has continued to thrive and expand since then.

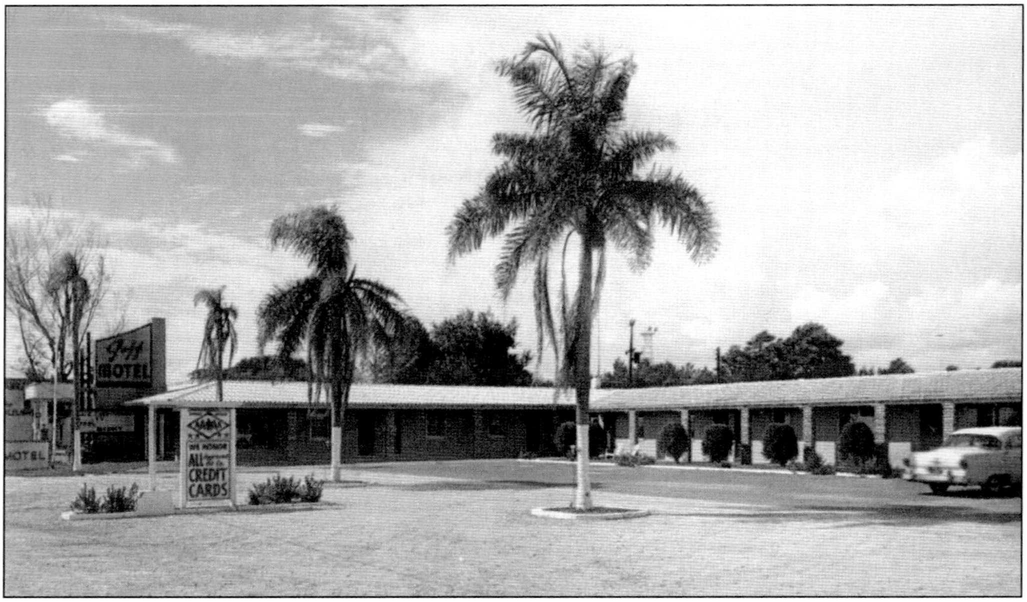

Built and opened in 1948 by Bill and Geneva Garvin, the Garvin Court was located near the Florida Power and Light Ice House on US #1. In those days, the highway was woodsy and a bit wild. The Garvin boys frequently found and skinned huge rattlesnakes. In 1955, US #1 was widened to four lanes. In 1957, the Goff family—Ed, Mary, Romeo, and Burma—purchased the motel. They operated it for many years as the Goff Motel, shown above.

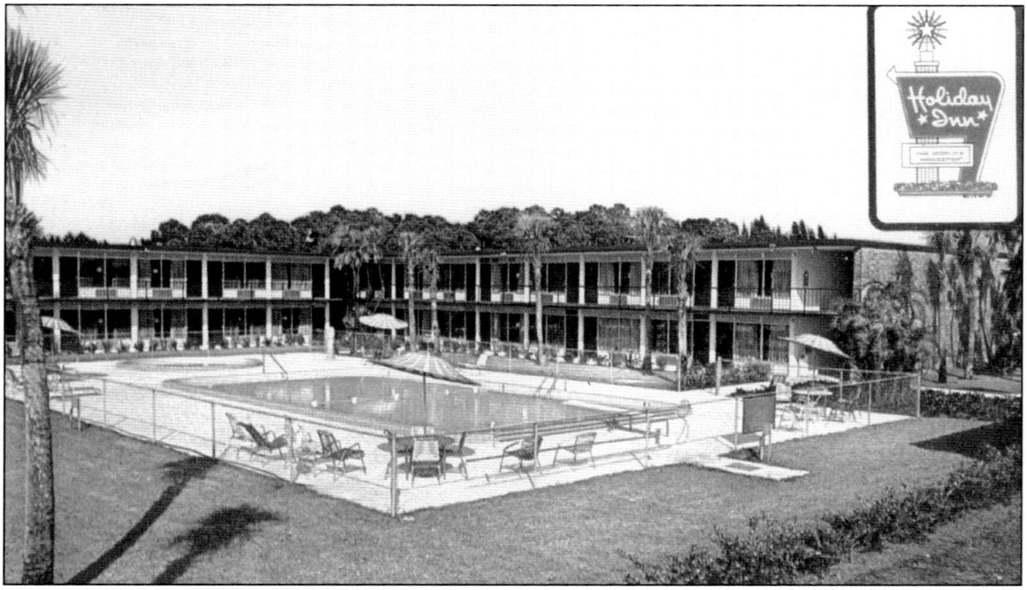

Melbourne and Eau Gallie's motel rows were on US #1, north of each city. As the population swelled, so did business at family-owned and operated motels. In the 1960s, larger motels in national chains began to move in. Melbourne's two-story Holiday Inn featured a swimming pool, restaurant, and cocktail lounge. Eventually, the smaller motels were sold and torn down as property on the river and US #1 increased in commercial value.

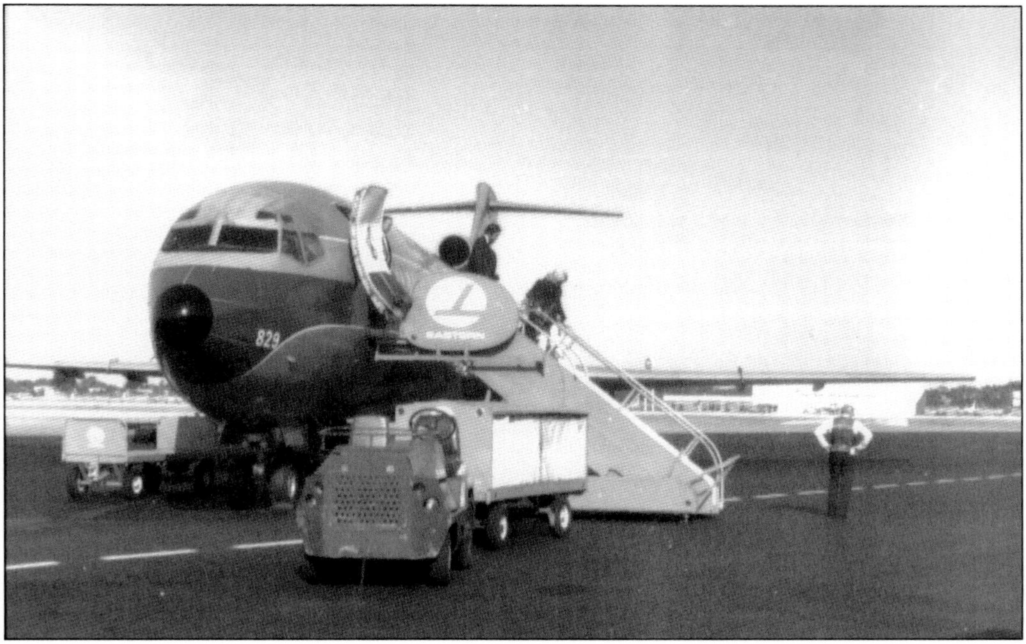

The Melbourne-Eau Gallie Airport was operated by the City of Melbourne as a municipal airport from 1947 until the Melbourne Airport Authority was chartered in 1968. By then, Melbourne Airport had emerged as a regional facility. The commercial airport closest to the Air Force Eastern Test Range, Melbourne International serves Brevard County and parts of Indian River, St. Lucie, and Osceola Counties. Commercial flights began in 1953 with service by Eastern Airlines. The first ticket, a round-trip to Jacksonville, was purchased by Louis Olsen. National Airlines began service in 1959. In 1960, the airport added a new passenger terminal at a cost of $150,000. In 1962, the Airport Authority spent another $750,000 to extend the runway and improve facilities in order to handle jet aircraft. Since then, the airport has continued to expand and now has 3 runways and almost 165,000 square feet of freight and passenger facilities.

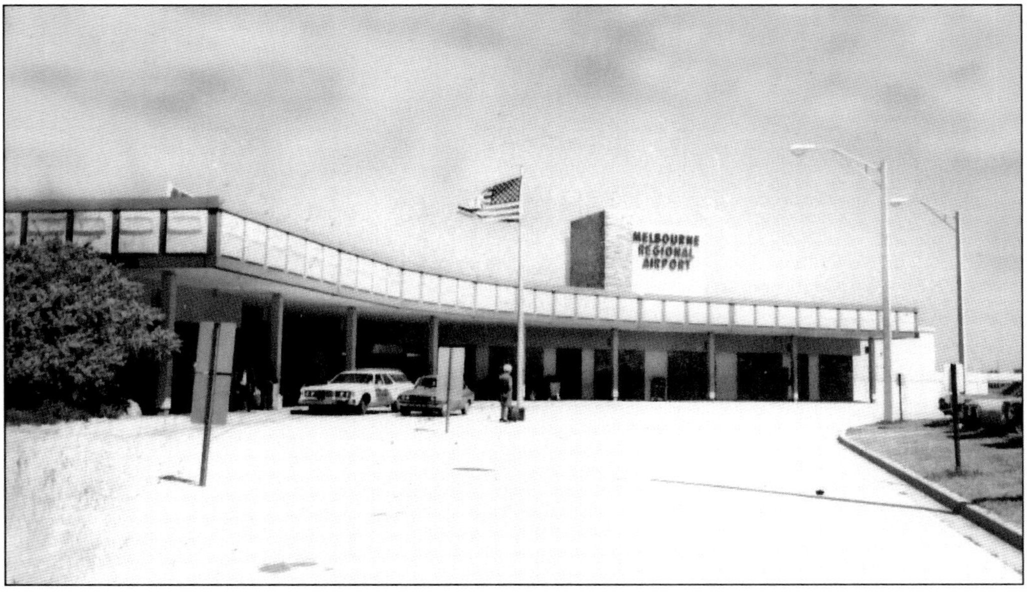

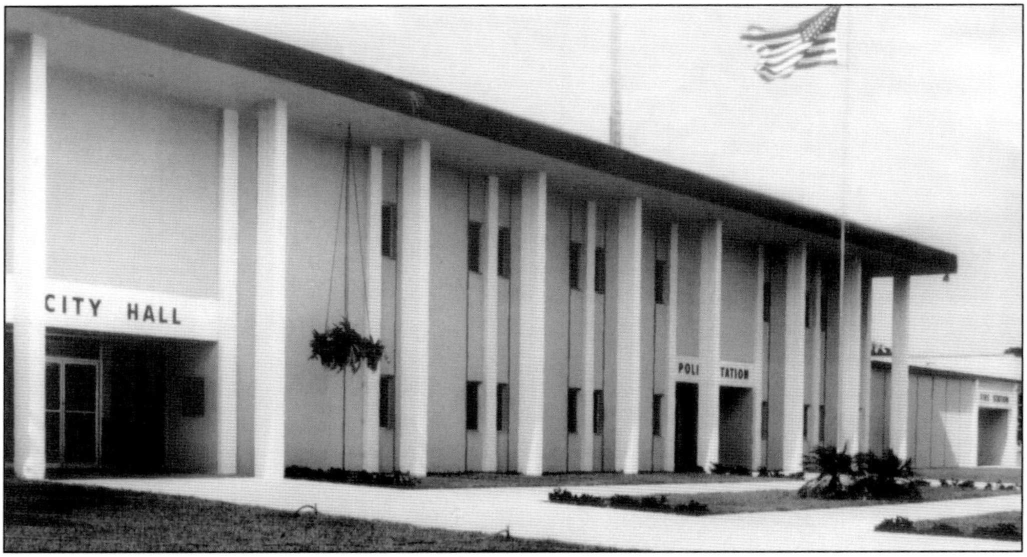

Above is Melbourne's municipal building, completed in 1964. Eau Gallie and Melbourne citizens voted to merge in 1969 and chose the name "Melbourne" for the unified city. The Interim Council chose this building for the city hall. Eau Gallie's municipal building housed the police station and municipal courtroom. Eau Gallie's seal and nickname, "the Harbor City," were adopted for the new municipality.

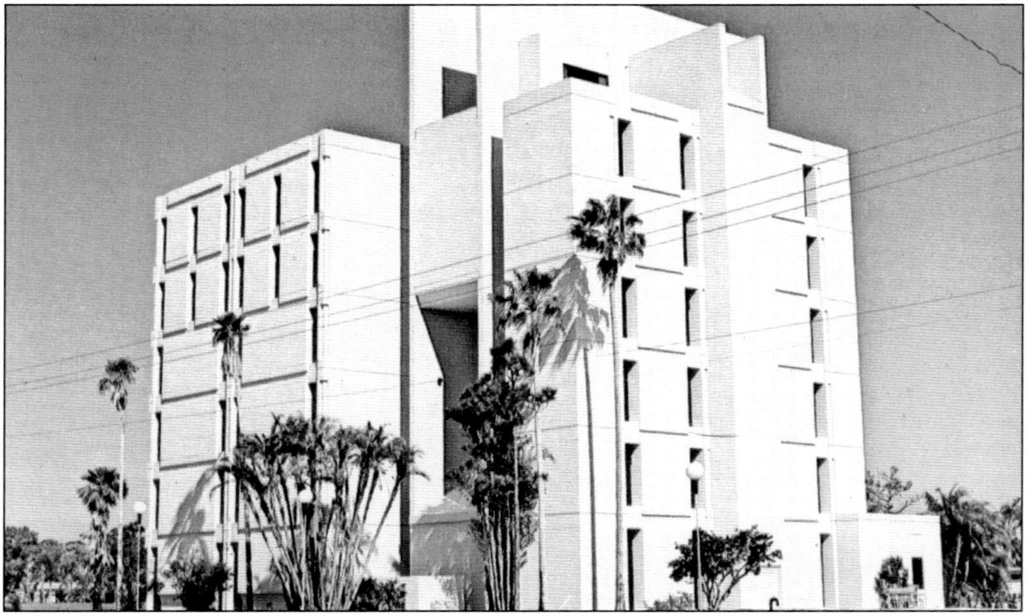

Above is the Science Building of Florida Institute of Technology (FIT), located in Melbourne. Founded as Brevard Engineering College in 1958, FIT (now Florida Tech) grew quickly due to enthusiastic local support and generosity. The first class graduated in 1966. At its inception, the university emphasized electronic engineering, sciences, mathematics, and space technology. Since that time, the curriculum, campus, and facilities have expanded considerably. In 1971, the South Campus of Brevard Community College opened on Post Road. It has also undergone a great deal of expansion. These institutions are vital parts of Melbourne's cultural and economic structure.